International Socialism 131

Summer 2011

Contributors

Anne Alexander is a writer and researcher on the Middle East. She is currently writing a book about the role played by the workers' movement in the Arab revolutions.

Ian Birchall is the author of *Sartre against Stalinism* and *Tony Cliff: A Marxist for his Time*.

Paul Blackledge most recently co-edited *Virtue and Politics* (University of Notre Dame). His *Marxism and Ethics* will be published by SUNY Press next spring.

Joseph Choonara is the co-author of *Arguments for Revolution: The Case for the Socialist Workers Party* and the author of *Unravelling Capitalism: A Guide to Marxist Political Economy*.

Simon Englert is a postgraduate student and activist at the University of Sussex.

Luke Evans is a postgraduate student and activist at Goldsmiths.

Tim Evans is a writer and activist living in Swansea.

Amy Gilligan is postgraduate student and activist at the University of Cambridge.

G Francis Hodge recently completed postgraduate work in war studies at Kings College.

Peyman Jafari is a member of the International Socialists in the Netherlands. He is a PhD candidate at the University of Amsterdam and the International Institute of Social History.

Gareth Jenkins is a frequent contributor to *International Socialism* and *Socialist Review*. He used to teach literature and culture at the University of Greenwich.

Richard Seymour is the author of *The Meaning of David Cameron* and the proprietor of the *Lenin's Tomb* blog.

Martin Smith is a leading member of the Socialist Workers Party.

Maina van der Zwan is the editor of *socialisme.nu* and a leading member of the International Socialists in the Netherlands.

Unsteady as she goes

Alex Callinicos

For a while the high priests of capitalism congratulated themselves on the robustness of the economic recovery. Financial markets soared and there was euphoria about the robust expansion of the "emerging market" economies of the Global South. But in the past few weeks it has begun to sink in that the world economy is locked into a crisis that is far from over.

This reality has penetrated even the inner sanctums of the economics profession, where it is rarely admitted that markets can do any wrong. Robert Lucas, who received what is (rather dubiously) called the Nobel Prize for Economics in 1995 for his services to the cult of the market, gave a recent lecture in which he noted that the American economy normally grows by around 3 percent a year. The Great Depression of the 1930s marked an enormous deviation from this trend—real gross domestic product fell by 34 percent between 1929 and 1934. But what Lucas calls "the current US depression" represents another major deviation, though not as great, since growth is just under 10 percent below trend: the "Depression of 1930s and the current one are both much deeper, more prolonged than typical". [1]

Lucas notes that, as in the Great Depression, the present crisis started in the banking system, though this time the American state didn't sit by, but pumped in vast amounts of liquidity, preventing total collapse. Lucas supports these policies, but he argues that business investment and consumer spending are being held back by the prospect of higher taxes,

---

1:    Lucas, 2011.

Barack Obama's healthcare reform and the imposition of very mild new controls on financial markets, all of which will turn the United States into a European-style welfare state. This is ridiculous. Gavyn Davies points out that, "as yet, there has been no increase in taxation, on the rich or anyone else. Nor have the Obama administration's medical and financial sector reforms really taken effect. It would take a remarkably farsighted private sector to have already reacted adversely to this set of long-term reforms, even if they might do so eventually".[2]

Figure 1: US recession: GDP deviations from trend
Source: Lucas, 2011

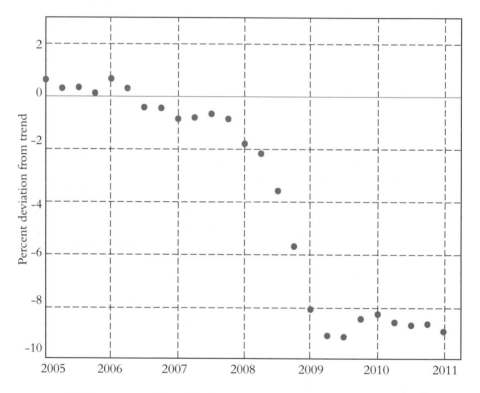

All the same, the global economic recovery does look like it's running out of steam. In recent weeks the US, the eurozone and Britain have all released data showing that growth is slowing. There is also

---

2: Davies, 2011.

increasing evidence that China, whose helter-skelter expansion has driven the recovery, is slowing down, though this means it is forecast by Goldman Sachs to grow at 9.4 rather than 10 percent this year.[3]

As Lucas points out, the problem isn't lack of money. Global profit margins are estimated to have risen by 40 percent in 2010, and are forecast to rise by another 11 percent in 2011.[4] So companies are flush with money. According to the *Financial Times*, "less than three years on from the dark days of the financial crisis, companies are sitting on a bulging war chest of several thousand billion dollars of cash". But it also reports that, burned by the financial crisis and worried about the future, they are wary about opening their coffers to spend on takeovers or new investments.[5]

The official explanation for the growth slowdown is the impact of various external "shocks"—the rise in the oil price, for example, and the disruption caused to global supply chains by falls in Japanese production after the Tohoku tsunami. No doubt these played a part, but the reality is that the world economy is still deeply constrained by the effects simultaneously of the crisis and of the measures taken to prevent it becoming even worse. The financial bubble that precipitated the crisis was driven by massive borrowing by states, banks and individual households. All are now trying to borrow less and save more. Since higher saving reduces effective demand for goods and services, the economic consequences are negative.

Thus take the American housing market, incubator of both the bubble and the crash. Figures released at the end of May show housing prices have suffered a double-dip—in other words, having fallen and then recovered, they are falling again. House prices are now 33 percent below their peak in 2006, a steeper fall than the 31 percent drop during the Great Depression. The problem is partly oversupply—ten million vacant homes, 2.3 million in foreclosure because their owners couldn't keep up their mortgage repayments. Demand is also falling because the high level of unemployment encourages young people to stay with their parents rather than buy their own home.[6] Rising house prices played a crucial role in driving higher consumer demand (since they allowed households to borrow and spend more) during the boom of the mid-2000s.[7] So an important engine of economic growth is broken—not just in the US, but

3:   http://blogs.ft.com/beyond-brics/2011/05/24/better-late-than-never-goldman-cuts-china-forecast/
4:   Jackson, 2011.
5:   Milne and Sakoui, 2011.
6:   Harding, 2011 and Kapner and Politi, 2011.
7:   See, for example, the data in Duménil and Lévy, 2011, chapter 10.

in countries such as Britain, southern Ireland and Spain that also experienced property bubbles in the previous decade.

The so-called crisis of sovereign debt falls into the same pattern. Financial markets have been targeting governments that they believe can't pay back their debts. This process has gone furthest in the eurozone, where Greece, Ireland and now Portugal have been placed under the supervision of the "troika" of the European Central Bank (ECB), the European Commission and the International Monetary Fund to ensure that they implement savage austerity policies in exchange for financial support.

These arrangements represent a significant restriction of national sovereignty: for example, the *Financial Times* reported in late May that "European leaders are negotiating a deal that would lead to unprecedented outside intervention in the Greek economy, including international involvement in tax collection and privatisation of state assets, in exchange for new bailout loans for Athens".[8] In fact, there are plenty of precedents from the 19th and early 20th centuries, when consortiums of European states took over financial control of indebted states such as China, Egypt and the Ottoman Empire.

Predictably, the "rescues" have simply made it harder for the victim states to repay their debts. Austerity measures cut economic output and so debt rises in comparison with national income, pushing the burden of repayment to impossible levels: the Greek economy is forecast to shrink by 3.5 percent this year, after contracting by 4.4 percent in 2010.[9] Greece is universally expected to default on its debts. This is a problem for the German and French banks that lent heavily to Greece and the other smaller eurozone states during the credit boom of the 2000s.

Moreover, if default spread beyond Greece, it might wipe out a large chunk of the capital of the ECB, the eurozone's ultra-orthodox guardian of stability. As part of the highly dysfunctional "rescue" of Greece in May 2010, the ECB agreed to prop up the weaker eurozone governments by buying their bonds. According to the *Financial Times*:

> Under the securities markets programme, it acquired €75 billion in government bonds, almost two-thirds of which are Greek. It also has on its books perhaps €150 billion in other financial assets put up as collateral by Greek banks, much of which is backed by Athens.

8:   Spiegel, Peel and Atkins, 2011.
9:   Hope, 2011.

Should Greece default, the value of those holdings would decline sharply. The ECB bought the bonds at market prices, which assumed some risk of default, so the immediate losses might be manageable. JPMorganChase calculates that, with €81bn in capital and reserves, eurozone central banks could withstand even a 50 percent "haircut", or discount, on Greek bonds. But if write-downs on Portuguese and Irish bonds followed, eurozone governments might be forced to provide billions of euros to rebuild the ECB's balance sheet.[10]

Both the eurozone crisis and the US housing double-dip demonstrate how badly damaged the global financial system was by the bubble and the crash. But we can also see how state policies—particularly the drive to austerity—have complicated the situation. Elsewhere government intervention has had different but also destabilising consequences. Chinese banks—under government orders—made $1.4 trillion worth of new loans in 2009, which helped to drive the economy, along with those supplying it with raw materials and components, out of recession.

The apparent success of China and other "emerging market" economies in weathering the Great Recession has played a critical role in boosting financial markets after their recovery from the crash. A fair chunk of the cheap money created by Western central banks has flowed into the big economies of the Global South, pushing up their exchange rates and thereby increasing the problems with which their industrial firms have to grapple in fending off cheap imports from China (whose currency is, of course, pegged against the dollar). Much of the excitement in the financial markets this year has been generated by firms trading in commodities—for example, the stock market launch of the Swiss-based trader Glencore.

Fast growth in the "emerging market" economies has helped to pull up the prices of food, oil, and other raw materials. In 2010 China became the largest consumer of energy, with 20.3 percent of global consumption (the US share was 19 percent).[11] The IMF commodity price index rose by 32 percent between July 2010 and February 2011, with the food price index rising even faster, by 41 percent.[12] The resulting pressure on living standards helped to precipitate the revolutionary wave in the Arab world. This is a political and economic problem as well for the countries at the heart of the recovery. The *Financial Times* recently reported: "Year to year figures for the latest months available show inflation in fast-growing BRIC nations of 6.5

10: Atkins, 2011.
11: Pfeifer, 2011.
12: IMF, 2011, pp30, 37.

percent in Brazil, 8.7 percent in India, 9.6 percent in Russia and 5.3 percent in China. The International Monetary Fund predicts this year's emerging market average rate will be 6.9 percent, compared with just 2.2 percent for the developed world".[13]

In China food prices are rising at twice the overall inflation rate, and a bubble has developed in the property market. The inflationary surge is stoking social tensions—thus higher fuel prices goaded lorry drivers in late April to go on strike, and blockade Shanghai's port of Baoshan, clashing with riot police. Then in mid-June migrant workers clashed with police in the southern factory town of Zengcheng after security guards attacked a pregnant street hawker. The government, nervous about the forthcoming handover to a new generation of party leaders, is trying to cool the economy down by, for example, increasing interest rates. But there may be a bigger bust on the way. Nouriel Roubini, respected for his accurate forecast of the financial crash, has been arguing for some time that China has been developing its own bubble:

> China's economy is overheating now, but, over time, its current overinvestment will prove deflationary both domestically and globally. Once increasing fixed investment becomes impossible—most likely after 2013—China is poised for a sharp slowdown... China has grown for the last few decades on the back of export-led industrialisation and a weak currency, which have resulted in high corporate and household savings rates and reliance on net exports and fixed investment (infrastructure, real estate, and industrial capacity for import-competing and export sectors). When net exports collapsed in 2008-2009 from 11 percent of GDP to 5 percent, China's leaders reacted by further increasing the fixed-investment share of GDP from 42 percent to 47 percent.

> Thus China did not suffer a severe recession—as occurred in Japan, Germany, and elsewhere in emerging Asia in 2009—only because fixed investment exploded. And the fixed-investment share of GDP has increased further in 2010-2011, to almost 50 percent.

> The problem, of course, is that no country can be productive enough to reinvest 50 percent of GDP in new capital stock without eventually facing immense overcapacity and a staggering non-performing loan problem. China is rife with overinvestment in physical capital, infrastructure, and property. To a visitor, this is evident in sleek but empty airports and bullet trains (which will reduce the

---

13: Wagstyl and Wheatley, 2011. In April South Africa joined the four original BRIC states (Brazil, Russia, India, and China).

need for the 45 planned airports), highways to nowhere, thousands of colossal new central and provincial government buildings, ghost towns, and brand-new aluminium smelters kept closed to prevent global prices from plunging.[14]

The fact that Roubini got the financial crisis right doesn't mean he will also get China right. There is an alternative scenario—very much pushed by the leadership of the Chinese Communist Party—according to which the economy will gradually reorient towards the domestic market on the basis of a new model that gives priority to consumption over investment and exports. But this isn't a simple matter of shifting policy. Institutionalised class interests are also involved. Herman Schwartz writes:

> The largest economic benefits from growth have gone to the children of the party elite, who have constituted themselves as a new economic elite... These children also hold 85-90 percent of the key positions in the five most important industrial sectors: finance, foreign trade, land development, large-scale engineering and securities. Their control over these positions has assured their wealth in a society in which markets largely function via contacts, not contracts. From their point of view, profitability ultimately rests on exports rather than on a brutal struggle in a Chinese market characterised by no brand loyalty, no product differentiation, and workers' emerging ability to push wages up.[15]

Now there are counter-trends. The Chinese authorities are nudging the renminbi very slowly up on the foreign exchanges and beginning to allow it to be used in bond issues and the like, primarily in Hong Kong, which still has its own financial system. Renminbi deposits in Hong Kong have risen from 90 billion in the middle of last year to 510 billion ($78.7 billion) at the end of April, though this still represented only 7 percent of total deposits.[16] These are essential steps if the renminbi is to join the dollar and the euro as an international reserve currency used by foreign investors, which would also require a move away to pegging it to the dollar at an exchange rate that favours exporters.[17] The sheer scale of China's growth is widening the domestic market, and encouraging both local firms and transnationals to fight for market share. But whether changes of this kind will turn the super-tanker of the Chinese export economy round quickly

---

14: Roubini, 2011.
15: Schwartz, 2009, p168.
16: Konyn, 2011.
17: See the analysis, sceptical about the claims that the renminbi is set to replace the dollar as the main reserve currency, in Eichengreen, 2011, pp143-147.

enough to avoid the crunch predicted by Roubini is quite another matter. And if China does suffer even a significant growth recession, where output doesn't fall but the rate of growth does, all bets are off.

Worries about the state of the Chinese economy were one factor in the abrupt sell-off in early May that saw the prices of oil and other commodities fall sharply (though oil rose again a month later after Iran and Venezuela blocked Saudi Arabia's attempt to get the Organisation of Petroleum Exporting Countries to agree to raise output). There is increasing evidence that the global commodities market is now well integrated in the financial markets. A recent study has found that the futures prices of non-energy commodities have tended to rise and fall since the early 2000s in line with the price of oil, something that hadn't been seen since the years of high inflation in the 1970s and early 1980s. Part of the explanation may be the increasing investment (up from $15 billion in 2003 to $200 billion in 2008) in bets on the commodities markets.[18]

Price movements in other words are becoming driven less by changes in supply and demand than by flurries of speculation—something that was already evident in the sharp fall in the oil price as the financial crash gathered pace in the autumn of 2008. The commodities sell-off is therefore a sign that the markets themselves are beginning to get worried.

This situation poses a dilemma for the US Federal Reserve Board and the other leading central banks that now play the main role in managing advanced capitalist economies. The uptick in inflation is putting them under pressure to move away from the ultra-cheap money policies that they embraced in response to the 2008 crash. The ECB has already started to push up interest rates. But an end to cheap money might kill off an already fragile recovery. The Fed's quantitative easing programme (QE2), under which it decided to pump $600bn into the financial system, is due to finish at the end of June. But, given complete gridlock in the US Congress (where Republicans who won control of the House of Representatives thanks to the Tea Party movement are demanding massive spending cuts), the electronic equivalent of printing money may be the only way of propping up the economy if it looks like sliding back into recession. There is growing talk of "QE3". The managers of global capitalism have a very limited set of options.

Britain: intimations of mortality?

Britain is very much part of this broader economic picture. In the first quarter of 2011 even the Greek economy grew faster. Growth in manufacturing,

---

18:   Tang and Xiong, 2011.

which had been stronger than in the rest of the economy because the 25 percent fall in the pound since 2008 has cheapened exports, is slowing down. The combination of spending cuts, wage freezes, tax increases and higher inflation is squeezing living standards brutally. Even the government's tame Office for Budget Responsibility predicts that spending in 2015 will be only 5.4 percent higher than the peak of 2008. The *Financial Times* commented:

> In fact, before the 1970s, you have to go back to the 1900s for a similarly slow improvement in living standards... Before the early 1900s, only the 1840s saw similarly slow spending growth, although figures available for the period are sketchy. A slowdown in international trade and a sharp reduction in overseas demand for British goods, combined with a series of poor harvests, helped to produce a deep recession from 1840-42.[19]

The rationale for the Conservative-Liberal coalition's austerity programme was that the economic slack creating by making sharp cuts in public spending would be taken up by more robust private sector growth. But all the signs are that the private sector is being dragged down by the squeeze in the public sector. By early June the *Observer* was reporting:

> Some of Britain's leading economists are warning the chancellor, George Osborne, that the economy is too fragile to withstand his drastic spending cuts and that he must draw up a plan B.
>
> Experts, including two former Whitehall advisers and two signatories of last year's high-profile letter backing the Tories' cuts, have told the *Observer* that they have profound concerns about the direction of Treasury policy.[20]

Osborne continues to dismiss the necessity of a plan B for stimulus measures if the economy slid back into slump, an idea first mooted by the cabinet secretary, Gus O'Donnell, in December. But the pressure on the government to change course is likely to grow. Its other big area of vulnerability is, of course, the National Health Service, where Andrew Lansley's proposals massively to extend the market have run into huge opposition. The Liberal Democrats have made rolling back these plans the test of their new assertiveness after the massacre they deservedly suffered in the May council elections.

19: Pimlott, 2011.
20: Stewart and Boffey, 2011.

But the Tories' hand within the coalition has been strengthened by the election results. After losing nearly 700 seats, the Lib Dems are in no position to threaten to bring the government down, since they would be massacred in the subsequent general election. Labour was the main beneficiary of the Lib Dem wipeout, ending up narrowly ahead in vote share, with 37 percent to the Tories' 35 percent and just short of a majority in the Welsh Assembly. But the Tories could still take some comfort from the results. Not only were they satisfied, as the most wholehearted opponents of the Alternative Vote, with the crushing victory of the No campaign in the referendum but, as John Curtice points out:

> At roughly 800 seats, Labour's net gains fell short of the target of 1,000 seats that some commentators suggested the party needed to show it really was back on the road to recovery. Part of Labour's problem was that its vote increased most in traditional Labour territory—the north and working class seats with relatively large levels of unemployment—a pattern that reduced the yield its advance produced in terms of seats.
>
> The Conservatives suffered in Scotland too, leaving the party with its worst ever result in Scotland. But in Wales the party enjoyed a modest increase in support and claimed second place in the Assembly from Plaid Cymru. Meanwhile its performance in the local elections was on a par with last year's. For every seat it lost to Labour it seemed to gain one from the Liberal Democrats, leaving the party with a surprise net increase in seats. For a party in government, the Conservatives will doubtless see this as an achievement.[21]

And of course in Scotland, where the polls initially predicted a Labour victory in the elections to Holyrood, instead it suffered a thumping defeat at the hands of the Scottish National Party. The result was a triumph for Alex Salmond's strategy of carefully positioning the SNP slightly to the left of a lacklustre Scottish Labour leadership, and therefore harvesting the strongly social democratic loyalties of the Scottish electorate. But it also underlined that the electoral base of the two big parties remains much weaker than it was in the decades immediately after the Second World War. Because they are less tightly bound to one of these parties, voters are much more volatile. Richard Seymour elsewhere in this journal emphasises the limits of the revival in Tory fortunes under David Cameron. Using Nick Clegg as the fall guy worked this time for the Tories, but it may not work again. A succession

---

21: Curtice, 2011.

of U-turns, over not just the NHS but also, for example, sentencing policy and benefit cuts, has underlined the fragility of the coalition despite the front offered by Cameron and Osborne.

All the same, Labour's less than stellar performance is increasing the pressure on Ed Miliband from the Blairite right. Never really reconciled to his victory in the leadership election last autumn, they continue to repeat the mantra that the only way to beat the coalition is to press on with Blair's agenda of neoliberal "reform". His response, to embrace the "Blue Labour" agenda of Jon Cruddas, Maurice Glasman and others, seems like an alternative way of tacking right, by adopting a Labourist version of Cameron's Big Society emphasis on community, and in the process pandering to the reactionary prejudices that the "Blue Labour" stereotype attributes to white working class people.[22]

This means the developing resistance to austerity can't look to the leadership of the Labour Party for support or direction—though huge numbers of Labour supporters are involved in this resistance. The trade union leaders, by contrast, have been forced to move because of the very direct threat that Osborne's cuts represent to large portions of their base. The giant TUC march on 26 March brought the organised working class onto the streets in unprecedented numbers. The critical question, as ever, remains whether the very broad opposition to austerity can be translated into real collective action in which workers use their economic muscle to block the coalition's offensive.

As Martin Smith shows elsewhere in this journal, the conservatism of the union bureaucracy remains a huge obstacle to such action developing. But the bureaucracy is itself divided and under pressure to act. As we go to press, large numbers of public sector workers are due to go on strike on 30 June, mainly in response to attacks by the government and employers on their pensions. The signs are that the British workers' movement is entering a more turbulent phase.

These developments coincide with a more general uptick in resistance in Europe, with the massive youth protests in Spain and Greece, and, of course, as Anne Alexander's article on Egypt reminds us, the revolutions in the Arab world continue. In Britain the same radicalisation that was expressed in the student protests at the end of last year has been in the efforts at direct action on 26 March and the wave of SlutWalk anti-rape demonstrations.

One striking feature of the Spanish protests was the rejection of political parties and even the trade unions. This no doubt has much to do with the fact—in Spain as elsewhere—that the political elite remains locked into the

---

22: Wintour, 2011. For a critique of "Blue Labour", see Rooksby, 2011.

neoliberal consensus, and with the failure of the union bureaucracy (despite last autumn's general strike) to mount sustained resistance to austerity.

But there is a broader factor at work as well. Recent mass struggles—including the student movement in Britain and the Arab revolutions—have been marked by the relative lack of involvement of substantial political forces (with the important, but complicated, exception of the Muslim Brotherhood in Egypt). The problem here isn't simply the general weakening of political parties, but also the fact that what were the great ideologies of emancipation in the 20th century—socialism (the workers' movement), nationalism (the anti-colonial struggles), liberalism (the revolutions of 1989)—have much less of a hold than they did a generation or two ago. Liberalism has been discredited by the experience of neoliberalism, and in the Middle East by its association with US imperialism; socialism has had to carry the burden of Stalinism and social democracy; and nationalism has been caught up in the failure of so many postcolonial regimes. These experiences are part of the story of the erosion of mass parties in recent decades.

None of these ideologies are in any way dead, and all are capable of revival. But the weakening of their influence means that mass movements tend not to have any clear ideological articulation. This doesn't mean that these movements are purely spontaneous or that no political activists are involved in them. On the contrary, revolutionary socialists, for example, can be proud of the role they have played in struggles as diverse as the British student movement and the 25 January Revolution in Egypt. But, for much wider layers, suspicion of all political organisation and the belief that movements can sustain themselves through their own horizontal networks have become a kind of common sense. This then helps to sustain the kind of illusions in social media so effectively criticised by Jonny Jones in our last issue.[23]

None of this alters the fact that we are experiencing an international renewal of struggle that continues the process of radicalisation beginning with the Seattle protests in November 1999. But revolutionary socialists have to recognise that this radicalisation doesn't automatically lead those affected towards Marxism in the way that tended to happen during its predecessors in the 1930s and the 1960s and early 1970s. We have to fight to make our voices heard. This is no great injury—no one has the right to imagine they are the voice of history, but it is a challenge.

23: Jones, 2011.

References

Atkins, Ralph, 2011, "Eurozone: Frankfurt's Dilemma", *Financial Times* (24 May).

Curtice, John, 2011, "Mixed Messages for Everyone—Except Salmond and Clegg", *Independent* (7 May), www.independent.co.uk/news/uk/politics/john-curtice-mixed-messages-for-everyone-ndash-except-salmond-and-clegg-2280334.html

Davies, Gavyn, 2011, "The Classical View of the Global Recession", 31 May 2011, http://blogs.ft.com/gavyndavies/2011/05/31/the-classical-view-of-the-global-recession/

Duménil, Gérard, and Dominique Lévy, 2011, *The Crisis of Neoliberalism* (Harvard University Press).

Eichengreen, Barry, 2011, Exorbitant Privilege: The Rise and Fall of the Dollar (Oxford University Press).

Harding, Robin, 2011, "US Home Price Double Dip Erases Post-Crisis Gains", *Financial Times* (31 May).

Hope, Kerin, 2011, "Greek Growth Expected to be Short-Lived", *Financial Times* (13 May).

International Monetary Fund, 2011, World Economic Outlook April 2011, http://www.imf.org/external/pubs/ft/weo/2011/01/index.htm

Jackson, Tony, 2011, "Soaring Profit Margins Are Hard to Sustain", *Financial Times* (15 May).

Jones, Jonny, 2011, "Social Media and Social Movements", *International Socialism 130*, www.isj.org.uk/?id=722

Kapner, Suzanne, and James Politi, 2011, "US Housing Glut and Weak Demand Depress Prices", *Financial Times* (1 June).

Lucas, Robert E, 2011, "The US Recession of 2007-201?" (19 May), www.econ.washington.edu/news/millimansl.pdf

Milne, Richard, and Anoushka Sakoui, 2011, "Corporate Finance: Rivers of Riches", *Financial Times*, (22 May 2011).

Pfeifer, Sylvia, 2011, "China Becomes Leading User of Energy", *Financial Times* (8 June).

Pimlott, Daniel, 2011, "Seven Years of Sluggish Growth Forecast", *Financial Times* (31 May).

Rooksby, Ed, 2011, "Don't Underestimate Toxic Blue Labour", *Guardian* (21 May), www.guardian.co.uk/commentisfree/2011/may/21/blue-labour-lord-glasman-conservative-socialism

Roubini, Nouriel, 2011, "China's Bad Growth Bet" (14 April), www.project-syndicate.org/commentary/roubini37/English

Spiegel, Peter, Quentin Peel, and Ralph Atkins, "Greece Set for Severe Bail-Out Conditions", *Financial Times* (29 May).

Schwartz, Herman M, 2009, *Subprime Nation: American Power, Global Capital, and the Housing Bubble* (Cornell University Press).

Stewart, Heather, and Daniel Boffey, 2011, "George Osborne Plan Isn't Working, Say Top UK Economists", *Observer* (4 June), www.guardian.co.uk/politics/2011/jun/04/george-osborne-plan-not-working?INTCMP=SRCH

Tang, Ke, and We Xiong, "Index Investment and Financialisation of Commodities", www.princeton.edu/~wxiong/papers/commodity.pdf

Wagstyl, Stefan, and Jonathan Wheatley, "Global Economy: A High Price to Pay", *Financial Times* (30 May).

Wintour, Patrick, 2011, "Ed Miliband Endorses 'Blue Labour' Thinking", *Guardian* (17 May), www.guardian.co.uk/politics/2011/may/17/ed-miliband-endorses-blue-labour-thinking

Britain's trade unions: the shape of things to come
Martin Smith

> The past has been
> A mint of blood and sorrow—
> That must not be
> True of tomorrow. [1]

From appeasement to coordinated strike action

Langston Hughes wrote the short poem "History" ,just as the US labour movement rose like a phoenix out of the ashes of the devastation of the Great Depression of the 1930s. Today Britain too is in the throes of an assault on the working class and the poor, the like of which we have not seen since the 1930s. Will it end in "blood or sorrow" or will we too see a sweet revenge? The half million strong Trades Union Congress demonstration against the cuts on 26 March 2011 marked a major turning point in that struggle. The process may have been slow, painful and one that is still fragile, but the organised working class has become a central player in the resistance to the government's austerity measures. Mark Serwotka, the general secretary of the PCS, summed up the mood of many when he said, "We have marched for the alternative. Now we have to strike for the

---

1:    Hughes, 2001, p140.

alternative".[2] As I write this article, four major unions are set to strike to defend their pensions on 30 June. If these strikes go ahead, it opens up the possibility of wider and more militant struggles to follow.

But if you cast your mind back to last summer, the picture was far from rosy. The TUC made it clear that it was opposed to an autumn national demonstration against the government's austerity measures, and not only that, it announced that David Cameron had been invited to address the TUC's annual Congress in September. A spokesperson said: "The TUC's general council gave overwhelming support for the invitation to the prime minister to address Congress. This was not to endorse his policies, but to ensure he addresses the concerns of people at work".[3] Many a union leader lined up to make it clear that they too opposed any talk of strikes and mass demonstrations. Derek Simpson, the then joint general secretary of Unite (Britain's biggest union), told the BBC that talk of an "autumn of discontent" would only help the government by deflecting attention away from the spending cuts and their impact. "I don't think that's the nature of the British public," he said. "We don't have the volatile nature of the French or the Greeks".[4] The rejection of a general strike was not confined to the trade union leaders. The national steering committee of the Coalition of Resistance (CoR), one of the national anti-cuts organisations, voted down a motion calling for a general strike. Some officers of CoR claimed it would upset Unite.

But by the time the TUC leaders arrived at their conference in Manchester last September the "volatile nature" of the Greeks and French seemed to have infected the conference delegates. I wrote at the time:

> I first attended a TUC conference in 1986 and have been going to them on and off ever since. Never before have I heard so such fighting talk. Talk of a national demonstration against the cuts and coordinated resistance has buoyed up many trade union activists. A massive protest next year could electrify the trade union movement and become the launch pad for militant action. September's TUC shows that when the trade union bureaucracy gives even the slightest nod in the direction of resistance it can dramatically alter the mood of key sections of the working class.[5]

The reason for this dramatic shift was threefold. Clearly the scale of

---

2:   *Socialist Worker,* 23 April 2011.
3:   *Guardian,* 8 July 2010.
4:   Interviewed by the BBC, 8 August 2010.
5:   Smith, 2010.

the cuts and the refusal of the government to enter meaningful talks gave the union leaders little space to manoeuvre and negotiate compromises. Also union leaders have always felt more comfortable resisting a Tory government than they do a Labour one. Secondly, by early autumn the pressure was building up from below. London firefighters organised very large and militant demonstrations in opposition to the cuts to their services, and joint strikes by rail workers belonging to the RMT and TSSA brought London to a grinding halt in September. Even workers at the BBC voted to take action against job losses. Lastly, during the summer of 2010, major divisions emerged inside the trade union bureaucracy. While union leaders like Simpson and Dave Prentis of Unison rejected out of hand any idea of a national demonstration, let alone strikes, others like Mark Serwotka (PCS) and Bob Crow (RMT) openly called for action. Fear of being outflanked by the smaller unions and of pressure inside their own unions forced the likes of Prentis and Simpson to support both the call for a national demonstration in the spring and the motion calling for coordinated action.

Two other movements outside the sphere of the "official" trade union movement also helped radicalise sections of the working class. First, as the cuts were unveiled a myriad of anti-cuts groups and protests grew up. Individual trade unionists played a key role in many of these. But it was the outburst of student militancy last winter that really showed how fragile the government was. The students smashed the idea that the cuts could not be resisted. Len McCluskey spoke for hundreds of thousands when he told the police at the 26 March demonstration to "keep your sleazy hands off our kids". Most important of all, the student protest destroyed the myth that the government's austerity measures were supported.

During March there were small signs of a growing militancy developing inside the working class. There was Day X, the protest that saw over a thousand student nurses and doctors take to the streets in London against the cuts in the NHS. This unofficial march was clearly inspired by the student protests. Then the University and College Union (UCU) took national strike action over pensions on 24 March 2011, and within days of the 26 March protest teachers in Camden, north London, and teachers and council workers in Tower Hamlets, east London, struck for the day against the cuts. Over 7,000 workers were involved. An interesting feature of the strikes was the spontaneous chanting for a general strike.[6]

The idea of a general strike was, in the run-up to and on the TUC demonstration on 26 March, a popular political slogan. Since then it has

---

6: See the online report at www.socialistworker.co.uk/art.php?id=24397

become a real possibility. Coordinated strikes set for 30 June and the possibility of further and more widespread action in the autumn mean that the working class is slowly nudging towards a major industrial confrontation with the government. It is no exaggeration to say that the trade union movement faces its biggest test since the miners' strike of 1984-5. The defeats of the past two decades and the very low levels of class struggle mean that two factors are going to be critical to the outcome of any future struggles. The first will be the role of the trade union bureaucracy and the second the confidence and organisation of union members and the shop stewards and reps. I want to look first at the strengths and weaknesses of the trade union movement in Britain today.

Figure 1: Trade union membership levels in UK from 1892 to 2009

Source: Labour Force Survey, Office for National Statistics; Department for Employment (1892-1974); Certification Office (1974-2007/08)

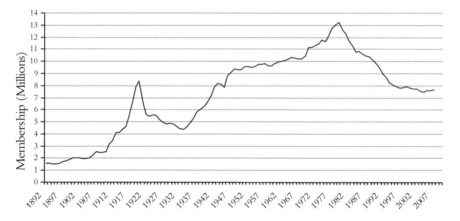

A question of organisation

The first thing that strikes you when you look at figure 1 is the sharp decline in union membership during the 1980s. This is primarily due to two related factors. The first is the high levels of unemployment that stalked the country during most of the 1980s. Unemployment reached its highpoint of 3 million people (12 percent of the working population) in 1983.[7] Industrial sectors like coal, steel and manufacturing were hit particularly hard; these bastions of the trade union movement were decimated. So even when the economy grew again, the growth often took place in sectors with little or no trade

---

7:    See www.statistics.gov.uk/articles/nojournal/Analysis.pdf

union organisation or tradition and therefore many unions did not even maintain their membership, let alone expand. There was one very big exception to this, the public sector, which has seen an expansion and strengthening of trade union organisation.

The second factor is that the working class in Britain suffered a series of major defeats during the 1980s. Although space does not permit me to go through a detailed history of the events that led up to those battles, a very brief outline does help put the movement's strengths and weaknesses in context.

The end of the Second World War ushered in an era of economic expansion and increased profitability in Britain. These favourable economic conditions enabled unions and in particular shop stewards to win increases in wages and improvements in working conditions. The shop stewards were the backbone of this movement. The Communist Party may have been relatively small, but it was politically dominant. By this time the CP had become a loyal Stalinist party, the years of the "revolutionary" shop stewards movement were long gone and these CP militants limited the struggle to the winning of concessions, a "DIY" version of reformism. The Peter Sellers film *I'm All Right Jack*, although mocking these shop stewards, and in particular the CP militant, gives a valuable insight into the shop floor politics of that period.

However, as a series of economic crises hit the world's economies from the late 1960s onwards, the British ruling class was forced to try and cut wages and conditions in order to increase profitability. Both the Labour government of 1964-1970 and the Tory government under Edward Heath of 1970-74 went on the offensive against militant shopfloor organisation. But determined trade union opposition beat both governments. The zenith of this movement was when the Heath government was brought down by waves of strikes. The historian Royden Harrison noted:

> The labour unrest of 1970-74 was far more massive and incomparably more successful than its predecessor of 1910-1914. Millions of workers were involved in campaigns of civil disobedience arising out of the resistance to the government's Industrial Relations Act... Over 200 occupations of factories, offices, workshops and shipyards occurred between 1972 and 1974 alone and many of them attained all or some of their objectives...

> But it was the coal miners, through their victories in the two Februaries of 1972 and 1974 which give a structure, a final roundedness and completeness which the contribution of 1912 had failed to supply to the earlier experience. First they blew the government "off course"; then they landed it on the rocks.

First, they compelled the prime minister to receive them in 10 Downing Street—which he had sworn he would never do—then they forced him to concede more in 24 hours than had been conceded in the last 24 years. Then two years later their 1974 strike led him to introduce the three-day week—a novel system of government by catastrophe—for which he was rewarded with defeat in the General Election. Nothing like this had ever been heard of before![8]

When the Labour government came to office in the spring of 1974 it made a tactical retreat before the workers' movement. It bought off working class discontent and also repealed the Tory anti-union laws. But this came with a price: left wing union leaders like Jack Jones of the Transport and General Workers Union and Hugh Scanlon of the Amalgamated Union of Engineering Workers (two unions which are now amalgamated as Unite) sold the Labour government's incomes policy, the "social contract", to their members. The purpose of the "social contract" was to keep wages low. The Labour government also introduced a series of measures to weaken shop stewards' organisation.

After three years of falling real wages and huge cuts in public expenditure, the dam broke and a series of official strikes labelled by the press as the "Winter of Discontent" rocked the government. But they did not have the same characteristics as the strikes of the early 1970s: they were very bitter and protracted disputes but they did not generalise politically. They were also firmly under the control of national union officials, not the rank and file. By the time of the general election of May 1979 Labour voters were demoralised. This was the political and economic background that enabled Margaret Thatcher and the Tories to come to office.

The primary aim of the Conservative government was to reverse the defeats the ruling class had suffered at the hands of the trade unions in the early 1970s. Unlike Cameron today, Thatcher proceeded cautiously at first, pursuing a strategy—devised by right wing Tory Nicholas Ridley in 1978—of isolating and defeating key groups of workers and slowly introducing anti trade union legislation. The first confrontations were with the steel workers in 1980 and the health workers in 1982. But the key battle took place in 1984-85 when the government and the state took on and beat the miners in a brutal year-long strike. Two more major industrial confrontations followed: the first was with the printers in 1985-86 and then the dockers in 1989. Thatcher won every one of these battles: however, they were all hard

---

8:    Harrison, 1978, pp1-2.

fought and during the miners' strike there were at least two occasions when the government came very close to losing.[9]

Figure 2: Number of stoppages and working days lost

Source: Economic and Labour Market Review, Office for National Statistics, June 2008.

	Working days lost (000s)	Working days lost per thousand employees[1]	Workers involved (000s)	Stoppages[2]	Stoppages involving the loss of 100,000 working days or more
1988	3,702	157	790	781	8
1989	4,128	172	727	701	6
1990	1,903	78	298	630	3
1991	761	32	176	369	1
1992	528	23	148	253	–
1993	649	28	385	211	2
1994	278	12	107	205	–
1995	415	18	174	235	–
1996	1,303	55	364	244	2
1997	235	10	130	216	–
1998	282	11	93	166	–
1999	242	10	141	205	–
2000	499	20	183	212	1
2001	525	20	180	194	1
2002	1,323	51	943	146	2
2003	499	19	151	133	–
2004	905	34	293	130	3
2005	157	6	93	116	–
2006	755	28	713	158	1
2007	1,041	38	745	142	4

1 Based on the September 2007 estimates of employee jobs.
2 Stoppages in progress during year.

As well as weakening the trade union movement, the defeat of some of the best-organised sections of the British working class had other serious knock on effects. Firstly, it severely weakened the confidence of workers to fight. From the late 1980s onwards there has been a sharp fall in the number of officially recorded stoppages. There had been an average of seven million officially recorded strike days per year during the 1970s and early 1980s. As

---

9:    Robertson, 2010.

Figure 2 shows the decline in the number of strikes over the last 20 years is severe and has only topped the million mark three times in that period.

This has been a tme when there has been a relative stalemate between the employers and the trade unions. There have been some important strikes but none have generalised into a wider fight and neither has any group of workers been smashed in the same way as the miners or printers were in the 1980s. This equilibrium is about to change: this government is desperate to ram through its austerity measures and it is just as apparent that a large section of the population are willing to stand up to it.

We shouldn't downplay the defeats of the last two decades, but there are a number of encouraging factors which should give confidence to our side. As Figure 1 clearly shows, over the last ten years the decline in union membership has halted and membership may even be increasing. Obviously if the government were to get away with its attacks it would be catastrophic for the working class. Although the trade union movement is half the size it was in 1979, it is nonetheless bigger than it was during the 1910-14 upsurge in militancy and bigger than at any point between 1926 and 1942.

Figure 3: Trade union density by gender and age bands, 2009
Source: Labour Force Survey, Office of National Statistics

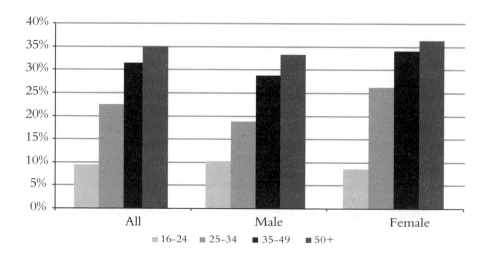

Another problem facing the Cameron government is that Thatcher only half finished the job. She did indeed defeat workers in key sections like mining, docks and steel. However, she left some big battalions relatively intact.

Figure 3 shows that union density levels in the public sector, sections of the service sector like transport and power, and core sections of the manufacturing sector remain relatively high. For instance, almost 75 percent of rail workers belong to a trade union and likewise 67 percent of all civil servants.[10] But even these statistics do not give a complete picture. There are big variations within sectors. Take, for example, Tesco, Britain's biggest employer: membership levels for shop workers are relatively low at 26 percent, but among warehouse workers levels reach 78 percent and among drivers 75 percent.[11]

The problem for the government is that if its austerity measures are going to succeed then it is going to have to defeat some of these core groups or persuade their leaders to hold down struggle. This is not going to be an easy task, as one journalist on the *Economist* noted: "Public-sector unions enjoy advantages that their private-sector rivals only dream of. As providers of vital monopoly services, they can close down entire cities. And as powerful political machines, they can help to pick the people who sit on the other side of the bargaining table".[12]

The government's strategy of massive cuts in wages, pensions and public services is certainly bold, but it may not be wise. As I stated above, the strategy being deployed by Cameron is in stark contrast to that adopted by Thatcher. Back in the 1980s the Tory government was very careful and only fought one group at a time; it never bit off more than it could chew. This time Cameron is taking on everyone at the same time. If he fails it will be the biggest defeat the ruling class has suffered since 1974, but if he is successful he will have inflicted a huge defeat on the working class.

Statistics that look at the number of strikes, membership levels and density of membership are an important tool, but they present a static and two-dimensional view of what is going on. Previously I wrote in this journal:

> Any debate about the nature of class struggle today in Britain has not only to discuss the economic situation but also look at the political and ideological dimensions of the struggle. There are many on the left who argue that an industrial upturn will come about out of a slow rising tide of trade union militancy. Industrial relations academics in Britain often cite the development of trade unions in car plants from the mid-1950s until the mid-1970s as an example of this. Of course this is one model of how an upturn has taken place, and of course this could happen again. But most industrial upturns have not

10: PCS, 2011.
11: USDAW, 2010.
12: *Economist*, 6 January 2011.

developed this way. For example the upswing of class struggle in Britain in 1889 and 1910, the sit-down strikes in the US in 1934-36, the May events in France in 1968 and the Italian hot summer of 1969 were a product of sudden explosions of anger.[13]

We have seen sudden and unpredicted explosions of anger in Britain over the last few months. The student protests are an obvious example of this and also the TUC's demonstration shows there are a large number of people who want to resist the government's cuts. But it is not all onwards and upwards: as well as anger, there is a great deal of fear inside the working class—people are scared of losing their jobs; they are apprehensive about being able to pay the mortgage or debts. Although this is hard to quantify, it does explain how the Scottish teachers' union, the EIS, can sell a wage cut to its conference delegates, or the reason why tens of thousands of workers are bullied by management into taking "voluntary redundancy" when there is little prospect of finding another job. The relationship between fear and anger is not a static one. Subjective factors like strong union organisation, reps urging a fight, anti-cuts groups campaigning to save a local community service can tip the balance away from fear and towards anger and action. Given the obvious weaknesses inside the trade union movement and the fact that workers generally lack confidence to fight, the trade union bureaucracy can be a critical factor in any possible fightback.

The trade union bureaucracy

Britain's trade unions have been in existence for over 120 years now. In all that time we have never had just one "big union" representing all workers. As it says on the tin, they are *trade* unions and therefore reflect the divisions imposed on them by the capitalist system. Because British capitalism is constantly evolving the unions mirror those changes.

If you were to look at the British trade union movement in 1933 there were just over 300 trade unions affiliated to the TUC and most were numerically smaller than many unions today. So the biggest union in the country in 1933 was the Miners Federation, which had half a million members, and the tenth biggest was the wood workers' union, which had 97,000 members.[14] In 1963 there were 183 TUC affiliated unions. The picture is now very different: by 1995 the TUC had 70 affiliated unions and today it has 58. The two biggest, Unite and Unison, have

---

13:   Smith, 2005, p113.
14:   Clegg, 1987, p570.

over 1.5 million members each and the third biggest, the GMB, has over 650,000 members.[15] Unison was formed in 1993 and Unite was created in 2007. These so-called "super unions" are a product of merger and not mass recruitment drives.

The rise of the "super unions" has not solved the question of retention and growth. Unite was launched in 2007 and it claimed it had over 2 million members. Now the union's website claims 1.5 million members, a fall of half a million. But the truth is it is even worse than that publicised. Unite has just produced a recruitment strategy document for its full-time officers. It makes depressing reading, and acknowledges that its membership now stands at 1,182,000 members, a fall of nearly 1 million.

Figure 4: Unite membership decline 2007-2010

Source: Unite union

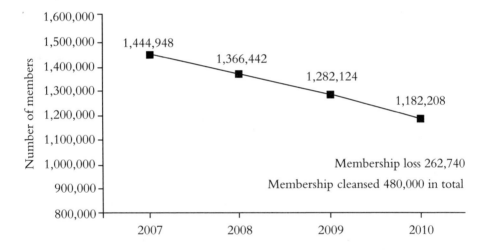

The problem with mergers is that, while they temporarily halt any decline in membership, they do not address the fundamental problems of union decline and do defer any mass recruitment campaigns. If history has taught us anything it has shown that unions expand in struggle and when they can prove they can win real improvements for workers. If a mass strike

15: www.tuc.org.uk/tuc/unions_main.cfm—as seen in Figure 4, Unite's membership actually stands at just under 1.2 million, but for consistency I have used the TUC's own figures in all cases.

movement emerges, I believe unions will see workers flock to join their ranks. In the run-up to the Tower Hamlets NUT strike, over 140 people joined the union, an increase of 10 percent in the membership. Again if we look to the past there is a strong case to be made that high levels of nation-wide strike activity brought with them rapid and powerful shop stewards movements in Britain, most notably between 1910-1920, 1935-1939 and 1968-1974. The growth of these large unions mirrors the restructuring of British capitalism which has seen the development of large national and global corporations and expansion of the public sector. Bureaucrats have followed a conscious policy of mergers in order to survive

The growth of the large public sector unions demonstrates the changing nature of work in Britain. Up until 40 years ago large professional associations in teaching and local government considered themselves to be superior to unions— they represented workers most of whom felt they were a cut above manual workers. However, as teachers' and local government workers' status, pay and conditions were undermined, their associations made the transformation from professional bodies to trade unions and affiliated to the TUC—the National Association of Local Government Officers (now part of Unison) in 1964 and the National Union of Teachers (NUT) in 1970.

Sadly many trade union leaders ape their rivals in other ways. I heard one left wing union leader make a throwaway comment that he was "the CEO" of the union. Figure 5 shows the annual salaries and benefits given to eight of Britain's union general secretaries and demonstrates how that off the cuff comment could be made. It is a graphic reflection of how far removed their lifestyle is from their members. The truth is all trade union officials who are working full time for the union are subjected to conservative pressures built into the union machine. A very well paid job, free from the daily grind of work, can be enough to subdue the instincts of the best militants.

The existence of a trade union bureaucracy, a social layer made up of full-time officials with material interests in confining the class struggle to the search for reforms within a capitalist framework, is not a new phenomenon. At the end of the 19th century Sidney and Beatrice Webb wrote a book charting the formation of a trade union bureaucracy. They noted, "During these years we watch a shifting of the leadership in the trade union world from the casual enthusiast and irresponsible agitator to a class of salaried officers expressly chosen out of the rank and file of trade unionists for their superior business capacity".[16]

16: Sydney and Beatrice Webb, 1919, p577-578

Figure 5: Annual salary and benefits of trade union secretaries 2009-2010

Source: Certification Office for trade unions and employers association[17]

Union	Salary	Benefits
CWU	£87,045	£1,393
GMB	£84,000	£28,000
NUT	£111,431	£22,400
PCS	£85,421	£27,213
RMT	£84,923	£28,088
Unison	£94,953	£35,156
Unite	£97,027	£89,599
UCU	£97,592	£15,827

Tony Cliff described the trade union bureaucracy as:

a distinct, basically conservative formation. Like the god Janus it presents two faces: it balances between the employers and the workers. It holds back and controls workers' struggles, but it has a vital interest not to push the collaboration with the employers to a point where it makes the unions completely impotent. For the official is not an independent arbitrator. If the union fails entirely to articulate members' grievances this will lead eventually either to effective internal challenges to the leadership, or to membership apathy and organisational disintegration, with members moving to a rival union. If the bureaucracy strays too far into the bourgeois camp it will lose its base. The bureaucracy has an interest in preserving the union organisation which is the source of their income and status.[18]

17: Certification Office for trade unions and employers association, Annual Report of the Certification Officer, 2009-2010, p66.
18: Cliff and Gluckstein, 1986, p27.

Put simply, the trade union bureaucracy balances between the two main classes in capitalist society—the employers and the workers. Precisely because union leaders' power comes from their ability to defend members' interests even the most right wing general secretary can be forced to call or support strike action. We have two very interesting examples of this at the moment. The Association of Teachers and Lecturers union is currently balloting its members to strike on 30 June. Traditionally it has been on the right of the trade union movement and last went on strike in 1979.[19] Likewise delegates at the Royal College of Nursing conference this year voted to take strike action if their pay was cut, even though the RCN has more in common with a professional association than a trade union.

Two other factors keep the trade union leaders in check. One is the union's machine—the headquarters, finances and organisation, of which Rosa Luxemburg wrote:

> There is first of all the overvaluation of the organisation, which from a means has gradually been changed into an end in itself, a precious thing, to which the interests of the struggles should be subordinated. From this also comes that openly admitted need for peace which shrinks from great risks and presumed dangers to the stability of the trade unions, and further, the overvaluation of the trade union method of struggle itself, its prospects and its successes.[20]

The same point was put to me rather more succinctly by a full-time official for the predecessor to PCS during an unofficial strike I was involved in at the Passport Office. She told us to "get back to work—we are not going to sacrifice the union for you lot!" That was 1986, and the fear of the bosses using the anti trade union laws has increased tenfold since then. The legislation strikes at the trade union leaders' Achilles heel. The fear that the courts will impose a heavy fine on the union if it fails to curb unofficial disputes has seen the unions shy away from leading the kind of militant fights that can win. An article published in the *Guardian* in 2010 noted that over the last five years there were "36 applications for injunction to the

---

19:   Mary Bousted is the general secretary of the ATL. Over 30 percent of her members work in private schools and by any criterion they are a conservative section. But even among these workers the anger is palpable. To get a flavour of the mood of the ATL conference and a taste of how a trade union bureaucracy can move to the left you can read her speech at the ATL website—www.atl.org.uk

20:   Luxemburg, 1970, pp214-215

high court to block strikes (almost all were successful), all bar seven against planned strikes in transport, the prison service or Post Office".[21]

The final conservative pressure on the union leaders is the link between the trade unions and the Labour Party. One feature of advanced capitalist economies is an apparently sharp division between politics and economics. To put it crudely, trade union leaders and the majority of members believe unions deal with economic issues like wages and conditions and the Labour Party deals with winning reforms through parliament. This blunts the struggle and reinforces the idea that negotiation and reform are the only avenues open to workers.

Some claim that Labour's link to the trade union movement is weakening. Two relatively small unions left the Labour Party in 2004. The RMT was expelled after deciding to allow branches to affiliate to organisations to the left of Labour, and the FBU voted to disaffiliate due to the betrayals of the Labour government during their 2002-03 dispute. But the latest figures published by the electoral commission show that Labour is still very much financially dependent on the trade unions. In quarter four of 2010 the party received £2,545,611 in donations (excluding public funds or "Short money"), £2,231,741.90 or 88 percent of which came from the unions, compared to 36 percent in the final quarter of 2009. Private donations have all but collapsed since Ed Miliband became leader, with just £39,286 raised from individual donations to Constituency Labour Parties. In total the unions were responsible for 62 percent of all Labour funding last year (up from 60 percent in 2009), with one union, Unite, providing nearly a quarter (23 percent) of all donations. Back in 1994, when Tony Blair became Labour leader, trade unions accounted for just a third of the party's annual income.[22]

Time and time again we have seen union leaders subordinate their members' interests to those of the Labour Party. This was patently clear during the Brown/Blair years in government, but the impulse is just as strong now Labour is in opposition. In the run-up to the TUC demonstration leaders of the GMB and USDAW (the shop workers' union) made it clear that the goal of the demonstration was to help get Labour re-elected and that any strike action that took place before the council elections on 5 May 2011 would damage Labour's electoral challenge in those elections. The lack of class confidence strengthens the hand of those who say wait for Labour.

As the possibility of large-scale strikes against the government's cuts

---

21: *Guardian*, 2 April 2010.
22: Electoral Reform Commission, 2011.

are being put on the political agenda, the division between left union leaders and right union leaders can play an important role in events.

Left v right

In 1998 a relatively unknown train driver from Leeds, Mick Rix, won the general secretary election in the train drivers' union Aslef. Within the space of five years the left won general secretary election after general secretary election. Bob Crow (RMT), Mark Serwotka (PCS), Billy Hayes (CWU), Andy Gilchrist (FBU), Tony Woodley (TGWU) and Jeremy Dear (NUJ) were collectively known as the Awkward Squad.[23] The rout of the right was complete when Ken Jackson, the head of Blair's favourite union Amicus (now part of Unite), lost to a relatively unknown regional officer, Derek Simpson, in 2002. John Edmonds, the former GMB leader, was not exaggerating when he said, "No Blairite can a win a trade union election".[24]

The election of these left wing officials and in a few cases activists from the rank and file represented a desire for change. I wrote at the time: "The Awkward Squad's enthusiasm for political movements like the Stop the War Coalition and the anti-capitalist movement, and its rejection of partnership with the bosses, were and continue to be a breath of fresh air for the trade union movement".[25] But international questions and political movements that take place "outside the trade union orbit" have always been the line of least resistance for the leaders and have been used as a safety valve for the anger of the members.

It was Andy Gilchrist, the leader of the FBU, who famously said: "It's a well known secret that many of us meet up to discuss. We'll support each other on specific issues and follow each other's lead".[26] Well, that was true up to a point; the problem was that this cooperation was confined to a fight within the union structures, to motion mongering at the TUC and, for those affiliated, Labour Party conference. Even in this environment it was a case of the left being pulled by the right.

The clearest example of this took place at the Labour Party conference in Bournmouth in 2003. That was the year Blair ordered the invasion of Iraq. All of the Awkward Squad opposed the war and it should have been the

---

23: The order of the election victories follows, Mick Rix 1998, Andy Gilchrist 2000, Mark Serwotka 2000, Billy Hayes 2001, Jeremy Dear 2001, Bob Crow 2002, Derek Simpson 2002 and Tony Woodley 2003. Paul Mackney, who was also one of those involved in the informal grouping, became Natfhe (now part of UCU) general secretary in 1996.
24: *Telegraph*, 7 September 2002
25: Smith, 2003, p2.
26: Vallely, 2002.

conference at which Blair was brought to task. But he wasn't—the motion opposing the Iraq war was pulled through lack of support. How could that happen? Derek Simpson and Amicus persuaded the other big unions, the GMB, TGWU and Unison, to unify around a motion on foundation hospitals and pull their support for a motion opposing Iraq. Blair was let off the hook and the most right wing elements of the Awkward Squad set the agenda. When Billy Hayes of the CWU spoke at a fringe meeting later in the week, his excuse was feeble to say the least: "We have to start to set priorities. We have to remember it took the Blairites ten years to take over this party; we have to be patient on what we can achieve".[27]

Members of the Awkward Squad have been involved in a number of key disputes over the past 11 years—the firefighters' dispute of 2002-3,[28] the national post dispute of 2007, the public sector pay revolt of 2008 and the BA cabin crew strike of 2010-11.[29] They have all been discussed in previous editions of this journal and its sister publications. Without repeating what has been written, in all cases the trade union leaders failed to promote the kind of action needed to win and as a group they shied away from encouraging solidarity action. However, another less pronounced feature of the last decade has been a small number of unofficial disputes—post workers (2003), BA check-in workers (2003), Shell tanker drivers (2008), the second wildcat strike by construction workers at the Lindsey oil refinery (2009) and the Visteon occupation (2009). The tactics deployed were in stark contrast to the official strikes mentioned earlier: they were militant, unofficial and with the exception of Visteon they all involved other workers taking secondary action.

The left in one form or another has won just about every major general secretary election since 1998 (Usdaw is the exception to this rule). It is an indicator that members want leaders who will stand up for their interests. Even when Rix lost the Aslef general secretary election to a right wing populist, Shaun Brady, in 2003, the status quo was soon restored when Brady was removed a year later and replaced by Keith Norman, a mainstream Aslef official and Labour Party member.[30] This trend continues. Last year left wing official Len McCluskey, won the Unite general secretary elections and Jerry Hicks, a lay member and someone who would be regarded as part of the hard left, came second with 52,000 votes.

The left's victories are not just confined to general secretary elections.

27: *Guardian*, 3 October 2003.
28: Smith, 2003, pp13-15.
29: Kimber, 2009, pp46-55.
30: If you are so inclined you can read a blow by blow account of the Rix/Brady battle at www.labournet.net/ukunion/0408/aslef21.html

The hard left has won a large number of national executive seats in unions like the PCS, NUT, RMT, UCU and Unite. In the NUT, PCS and UCU these activists have played a pivotal role in getting the 30 June action off the ground and in the case of the UCU, the national strikes in the lead up to 26 March.

Sharp divisions are once again opening up inside the TUC. The sheer scale of the government assault on trade unions has opened up debates among the leaders of the unions. A small group of unions, ATL, NUT, PCS and the UCU, are pushing for strikes against the cuts in pensions now. Others like Unite and Unison say they will be ready to fight in the autumn. Behind the scenes Paul Kenny of the GMB and Dave Prentis of Unison are complaining that the smaller unions are trying to bounce them into taking action. Socialists should not be neutral in this fight. When a section of the bureaucracy want to fight it makes it easier to win action and, importantly for activists in the unions where their leaders are shying away from action, it makes it easier to point the finger and say, "If that union can fight, why can't we?"

At the same time it is important not to sow illusions in left wing officials. A J Cook is a name to evoke powerful memories. He is remembered as the man who led the miners during their bitter struggles in the 1920s. He is regarded by many as the most left wing leader Britain has ever had. The Russian revolutionary Leon Trotsky wrote a series of brilliant polemics about Britain in the run-up to the General Strike of May 1926. He made absolutely no concessions to any of the left union leaders—even Cook. For example, Trotsky wrote:

> Both the right and the left, including of course both Purcell and Cook, fear to the utmost the beginning of the denouement. Even when they in words admit the inevitability of struggle and revolution, they are hoping in their hearts for some miracle that will release them from these perspectives. And in any event they will stall, evade, temporise, shift responsibility and effectively assist Thomas [the right wing leader of the rail workers] over the really major question of the British labour movement. [31]

Trotsky was absolutely right. Cook was a prisoner of the trade union bureaucracy. He was a tireless fighter for the miners' cause, but that alone was not enough. When it became clear that the other union leaders were going to leave the miners to fight alone, Cook was never willing to go over the head of the TUC and call on workers to defy their own leaders' treacherous behaviour. He was trapped in his own bureaucratic straitjacket .

31: Trotsky, 1973, p167.

On a much lower scale, but much more recently, we have seen the same kind of pressures applied to the left union leaders over the last nine months. It was obvious during the summer of 2010 that the TUC was not going to call a demonstration in the autumn. A number of unions began to discuss the idea of holding an autumn demonstration if the TUC failed to organise one. This was absolutely the right response, but the demonstration never materialised. As soon as one leader got cold feet and withdrew support for the demonstration, the others pulled out one by one. In other words, rather than the left pulling the right towards resistance, the opposite occurred. A similar situation occurred earlier this year when some unions tried to set a date for coordinated action around the time of the 26 March TUC demonstration. If hundreds of thousands had gone on strike in the run-up to the demonstration, it would have electrified the trade union movement, but again, with the exception of the UCU, no other union took action. Indecisiveness ruled the day—union officials in the PCS told me that the UCU strike was not "big enough", while NUT officials said they needed to wait for another teaching union to commit to action before they called a strike ballot. The UCU was different because revolutionary socialists on the NEC pushed the bureaucracy to call the action.[32]

There is no better guide to how socialists should relate to the trade union bureaucracy than the statement put forward by the Clyde Workers' Committee in November 1915:

> We will support the officials just so long as they rightly represent the workers, but we will act independently immediately they misrepresent them. Being composed of delegates from every shop and untrammelled by obsolete rule or law, we claim to represent the true feelings of the workers. We can act immediately according to the merits of the case and the desire of the rank and file.[33]

Leon Trotsky put it even more succinctly when he wrote: "With the masses—always; with the vacillating union leaders—sometimes but only as long as they stand at the head of the masses. It is necessary to make use of the vacillating leaders while the masses are pushing them ahead, without for a moment abandoning criticism of those leaders".[34]

32: The discussions about an alternative demonstration or coordinated strikes in March have only been covered in *Socialist Worker* (23 April 2011) and *Socialist Review* (April 2011). I have spoken to officials in both the PCS and NUT who have confirmed the events I have outlined.
33: Hinton, 1973, p296.
34: Trotsky, 1973, p172.

The last sentence is of particular importance today for socialists. Right now Britain's union leaders are being forced to fight. When those leaders are pushing a fight we should support them and work with them. This is a doubly important point at this critical stage in the struggle against the government's austerity measures. There would have been no mass demonstration of half a million against the cuts unless the TUC had called it; in that situation it was right for socialists to build the demonstration. Secondly there is no possibility of getting 800,000 workers to strike against the cuts independently right now. The fact that a section of the bureaucracy has called action makes it possible. In this situation socialists should support those leaders who want to fight and criticise those that don't. But that cannot be all: socialists have to push the action to the next level and be prepared to challenge those leaders who are not prepared to go further. Historically, Britain's shop stewards/union reps have played a critical role in struggles. Are they still a force to be reckoned with? Have they been incorporated into the union machine? These are going to be crucial questions in the time ahead.

Union reps: the backbone of the trade union movement

Shop stewards and union reps have played a distinctive role in the British trade union movement. On a local level they hold union organisation together and lead almost every local dispute. They are also the key link between the national union officials and the members. Shop stewards played a pivotal role in a number of important disputes in the last century. In 1919 they led strikes that brought Britain to the brink of revolution and in 1974 the disputes they organised brought the Tory government crashing down. The shop stewards movement has become synonymous with the idea of trade union militancy.

However, there has been a severe weakening of union organisation over the last 35 years. This is reflected in the declining number of shop stewards/union reps, the fact that in many workplaces their bargaining powers have been seriously reduced and that there has be a concerted attempt by both management and union officials to bureaucratise these activists. Any serious assessment of shop stewards and union reps organisation needs to look at both its weaknesses and its strengths.[35]

The decline of union reps over the last 25 years is worrying, but it is explainable. In 1970 there were around 200,000 stewards in Britain; by 1984

35: For this section I have borrowed very heavily from Ralph Darlington's excellent article—Darlington, 2010, pp126-134.

they had reached the 335,000 mark. This dramatic increase was due to the rising levels of militancy and the growth of trade unionism in the white-collar sectors—local government, civil service and health.[36] There then followed a sharp fall in union membership and an even bigger fall in the number of shop stewards. As Ralph Darlington points out, recent estimates vary considerably: some believe that the number of stewards in 2004 was around 100,000,[37] others as high as 200,000.[38] Whatever the truth, it is a serious decline and one rooted in the defeat of key sections of the working class in the 1980s and the decline in industries with strong union representation.

Figure 6: Number of trade union lay representatives 1980-2004
Source: Charlwood and Forth, 2008, p6

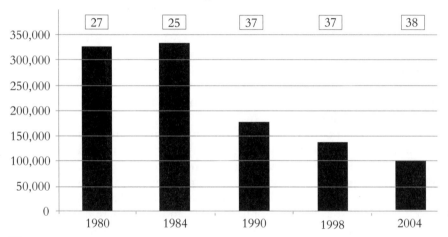

■ Number of shop stewards of recognised unions
☐ Number of members per steward

The picture is uneven: in the public sector 67 percent of employees work in a workplace with an on-site union rep, whereas in the private sector it is only 17 percent.[39] Even within unions there are wide variations. Take for example, the PCS, one of Britain's better-organised unions—it has an average

---

36: Charlwood and Forth, 2008, pp3-4.
37: Darlington, 2010, p127.
38: BERR, 2009, p2.
39: DTI, 2007

union rep to member ratio of one rep to every 26 members. However, in some sections like aviation it is as high as one in ten and in others like Siemens it is as low as one in 49.[40] Statistics alone don't really tell you how active the stewards are. Frustratingly, there are no major studies in this area and so a few anecdotes will have to do. During the early part of the year I was involved in building support for the Tower Hamlets Unison strike. The branch has 3,500 members and delivered a very solid strike on 30 March 2011. The branch secretary and assistant branch secretary told me that on average around 25 stewards attend their monthly meeting. They believed that in an ideal world they needed three times that number. Likewise when I was the branch secretary in the London Passport Office in the early to mid-1980s, on average 16 reps attended branch committee meetings. Today it is half that, though the union now incorporates even more workers because the union is open to higher and lower grades.

Passivity is one problem and obviously management offences against trade unions are another. But management are deploying the carrot as well. Alex Callincos wrote: "While capitalist democracy permits the development of working class organisation (not simply trade unions but also the parties linked to the unions, like Labour in Britain), it also seeks to contain those organisations".[41]

In the wake of the Donovan Commission's recommendations (Royal Commission on Trade Unions 1968), employers encouraged a massive expansion in the number of stewards on full-time release. Today it is estimated that 13 percent of all stewards are on full-time facility duties. Ralph Darlington believes that it could involve between 16,000 and 18,000 union reps.[42] In the most extreme case I have found, in Usdaw there has been a 28 percent decrease in shop stewards since 1997, but a 50 percent increase in the number of reps on full-time facility time.

This significant increase in full-time facility time for stewards has led to what some industrial studies experts call "steward bureaucratisation". This is a situation where management are granting convenors/branch secretaries 100 percent facility time to cover large workplaces, often across many sites. Instead of bargaining over wages and conditions (which has in most cases been handed over to national officials) more and more of their time is spent dealing with grievances and disciplinary cases. The effect of this is to remove them further and further away from the shop floor or office. If activists are not

40: PCS, 2011
41: Callinicos, 1995, p15.
42: Darlington, 2010, p128.

careful a gulf can arise between themselves and the members they represent. This is not just confined to stewards on full-time facility time as Waddington and Kerr have noted:

> The severe weakening of workplace union organisation today compared with the past has been reflected in the way that many stewards/reps, whether full-time or otherwise, spend less time than previously on collective bargaining issues such as wages and conditions and more time on representing individual members in relation to welfare work, grievances and disciplinary cases. Even though many stewards have undoubtedly displayed an extraordinary level of commitment to holding together workplace union organisation (spending on average 6.3 hours a week on union duties), some of them have also, as a result of often feeling beleaguered and defensive in relation to employers, become fairly cynical towards their members, reflected in an unwillingness to make attempts to mobilise them into taking action. The seeming paralysis of the shop stewards' network within the car industry—where representation is firmly based in companies such as Vauxhall, Land Rover, Jaguar, Toyota, Nissan and Honda—and an inability to resist wage freezes, lay-offs and redundancies during the current economic recession has underlined the atrophy of organisation. Meanwhile, one of the weaknesses of union organising campaigns in recent years, given the characteristic lack of integration with bargaining agendas, has been the limited extent to which some lay union reps have been involved, with the most bureaucratised reps effectively operating as a barrier to union recruitment and renewal initiatives in some contexts.[43]

This is not a reason to resist becoming a workplace rep or even a branch officer—precisely the opposite. The union movement needs more activists—abstaining will not strengthen the movement. But activists have to be aware of the dangers; they have to be accountable to the members, fight the pressures that turn them into another "hack", and encourage strikes. At all times socialists who are reps should put the interests of the rank and file before the needs of the boss or for that matter the union machine. As for the taking of positions with 100 percent facility time, two basic rules should be applied: first, activists should only stand if they have a base and, secondly, why not share the facility time with another activist? There is nothing like working on the shop floor or in the office to keep your feet on the ground.

But it is important not to exaggerate the moves towards "stewards bureaucratisation". The vast majority of stewards and union reps have held

---

43: Waddington and Kerr, 2009, pp27-54.

union organisation together through very difficult times and the fact remains that one in ten union reps get no paid time off at all to carry out their duties.[44] Also, while it is true that in many industries there has been a centralisation of union power, in other sectors, for example in further education, the civil service and on London Underground, recruitment strategies have been adopted which have encouraged the rebuilding of stewards' organisation and the decentralisation of negotiating powers.

Yes, today's stewards/branch reps are too male, pale and stale. But if they are going to revive they need an injection of younger activists. History has taught us that unions and union organisation have grown out of victorious struggles, particularly where struggle has been accompanied by a political strategy to develop such organisation. If you go back to Figure 1 you can see that the revival of union membership coincides with periods of high levels of class struggle: 1910-26, 1936-38 and 1968-84. Conversely, membership and union organisation have tended to fall after major defeats—1926 and 1985 are two obvious cases in point. What are the prospects for such a revival today and what should socialists be arguing?

Where next?

When Bob Dylan's album *The Times they are a-Changin* was released in 1964, it captured the spirit of social and political upheaval that characterised much of that decade. If the album had been recorded today it would be just as relevant. Across the Middle East workers, students and the poor have driven out tyrants like Hosni Mubarak in Egypt and **Zine El Abidine** Ben Ali in Tunisia. The revolt is not confined to North Africa and the Middle East. The spread of austerity across Europe in 2010 has brought with it general strikes in Greece, France, Spain and Portugal, and the explosive emergence of a mass movement in Wisconsin. Not even China is immune: in April 2011 three days of strikes and protests by Shanghai truckers over rising fuel prices shocked the Chinese government, provoking new fears that social discontent over inflation will ignite broader movements of the working class.

Britain is part of this process: last year's student revolt is evidence of this. But the resistance is now taking a different form—it is moving away from the street and into the workplace, where workers wield power as an organised force. Just like in the 1980s we face a nasty government, but unlike then it is a weak and increasingly divided government. Unlike Thatcher who picked off one group of workers at a time, Cameron is

---

44: TUC, 2007.

taking everyone on at the same time—even many on his own side think this is a dangerous strategy.

We have to see the economic crisis as a process, not an event. It will be the dominant factor shaping British and world politics for years to come. In Britain over the coming months the possibility of large groups of workers striking together is going to be discussed in workplace after workplace. It is imperative that activists push as hard as they can to make the demand for coordinated action a reality. If the 30 June strikes take place there will be further pressure on the "big battalions" of Unison, Unite and the GMB to join any future action. From this kind of development you can see how a general strike could develop and therefore why it is important to raise it as a demand.

As I write this article Dave Prentis has told the press, "Unless the government changes direction it is heading for industrial action on a massive scale".[45] Fine words indeed, but we have a responsibility to turn them into action. In concrete terms, that means every trade unionist should be building support for the idea of mass strikes against the cuts in their workplaces. In unions where the leadership is trying to stall any joint action, we need to exert as much pressure on them as possible. But we also have to acknowledge another problem: the gap between the political anger in Britain and the level of class struggle is large. There is a real need right now to bridge the gap between the anti-cuts campaigns and students and the organised working class. This cross-fertilisation will strengthen the entire working class movement.

Individuals matter—they can make a real difference to the outcome of any fight. National coordinated action is one route that may be taken in the struggle to defeat the government's austerity programmes. But there is also a realistic chance that branch and local disputes may set the pace or run parallel with national action. The nature of the assaults means that there is a local dynamic to the fight. In recent months there have been a number of strikes in local Unison and NUT branches and sections of the civil service. In all of these examples socialists have led the disputes. Every demonstration, every stunt and every community action must be supported and encouraged.

This means that socialists have to raise the big political questions like the call for a general strike and united strike action, but at the same time serious attention to detail has to be applied. Every steward should be recruiting to the union—in particular women, black and young people

---

45: *Telegraph*, 2 May 2011.

should be encouraged to become shop stewards/union reps. At the Tower Hamlets strikers' rally it was encouraging to see the branch officials calling for a general strike, but it was just as impressive to see them afterwards behind a table encouraging strikers to become union reps. We have to ensure over the coming months that we build support for the fight from the bottom up. There is a mood for coordinated action, but that doesn't mean it will happen. The union leaders' record is not a good one, the history of the British trade union movement has been one of shoddy compromise and sell out. Today it is no secret that many are nervous about the proposed strikes.

Historically, rank and file organisations have been launched in an attempt to overcome the conservative nature of the trade union bureaucracy. The most famous examples of these movements in Britain developed primarily on the Clyde and in Sheffield among engineers during the First World War, on the buses and in the aircraft building industries during the 1930s and in the mines during the early 1970s.[46] This type of organisation also arose in Italy during the "Red Years" of 1918–1920 and the US in the 1930s.

Rank and file organisations develop during high levels of class struggle and more often than not along workplace lines. But their key feature is that although they often exist within official union structures, because they arise from and are a direct expression of the will of the shop floor, they are militant and soon come into conflict with the trade union bureaucracy. But as the Clyde Workers' Committee's first leaflet made clear, they are both prepared to work with the unions, but also to act independently if the union leaders fail them.

I do not believe the creation of a national rank and file movement is possible right now, but, as history teaches us, the situation can change rapidly. The weakness of shop floor organisation, the dominance of the trade union leaders and the lack of confidence of the rank and file to fight make the building of such a movement impossible at the moment.

The terrible record of the trade union leaders does not mean socialists should refuse to have anything to do with them—right now those leaders urging a fight are helping to strengthen the movement. That means we will have to build a working relationship with those officials who want to fight as a means of getting a mass movement off the ground. But we must learn from history: tailing these leaders will not do. We have to ensure that we pull in the direction of strengthening the rank and file and not

---

46: Fishman, 1995, provides a very useful analysis of the development of rank and file groups on London buses and in the aviation industry,

subordinating the struggle to the official machine. When debating with British Communists in the run-up to the 1926 General Strike, Trotsky cited Lenin: "Lenin allowed the possibility of a temporary bloc even with opportunistic leaders under the condition that there would be a sharp and audacious turn and a break based on actions of the masses when these leaders began to pull back, oppose or betray".[47]

The last task is in some ways the most important. Socialists have always been at the heart of any revival of working class militancy. Eleanor Marx and Ben Tillett played a central role in the great unrest of 1889, which led to the formation of mass general unions in Britain. Revolutionary socialists like Willie Gallagher and J T Murphy were central to the first shop stewards movement on the Clyde and in Sheffield, and the Communist Party helped to organise the revival of the trade unions in the 1930s. Today socialists have to throw themselves into the developing struggles. The wave of strikes which engulfed Britain in 1889 were predicted by no one and led by unorganised workers. The following year a massive May Day demonstration was held in London, Frederick Engels, Marx's lifelong collaborator, was there and wrote: "The English working class, rousing itself from 40 years of winter sleep, rejoined the movement of its class".[48]

Maybe, just maybe, this sleeping giant is awakening again.

47: Trotsky, 1973, page 256.
48: www.marxists.org/archive/marx/works/1890/05/23.htm

References

Achur, James, 2009, *Trade Union Membership 2009* (Office for National Statistics).

BERR, 2009, *Reps in Action: How Workplaces Can Gain From Modern Union Representation*, (Department for Business Enterprise and Regulatory Reform).

Callinicos, Alex, 1995, *Socialists in the Trade Unions* (Bookmarks).

Charlwood, Andy, and John Forth, 2008, "Workplace Employee Representations 1980-2004", NIESR discussion paper, www.niesr.ac.uk/pdf/240708_152852.pdf

Clegg H A, 1979, *The Changing System of Industrial Relations in Great Britain* (Blackwell).

Clegg, H A, 1987, *A History of British Trade Unions since 1889, volume 2: 1911-1933* (Clarendon).

Cliff, Tony, and Donny Gluckstein, 1986, *Marxism and Trade Union Struggle, The General Strike of 1926* (Bookmarks).

Darlington, Ralph, 2010, "The State of Workplace Union Reps' Organization in Britain Today", *Capital and Class*, volume 34, number 1, http://cnc.sagepub.com/content/34/1/126.full.pdf+html

Department of Trade and Industry, 2007, "Workplace Representatives: A Review of Their Facilities and Facility Time", www.berr.gov.uk/files/file36336.pdf

Electoral Reform Commission, 2011, "Political Parties' Latest Donations and Borrowing Figures Published", www.government-news.co.uk/electoral-commission/201102/political-parties-latest-donations-and-borrowing-figures-published.asp

Fishman, Nina, 1995, *The British Communist Party and the Trade Unions 1933-45* (Scolar).

Harrison, Royden, 1978, *The Independent Collier* (Harvester).

Hinton, James, 1973, *The First Shop Stewards Movement*, (George Allen and Unwin).

Kimber, Charlie, 2009, "In the Balance: the Class Struggle in Britain", *International Socialism 122*, www.isj.org.uk/?id=529

Hughes, Langston, 2001, *The Collected Works of Langston Hughes*, volume 1 (University of Missouri Press).

Luxembourg, Rosa, 1970, *Rosa Luxemburg Speaks* (Pathfinder).

PCS, 2011, "National Organising Strategy 2011" (PCS).

Robertson, Jack, 2010, "25 Years After the Great Miners Strike", *International Socialism 126*, www.isj.org.uk/?id=640

Smith, Martin, 2003, *The Awkward Squad, Let's Go to Work: New Labour and the Rank and File* (SWP).

Smith, Martin, 2005, "Trade Unions: Politics and the Struggle", *International Socialism 105*, www.isj.org.uk/?id=55

Smith, Martin, 2010, "Everything to Play for", *Socialist Review* (October), www.socialistreview.org.uk/article.php?articlenumber=11406

Trotsky, Leon, 1973, *Leon Trotsky on Britain* (Pathfinder).

TUC, 2007, "Workplace Representatives: A Review of their Facility Time—TUC Response to DTI Consultation Document" (TUC).

Unite, 2011, "A Union-Wide Strategy to stop decline and grow Unite" (Unite the Union).

USDAW, 2010, "Going for Growth" (USDAW).

Vallely, Paul, 2002, "Profile: Andy Gilchrist", *Independent* (23 November), www.independent.co.uk/news/people/profiles/profile-andy-gilchrist-609260.html

Waddington, J, and A Kerr, 2009, "Transforming a Trade Union? An Assessment of the Introduction of an Organising Initiative", *British Journal of Industrial Relations*, 47/1:27.

Webb, Sydney and Beatrice, 1919, *The History of Trade Unionism 1616—1920* (Edinburgh).

WERS, 2004, "Workplace Employment Relations Survey", www.wers2004.info

The Tories: An anatomy

Richard Seymour

After 13 years of exile the Conservative Party has returned to office, but weaker than ever and dependent on a coalition with the Liberals. Amid a global crisis, with a weak incumbent and against a widely disliked government, the Tories only managed to add 3 percentage points to their 2005 share of the vote, bringing them up to 36 percent. This took place amid the ongoing boycott of elections by millions of disappointed Labour voters. As Ed Miliband has acknowledged, most of the five million voters lost by Labour between 1997 and 2010 didn't switch to other parties, but stayed at home. Still the Tories, under a "modernising" leadership which styled itself as socially liberal and distanced itself from the Thatcherite past, barely exceeded a third of the vote. What explains the Tories' weakness?

Part of the answer, perhaps, is that the Tories "turned nasty" again following the 2008 recession, talking spending cuts and targeting welfare recipients in their election propaganda. But this raises further questions. Why did it take the Tories so long to adapt to the new terrain, adopt a "moderate" leadership and attempt to carve out a conservatism occupying much the same ground as New Labour had staked out since 1994? And why would it squander the fruits of this effort, which had seen the Tories restored to over 40 percent of popular support in polls for the first time since the early 1990s? Why are they determined now, governing with weak legitimacy, to impose widely unpopular policies such as privatisation in healthcare and tuition fee rises, which hurt parts of their electoral base? The answers must be sought in the Tories' relationship to capitalism, its crisis, and their long-term decline.

A bourgeois party

To understand the Tories' dilemma, it is necessary first to comprehend what the Conservative Party is. In the Marxist idiom, the Conservative Party is a *bourgeois* party—that is, one which exists to wage political struggles on behalf of the ruling class in the representative institutions of a capitalist democracy. Of course, the state is the strategic base for launching any major transformation or development in productive relations within a national territory, and the bourgeoisie will necessarily work hard to impregnate the state with its imperatives regardless of who is in office.[1] However, political parties concentrate determinate social interests (classes and class fractions) in their composition and ideology, and provide moral and intellectual direction to those interests. In the Tories' case, the party comprises a coalition between a ruling financial and business bloc, and a subordinate petty bourgeois layer. As such, the Conservative Party condenses within itself the strategic perspectives and wider social purview of these interests, and gives those a particular ideological articulation.

The Conservative Party became the dominant bourgeois party in British politics through a tortuous process of adaptation to the rising power of industrial capital in the 19th century. Initially a faction representing the landed interest, the Tories operated as the vanguard of counter-revolution during the late 18th and early 19th centuries. They were, in the Duke of Wellington's words, a party of "the Bishops and clergy, the great Aristocracy, the landed Interest, the Magistracy of the Country, the great Merchants and Bankers, in short the *parti conservateur* of the Country". However, through the leadership of a pro Free Trade Peelite faction, the Tories were compelled to adapt to changes reflecting the interests of industry—the Great Reform Act of 1932, and the repeal of the Corn Laws, for instance. By the late 19th century they were known as the "brewers' party" due to their alliance with the larger sectors of industry.[2]

However, there is no automatic translation between a determinate ruling class interest and Tory policy, since different ruling class fractions have conflicting interests. Even these fractions will divide over a variety of short and medium-term issues as well as the finer points of policy. Even if there *were* only one ruling class interest, there would be competition over which strategy

---

1:   On the question of the ruling class and the capitalist state, see Therborn, 2008.
2:   The landed interest in the Tory party continued to be important, however, at least in part because that was that was where the greatest concentrations of wealth were to be found, well into the 19th century. See Scott, 1982, pp34-42; Ross, 1983, pp32-33 and 46; Wellington quoted in Ramsden, 1998, p29. On Peel and the Tories, see Evans, 1991; on the Tories and the Corn Laws, see Ramsden, 1998, pp50-76

would most effectively meet that interest. The Tories must therefore operate as a vehicle for ideological contestation, with rival factions competing to provide leadership to the ruling class as well as to society as a whole.

But the second element of the bourgeois party is that it must have a popular base in order to make its programme effective. The Tories have had to operate since 1867 in a parliamentary system numerically dominated by working class voters. They have therefore been compelled to seek a mass membership base, without ceding strategic control over the party's decision making, while incorporating popular demands and themes into their policy platforms. This was pioneered in the "popular Toryism" of Benjamin Disraeli, which combined some social reform with an attempt to mobilise workers through imperialist and Unionist ideology. As the working class moved to the left in the early 20th century and the Labour Party emerged, the Tories decisively replaced the Liberals as the main bourgeois party and commandeered an anti-socialist political bloc that necessitated grudging concessions to popular interests combined with repression. Such concessions included the extension of the franchise to women during Stanley Baldwin's administration, while repression included concerted efforts along with industry to smash post First World War strike waves. This paid dividends electorally, with the Tories' share of the vote rising from the 1870s to the 1930s, during which decade it peaked at approximately 55 percent.[3]

The first major crisis of Tory dominance came in 1945, when social democracy finally emerged as a viable electoral bloc, and decisively altered the political terrain by introducing a strong welfare state, a sizeable public sector and a measure of economic "planning". It also incorporated the trade unions into a new corporatist settlement, with incomes policies determined by union leaders, bosses and the government of the day. Reluctantly, the Tories accepted the new settlement, since it was the only way to maintain the support of popular constituencies—these, for the Tories, usually being the lower middle class and a segment of skilled workers. This model came to be known as "One Nation" conservatism.

But a crisis of the post-war system, beginning in the 1960s, threw that strand of Tory praxis into turmoil. Ted Heath's 1970-4 government attempted to rule in the interests of capital, but it could not maintain popular consent in doing so. Enoch Powell, though his personal ascendancy was brief, worked as a pathfinder for a "New Right", which was piloted

---

3:    On the Tories and the enfranchisement of workers, see Cowling, 2005. On Disraeli's appeal to empire sentiment, see O'Gorman, 1986, pp146-147; on "popular Toryism", see Lee, 1979; Pugh, 1988; Cornford, 1963; on Baldwin's patrician Toryism, see Seldon, 1994.

into office by Margaret Thatcher. The novelty of this brand of conservatism was that it could mobilise a popular base without endorsing the welfare state, public spending or any of the traditional amelioration through which governments had sought consensus.[4] Despite its enduring political successes Thatcherism's moment passed, and the Tories have since had to contend with the continued secular decline in their popular base. If post-war Tory governments were usually elected with between 46 and 50 percent of the vote, Thatcher maintained support at between 40 and 44 percent of the electorate—but since 1992 support has tended to hover between 30 and 35 percent, a non-viable electoral coalition.[5] This is one of the key problems which David Cameron's triangulations are intended to overcome.

The Conservative Party today is facing long-term eclipse if it does not succeed in reviving British capitalism, and restoring its dominant position within that system partly by re-composing the electorate in favourable terms. The austerity project can be seen, in this light, as a strategy both to preserve ruling class dominance and to revive the Conservative Party. To understand how, it is necessary to understand the deep changes in British society wrought by Thatcherism, and its limited successes in staving off the forces undermining conservatism. The remainder of this article will look at the crisis of conservatism since the late 1960s, beginning with Heath and his ultimately failed attempt to re-orient British capitalism while retaining the broad lineaments of social democracy; proceeding through Thatcher's attempt to articulate a new hegemonic project, which ultimately gave way to the further fragmenting and contraction of the Tory base under Major, and the long period of opposition; and finishing with a look at Cameron's leadership.

Heath and the New Right

The Conservative Party under Ted Heath was one in the process of transformation. There was an emerging radical right in the party that sought to break with important elements of the post-war settlement. In the 1960s the first serious anxieties about Britain's post-war economy began to emerge. British capitalism was declining relative to other advanced capitalist states, Fordist industries were suffering from stagnant profits, and corporatist remedies controlling incomes and prices seemed to offer no solution. In this context, a right wing opposition centred initially on figures such as Enoch Powell and Keith Joseph began to develop in the Conservative Party.

4:   On the Tories' often grudging adaptation to social democracy, see Harris, 1972; Seawright, 2005; Zweiniger-Bargielowska, 1994
5:   On post-war Tory results, compared with Thatcher's, see Ross, 1983, pp5-9.

When Ted Heath held a press conference in 1970 at the Selsdon Park hotel, announcing that an incoming Tory government would be tough on crime, union reform, and immigration, it was heralded as the arrival of a neo-reactionary "Selsdon Man". Yet Heath did not attempt to break fully from the post-war settlement. He took as read the idea that government policy should seek to create relatively full employment and maintain a strong welfare state. His main strategy upon being elected was to orient British capitalism more towards Europe and away from the US, and to introduce tougher market conditions and weaker unions to reduce wages and improve competitiveness.[6]

Among the most pressing concerns for the incoming Heath government in 1970 was to combat shop steward militancy. Labour had attempted its own measure with Barbara Castle's "In Place of Strife" White Paper, but this had foundered on successful union opposition. Heath's Industrial Relations Bill was essentially the same kind of remedy—a corporatist device that would regulate and limit trade union activity, while still conceding that unions and collective bargaining were vital to the conduct of economic policy. By taming the unions, Heath believed, it would no longer be necessary to maintain an incomes policy. By freeing industry from the burdens of intervention, the government could dispense with expansionist nostrums such as the Ministry of Technology headed by Tony Benn under Wilson. But it was all to come to nought. The bill was broken on a wave of unprecedented militancy, on a scale arguably greater than 1926, and much more successful. 1972, the year in which the Industrial Relations Act was left dead in the water, was on the whole the most mortifying year in Conservative Party history. Heath returned to expansionism even earlier, forced to nationalise Rolls Royce in 1971, before increasing public spending in 1972, awarding sweeping powers to the secretary of state for industry, with the Industry Act of 1972, and imposing a statutory incomes policy in defiance of his previous commitments.[7]

In addition to defeats inflicted on Heath by the labour movement, the administration was blind-sided by the 1973 oil shock and by the global recession of 1974. By the mid-1970s British capitalism was on the precipice. Heath's promised reforms could not secure consent, while social democratic planning and corporatist instruments were proving incapable of reversing Britain's relative economic decline, or of reversing the long-term decline in profit rates which had began to manifest itself in the late 1960s. Nor could they contain working class militancy, or restore to managers lost authority

6:   For the best analysis of the Heath administration's programme, see Blackburn, 1971.
7:   Gamble, 1994, pp82-88; Darlington and Lyddon, 2001; Dorey, 1995, pp65-91.

with respect to shop stewards. This was the "crisis of authority" presciently diagnosed by Stuart Hall. In Gramsci's terms, a "crisis of authority" is the inability of the ruling class to operationalise public consent for its goals. It is a crisis of hegemony, radiating through every dominant institution, through every aspect of productive and ideological relations, and notably through the parliamentary political field itself.[8] In such circumstances, opportunities arose for a right wing opposition.

Enoch Powell was the first to show how a minority "free market" agenda could become an election winner. Powell's journey from High Tory imperialist to low racist demagogue needs little elaboration here. It is sufficient to note that, at some point after he lost the 1965 leadership contest to Edward Heath, Powell decided that immigrants to whom he had expressed no hostility before were suddenly a pressingly urgent political problem. He maintained that their problem was not the inferiority of the immigrants' "race", but with the inability of people of different cultures to integrate into the white British mainstream. Pioneering what was later dubbed the "new racism", Powell gained popularity and proved that it was possible to challenge the entire basis of the post-war compromise by mobilising anxiety over Britain's declining global status and the perceived laxities that made this possible. One could appeal to the working class not on the basis of immediate bread and butter issues, but on the basis of nationalism. In this outlook, trade union power, criminality, welfare largesse and immigration were weakening Britain's competitiveness and the authority of its sovereign state.[9]

Powell, though he had his admirers in the party, including Margaret Thatcher, was hung out to dry by Ted Heath and ended up traversing the unpromising terrain of Ulster Unionist politics. Nevertheless, the racist authoritarianism which he pioneered energised the right, and a series of racialised moral panics about "mugging" fed into a wider right wing dissatisfaction with disobedience among the lower orders. By the early 1970s the right's new dynamism seemed to be influencing the leadership of the Conservative Party. Beyond Powell, the patriarch of the Tory right was Keith Joseph, a baronet and son of a finance-capitalist whose free market ideology had contributed much to the policies announced at Selsdon. Joseph, derided by his opponents as "The Mad Monk", had been a member of the "One Nation" group in his early years, in which he expressed his support for the welfare state. In his ministerial roles had made free use of the state he was to belittle in later years. As minister of housing, he had been responsible for building 400,000 new

8:    Hall, Critcher, Jefferson, Clarke, and Roberts, 1978, pp218-72; see also Gramsci, 1971.
9:    Gamble, 1994, pp77-81; Seymour, 2010.

council homes. Yet he always hankered for the restoration of free market rule, and voted for pro-market legislation where he could.[10]

Together with Margaret Thatcher, Joseph articulated the critique of the post-war settlement that had long been propagated by the middle class right, and in think-tanks such as the Institute for Economic Affairs. They also set out to create new vectors for ideological dissemination, creating the Centre for Policy Studies to provide an alternative source of policy to that of the Conservative Research Department. With the political philosophy of Friedrich Hayek, Milton Friedman's monetarist ideas, and the new ideology of "public choice" economics, they developed an intellectual basis for the restoration of markets not merely as the chief way in which social relations were mediated, but as a positive good, an alternative to the failings of the consensus.

The rise of Thatcherism

In February 1974, amid renewed strike action by the mine workers, Heath went to the country to ask whether it should be run by the Tories or the miners. Labour won a slight plurality in parliament on a manifesto containing elements of the Alternative Economic Strategy devised by Tony Benn and his allies. But this would not have been sufficient to give them office had the Ulster Unionists not refused to take the Conservative whip. Notwithstanding the Heath administration's role in breaking the Northern Ireland Civil Rights Movement with the massacres of "Bloody Sunday", the Tories' long standing ties to Unionism had been severed by Heath's imposition of direct rule on Stormont, usurping the power of the gerrymandered Unionist rulers. The Liberals were also unwilling to enter into coalition with the Conservatives. Under Jeremy Thorpe, they were positioning themselves as a left of centre party defending the consensus that underpinned British politics in the post-war era. The Tories, allied to producers, could not control prices; Labour, beholden to unions, could not control wages; the Liberals alone, as a non-class party, could keep the system afloat.[11] Such was the political basis of the later Liberal-SDP alliance resulting from the right wing breakaway from Labourism in 1981.

Having taken office, and won a second election with a clearer mandate in October 1974, Labour—with more alacrity than usual—began to break every single promise on which they had been elected. Using the institutions of corporatism to contain wage rises and union militancy more effectively than the Tories had, they also commenced a programme of

---

10:   Denham & Garnett, 2001, pp97-106; Jessop, Bonnet, Bromley, & Ling, 1984.
11:   On the Liberals' articulation of consensus politics in 1974, see Dale, 2000, pp145-182.

deep public spending cuts, and under chancellor Denis Healey were the first to implement monetarist policies. This was not merely a betrayal. It was a logical and inevitable result of their commitment to a programme of ambitious reform that gave no consideration to the inevitable resistance of capital, and the state apparatus itself.[12] The Labour government was also susceptible to pressure from business, which was increasingly involved in direct political activism. In the post-war system there had been a steady growth in class-wide business cohesion, which enabled them to face down unwanted Labour reforms such as the Bullock Report advocating the piecemeal extension of industrial democracy in some enterprises. A member of the Confederation of British Industry group established to defeat the measure described how, after their victory, "CBI members woke up to the fact that they have greater strength than they realised".[13]

The decisive moment that broke the government, however, was the "winter of discontent". This is the period from 1978-9 in which the "social contract" between the government and the union bureaucracy, holding wage increases at well below the rate of inflation, broke down. In September 1978 both the TUC and the Labour Party voted to oppose a new pay increase norm of 5 percent, and strikes broke out in a number of industries, with secondary picketing compounding the disruption. However, Labour enjoyed more success than the Tories in blunting militancy, particularly that of the shop stewards. A 1968 report on shop steward militancy had recommended drawing shop stewards into the full-time union apparatus to distance them from the shop floor, and imposing productivity deals that would sidestep the stewards' role in negotiating wage rates. Under the Wilson-Callaghan government this process was accelerated, with the effect of encouraging sectionalism and scabbing. In addition, the government used troops to break strikes. For all its militancy, the organised working class had not broken with Labour, and the participation of "their" government in smashing their struggles was a shattering experience that broke the loyalty

---

12: Gamble, 1994, p83; Coates, 2003, pp137-154; Seldon and Hickson, 2004, pp207-208.
13: Partially this enhanced class cohesion was assured by the development of what the sociologist Michael Useem calls an "interlocking directorate", in which the largest companies developed the practice of accepting non-executive directors on their boards while sending their own favoured managers onto the boards of other companies. This enabled them to get a "scan" of the business environment, and created ties between financial and non-financial corporations, allowing the former to acquire better information and act as "nerve centres" of capital accumulation. But it also created networks of solidarity when business interests were threatened—Useem, 1984, pp38-58; 157-159; on growing links between financial and non-financial corporations in the same period, see Scott, 1979, pp75-104.

of many union members for good. At the end of this dismal period of government, with a rightward moving Labour shored up by a pact with the Liberals, business decisively swung behind the Tories, the electorate moved to the right and the Labourist coalition was fatally undermined.[14]

The humiliation of the Heath government, meanwhile, had galvanised the Tory right. Heath had won a mere 36 percent of the vote in October 1974 and there was growing pressure for him to step down. In February 1975 Thatcher challenged for the leadership, and won the backing of much of the right wing press in doing so. Thatcher had become the right's candidate after Keith Joseph dropped out, following a blunt speech sounding a eugenic alarm over the rise of the "underclass". Having made few enemies as yet, she channelled dissatisfaction with Heath as much as outright reactionary sentiment. Partly because of this, Thatcher still had to spend many years winning the Tories to her agenda before she could properly implement it. Even an ousted and weakened Heath could galvanise dissent when he chose to attack the new leadership and its policies in public. Yet the solutions of the Thatcherites had obvious advantages for a party in danger, as fellow New Rightist John Biffen complained, of being a "middle class party of the shires". If recessionary pressures intensified the drift towards corporatism, then Labour would benefit as it had the advantage of its relations with the trade union leadership. If the Tories could not keep union consent, they could not deliver in such circumstances. Breaking with corporatism and attacking union militancy should provide a route out of this impasse.[15]

The Hayekian doctrines guiding the Conservative leadership under Thatcher had long been the *cri de coeur* of the middle class. However, they also contained a serious analysis of, and remedy for, the "British disease". If Powell had shown that it was possible for the Tories to build a mass base without accepting social democracy, it would be no good doing so if the Tories could not by these self-same means effectively restore British capitalism and act as the main bourgeois party. Since this ability was already in question, the Tory leadership was prepared to take a gamble on a radical new policy mix. Thatcher knew that the corporatist state depended on healthy revenue streams, but that its ability to intervene and generate those revenue streams was by then seriously weakened. Higher public spending did not reduce unemployment. It just added to inflation. Price controls were ineffectual, and the "winter of discontent" of 1978-9 would later show that wage controls were just as ineffectual. In their place, capitalist freedom would be

---

14: Cliff and Gluckstein, 1996, pp328-31 and 343-344; Grant, 1980.
15: Joseph, 1974; Gamble, 1994, pp90-104.

restored. Collective bargaining was out; incomes policies and price controls were out; demand management and job-creation were out.[16]

In the new neoliberal statecraft, the government would spend less, and such money as was spent would be channelled through market-based delivery mechanisms and undemocratic bodies such as quangos. Just as the 18th century conservative thinker Edmund Burke argued that the aristocracy was the reasoning executive of the social body, so the Thatcherites seem to have believed that there was no area of expertise that businessmen could not turn their hand to. This meant that the bosses of Sainsbury's and Marks and Spencer were as good as anyone to write a report which led to the introduction of internal markets in the NHS, inflating administrative overheads dramatically.[17] Businessmen had always been brought in to assist in the management of nationalised industries and the public sector, but generally this was in areas where they already had expertise. Under the rubric of public choice theory, however, the government believed that no matter what the institution it could be made more efficient by being refashioned in the image of business.[18]

Thatcher might be known chiefly as a failure had she not maintained a plurality in the 1983 general election. Her first term was characterised by tremendous social conflict and soaring rates of unemployment in the context of a global recession. The government's remedy depended on freeing up capital, creating a stable currency, removing exchange controls and privatising public assets. But perversely—so it seemed then—this entailed the Thatcher government insisting on austerity in a time of economic weakness. So VAT was increased, interest rates were pushed up and public spending was slashed, ostensibly in order to balance the budget and cut inflation. However, the soaring value of the pound reduced the competitiveness of British exports and contributed to the deepening severity of the recession.

This meant that even the dramatic split in the Labour Party, with a liberal, right wing section taking off to form the Social Democratic Party, did not benefit the Conservative Party. On the contrary, the Liberal-SDP Alliance became a primary beneficiary of disaffection with the Tories, and even took seats from them. Moreover, if the government was supposed to help business by curtailing union militancy, its early reforms in this direction were relatively mild. It would have seemed as if a doctrinaire Tory party was governing in ways contrary to the interests even of its narrow business base.[19]

16: Gamble, 1994, pp88-138; Grant, 1980.
17: Mayston, 1996, p11.
18: Atkinson and Wilks-Heeg, 2000, pp58 and 72; Evans, 2004, pp53-64 .
19: Gamble, 1994, pp105-9.

Yet by mid-1982 the polls had reversed, and Thatcher was riding high. She won re-election the following year with 42 percent of the vote. In effect, the Tories had succeeded in escalating the crisis, policing it and riding it out.

It is commonplace to attribute the reversal to the effect of the Falklands conflict. In April 1982 the forces of the Argentinian dictator General Galtieri took control of territories in the South Atlantic known to Argentina as the Malvinas, and to Britain as the Falkland Islands. Until this point the Thatcher government had shown little interest in the islands, which were hardly of great strategic significance to British capitalism. Yet Thatcher embarked on a war to re-conquer the islands, carefully avoiding diplomatic exits, and appeared to have soared by some 15 percentage points in the polls while the war was taking place. Much of the left was convinced that this constituted the revival of, in Tom Nairn's words, "semi-permanent reaction".

Indeed, it is striking just how enduring and deep this strand of left opinion expected the Falklands legacy to be. Polling evidence suggests, however, that the impact of this war on the electorate was hugely over-stated by these analyses. Thatcher's popularity had already been recovering in the light of rapidly improving economic fortunes, as a global recovery got under way in early 1982, combined with a budget stimulus implemented by the Tories in the same period. The "Falklands factor" added about 3 percentage points to the Tories' lead, and the effect faded after the capture of Port Stanley. The humiliating defeat for Labour in 1983 was far more the result of the historic split in the Labourist coalition, as well as a recovery in the economic fortunes of potential Alliance voters, than it was the result of jingoism. What does seem to be the case is that the Falklands conflict consolidated Thatcher's position within the Conservative Party, and enabled her to briefly enjoy a relationship with the public that spoke over the heads of more staid bourgeois opinion.[20]

It was only after Thatcher's 1983 success, which further consolidated her dominant position in her party, that her government began to embark on major conflict with the unions. The chief macroeconomic objective of government was to control inflation by suppressing wage claims. That was to be achieved primarily through the acceptance of high unemployment—with right wing economists such as Milton Friedman arguing that there was a "natural" rate of unemployment and that any government action to push unemployment below that level would only increase the rate of inflation—and a coordinated attack on the bargaining power of labour.

Defeating the unions through a series of set-piece battles laid out in

---

20: Nairn, 1983; Sanders, Ward, Marsh & Fletcher, 1987.

a strategy by Nicholas Ridley achieved this latter objective. This involved taking on weaker unions first and defeating them, while making concessions to more powerful unions to prevent them from joining in the struggles. Having notched up a string of successes and demoralised its opponents, only then should the government proceed to attack the big battalions. In the case of the miners, this meant building up a state capable of out-flanking one of the best organised and combative groups of workers before provoking a conflict. As Huw Beynon and Peter McNylor pointed out, it was the spectre of the 1972 miners' strike, and the closure of the Saltley coke depot by tens of thousands of NUM "flying pickets" out-manoeuvring fewer than a thousand police, that provided the animus for this retooling. The Tories' success in defeating the miners also had the intended effect of devastating the social forces best placed to resist Thatcher's agenda and obstruct social democracy's adaptation to the new order. After the calamitous defeat of the miners' strike in 1985 the right wing within the trade unions and Labour imposed a "new realism" based on non-confrontation, sweetheart deals with employers and support for free markets. One recent account of the miners' strike notes that before the strike an anti-union Labour leader, such as Blair was, would have been "a contradiction in terms".[21]

The attack on wages and the long-term crisis of profitability in industry required a remedy to sustain both. The government found its remedy in the revival of the rentier and the replacement of cheap money with "sound money"—a strong currency sustained through low inflation. The City's speculative activities would drive capitalist investment by increasing the rewards of such investment, while integrating a section of the working class by allowing them to borrow against their property - which, owing to rationing in the provision of housing after 1983, would perpetually increase in value. Owner occupation increased to 72 percent. Enough people would feel wealthy enough to form a viable political constituency in favour of the new settlement. This constituency did not have to comprise a majority.

Until 1989 Thatcherism could command between 42 and 44 percent of the vote, a recovery from Ted Heath's 1974 low of 36 percent, but still well below not only the peaks of Conservative success under Baldwin, but also the average post-war performance—in fact, votes on the Thatcher scale would have resulted in defeats in the 1950s and 1960s. And had the global economy not recovered in 1982, the Thatcher government might well have gone down as the unpopular and short-lived pathology that Labour figures

---

21: Thompson, 1986, pp70 and 98; Saville, 1985; Cliff and Gluckstein, 1996, pp374-378; Beynon and McNylor, 1985, p71; Beckett and Hencke, 2009, p249.

hoped it would be. At every step the government was taking risks, and things could have worked out very differently.[22]

Thatcher did not command universal support for her project among capitalists either. Initially she was suspect because her agenda was seen as pandering to a middle class protest vote, not dissimilar to the United Kingdom Independence Party (UKIP) today. Why back an "extremist" option, many business leaders reasoned, when Labour was delivering, with the support of the trade union bureaucracy, higher levels of unemployment and deeper wage cuts than any government in the post-war era? It was only when the "winter of discontent" proved that the corporatist instruments refined over the last two decades could not contain working class militancy that they turned to Thatcher's remedy. Even then they tended to swallow unpalatable measures such as the destruction of manufacturing largely due to their greater fear of Labour taking power and turning to the left.[23]

Class struggle and hegemony

The great bulk of literature on the British Conservative Party concerns the perplexing phenomenon of Thatcherism and its considerable successes. Thatcherism has, in some senses, enjoyed what Stuart Hall refers to as "a long historical occupancy of power".[24] To adapt an old phrase, it might be said that "whoever is in office, the Thatcherites are in power". The forms of statecraft practised by all governing parties today follow the neoliberal logic institutionalised by Thatcher, and the current coalition is operating firmly within its radius. It has sometimes been argued by Tory "wets",[25] such as Ian Gilmour, that Thatcherism was an "ideological" deviation from the "pragmatic" traditions of British conservatism, a "retreat behind the privet hedge into a world of narrow class interests and selfish concerns".[26] The novelty of Thatcherism, though genuine, can be overstated. What was distinctive about Thatcherism in ideological terms was the new articulation it gave to the "individualistic, laissez-faire, anti socialist, and nationalist strains always present in 20th-century conservatism".[27] It would be difficult to account for Thatcher's successes if it were merely an "ideological" retreat from "pragmatism". Condensed in Thatcherism was a set of answers to the British experience of capitalist crisis, interpreted in the ideologically charged language of "British decline".

22: Coates, 2005, p8; Mullard, 1993, p222; Wallop, 2010; Wilenius, 2004.
23: Grant, 1980; Kavanagh, 1987, pp118-119.
24: Hall, 1987.
25: A Thatcherite idiom for the Tory "left".
26: Evans, 2004, pp4-5, 14.
27: Sofer, 2009, p290.

During the 1980s a number of powerful, competing left wing inter-pretations of Thatcherism were pioneered. The most well known of these were Eric Hobsbawm, Andrew Gamble and Stuart Hall, though distinc-tive contributions also emerged from Bob Jessop, Anthony Barnett and, in the SWP tradition, Tony Cliff.[28] The first three of these theorists were concerned, in different ways, with Thatcherism's hegemonic operations, its ability to change the terms of popular discourse, and its way of winning over a segment of workers to conservatism.

Stuart Hall, associated with the *Marxism Today* magazine, character-ised Thatcherism, adapting a coinage from Nicos Poulantzas, as a form of "Authoritarian Populism". Poulantzas had argued that capitalism in the late 1970s was shifting from consensual to more coercive forms of rule. Though still operating in the terrain of democratic class politics, the state was accumulating more repressive power—a form of government he called "Authoritarian Statism". But for Hall, Thatcherism was distinguished by its ability to mobilise popular elements of discontent with the state as a basis for its authoritarian remodelling of society. In the magisterial book, *Policing the Crisis*, Hall outlined the way in which British capitalism had experienced a "crisis of authority" affecting all of its dominant institutions since the 1960s. In response to this, the forces of "law and order" had developed a number of discourses to allow a reassertion of authority with a popular mandate. This came centrally in the form of a moral panic about "mugging", crimi-nalising young black males and mandating a racist crackdown, but it tied into a wider theme concerning British decline and the perception that this was a result of a lax moral and economic climate. The social democratic state, it was held, had corrupted a previously robust, entrepreneurial nation, spending beyond its means, subsidising poor industry and allowing a slack-ening of the moral fibre through ill discipline.

Thatcherism, operating on many of the same ideological vertices as Powellism, thus summoned a degree of support for an attack on the welfare state, corporatist public spending projects and the trade unions. This won the backing not only of the petty bourgeois rightist bedrock, and not only of big business—which, as we have seen, was partial and hesitant—but also of sections of the working class. This was possible, Hall argued, because certain of the petty bourgeois ideological themes of Thatcherism could resonate with popular ideas, and more particularly because the Thatcherite critique of social democracy built on real points of discontent with a system that was experienced by large numbers of people

28: The best synthetic analysis of these positions can be found in Blackledge, 2002.

as repressive rather than benevolent. With racism articulating these contradictory ideological elements, Thatcher embarked on an authoritarian transformation of British capitalism—using Gramsci's term, Hall described this as a "passive revolution"—with a measure of popular support.[29]

Hall's work was controversial because of its narrow focus on ideology, its often pessimistic conclusions, wherein he exaggerated the degree of popular support enjoyed by Thatcherism, and the problematic use of the concept of "passive revolution" to describe Thatcher's reign, which was more akin to a war of attrition.[30] Andrew Gamble, writing for *Socialist Register*, placed much more emphasis on political economy in his explanation. He coined the phrase "the free economy and the strong state" to describe what Thatcherism represented. While the Thatcherites ostensibly set out to "roll back the frontiers of the state",[31] what was actually involved was a rolling back of the state's involvement in welfare and the economy, coterminous with a rolling forward of the state's coercive power. This was a political-economic response to a crisis of British capitalism, and particularly of the social democratic settlement that had reigned since 1945. Modernisation through public spending projects had turned out a series of lame ducks, and the productive capacity of British capitalism could no longer sustain a strong welfare state while maintaining a healthy rate of profit.

This movement was articulated in a politics of "the nation", in which British decline could ostensibly be reversed on multiple fronts through a restoration of market discipline and law and order. For Gamble, however, the Thatcherites were riven by antagonisms, with relatively liberal and conservative wings vying for influence. The former, influenced by the neoliberal political economy of Milton Friedman and Friedrich Hayek, were less motivated by the restoration of authority, and far more so by the institutionalisation of sound money policies, public spending restraints and supply-side economics. The latter, by contrast, were social authoritarians driven by hostility to "enemies" within and without—the USSR, the IRA, "strikers, criminals, demonstrators and vandals". These tendencies, which one analyst has dubbed "mods" and "rockers" of Thatcherism,[32] could be seen loosely as representing, respectively, the bourgeois and petty bourgeois elements of the Thatcherite coalition. These antagonisms aside, Thatcherism successfully "disrupted the old commonsense of social democracy and established

---

29: Hall, Critcher, Jefferson, Clarke and Roberts, 1978; see also Hall, 1983; Hall, 1985; and Poulantzas, 2000.
30: On these criticisms, see Blackledge, 2002.
31: Green, 2004, p216.
32: Driver, 2009, p84.

a new commonsense in its place" with the market "reconstituted as a major ideological force, and crucial distinctions between the productive and unproductive, private and public, wealth creating and wealth consuming" forming the new "yardsticks for judging policy".[33]

From the Communist Party right, Eric Hobsbawm argued that Thatcherism had enjoyed such considerable success because class consciousness was on the decline. He maintained that Marxists had underestimated the difference in consciousness between white collar and blue collar workers. The result of the expansion of white collar employment was that "the class on which our movement was built has shrunk", and the forward march of labour had been halted. Thatcherism was thus taking the opportunity to "eliminate the entire labour movement, the Labour Party, and the entire left as a serious factor in politics". Moreover, in response to the Falklands crisis, Hobsbawm argued that patriotism was a genuinely popular reflex in some parts of the working class, and not entirely incompatible with political radicalism. If the left did not find a way to relate productively to this, then the right would monopolise patriotism with jingoistic and xenophobic strains. The clear implication of Hobsbawm's argument and language was that there was something almost fascistic about Thatcherism—indeed, he flirted with the terminology, hesitating "only just" to describe Thatcherism as "semifascist", something like but just shy of "fascism of the old kind". The consequence of this analysis was that the left should follow the trend established by Eurocommunism and relegate class as an organising principle in place of a strategy of Popular Frontism, organising a "coalition of all democrats" around the "mass parties of the left".[34]

Thatcher did not succeed in wiping out the labour movement, or the Labour Party, or indeed the entire left—but did it succeed in creating a hegemonic formation? And if Thatcherism was not fascist, did it not nonetheless fundamentally alter the mode of domination, as suggested by the formula of "authoritarian populism"? To answer this, it is first necessary to understand what is meant by "hegemony". In a conventional interpretation of Gramsci, relevant here, hegemony refers to the construction of consent for a social group's dominance, which operates in the sphere of civil society, through ideology and persuasion rather than repression.[35]

33: Gamble, 1979; Gamble, 1994.

34: Hobsbawm, 1989, pp9-22, 57-61, 80-81, 103-118 and 192; see also Birchall and Carlin, 1983.

35: In fact, this is a misleading interpretation of Gramsci's concept, which includes coercion towards subordinate social groups, alongside the securing of consent among allied groups. See Thomas, 2009, pp159-197.

In fact, while Thatcher took the ideological battle very seriously indeed, and had some successes in this respect—this is the strongest part of Hall's analysis—the key questions were not settled through consent, but through open class struggle. Public attitudes on the key issues of public spending, redistribution and welfare remained stolidly reformist, and on a number of central questions the public moved to the left during Thatcher's three successive administrations. As the historian Tim Bale put it, "Thatcher didn't win elections because she converted a majority of citizens to her cause (she didn't) or because she was personally popular (she wasn't)." Her successes were owed to the weakness of the opposition and, in part, to her governments' successful macroeconomic manipulations leaving a sufficient number of people feeling wealthy for long enough at election times. If Thatcher successfully imposed a new neoliberal commonsense, this was largely because she compelled social democracy to adapt to it by defeating opposed social forces in struggle. In fact, the evidence is that New Labour has done much more to move public attitudes to the right on public spending and welfare than the Tories did.[36]

And this is suggestive of the answer to the second question, viz, that while Thatcherism was a novel political formation, the form of state that it commandeered was not. Thatcher's strategy was not to destroy the labour movement, as Hobsbawm suggested, but to eradicate its militancy while maintaining the bureaucracy as an apparatus for securing the acquiescence of the working class through negotiation; not to destroy the Labour Party, but to destroy its left wing—a point that is worth bearing in mind today as the Tories seek to co-opt the trade union leadership into the cuts process, and the Labour right seeks to resist mobilising against austerity.[37]

What of the argument that the Tories were the beneficiaries of a decline in class conscious voting? In a manner similar to Hobsbawm, some psephologists argued that the 1980s were witnessing a trend of "electoral dealignment" in which voters ceased to vote on a class basis and became more like consumers, shopping around for parties based on value preferences. This, it was argued, was because many workers had become better off, and thus tended to favour Tory policies such as tax cuts. The evidence for this is based on an outmoded index of "class voting" known as the "Alford Index", which depicts the working class exclusively in the terms of manual labour, and in such a way as to include in the category self-employed traders,

---

36: Bale, 2010, p23. On social attitudes after Thatcher, see Cliff and Gluckstein, 1996, pp379-381; on New Labour's impact, see Asthana, 2010.
37: Such was the contemporary analysis of this journal. See Callinicos, 1985; these and other counterpoints to Hall, Hobsbawm and others are summarised in Blackledge, 2002.

small businessmen and "foremen and technicians", social groups who would properly belong to the middle class. More sophisticated studies of social attitudes and class find that class continues to strongly determine ideological outlook on core political issues such as privatisation, welfare and big business. If many working class voters broke with Labourism in the early 1980s, this was at least in part to do with Labour's failures in office, and particularly its use of corporatist instruments to break working class militancy and impose reduced living standards on the majority.[38]

The unstable formation that underpinned Thatcherism was already fragmenting by the time the legislation introducing the Community Charge, to replace local rates, was passed in 1988. The combination of Thatcher's increasingly "Eurosceptic" policies which was seen as pandering to petty bourgeois nationalism, the public disorder arising from the imposition of the poll tax, and the Tories' slump in the polls as the 1980s drew to a close led a faction of the Conservative leadership to move against her and try to rescue the party from what seemed to be a likely thumping in the next general election.

Divisions over Europe had started to come to the fore in the late 1980s over the Exchange Rate Mechanism (ERM) and moves towards a single currency, which Nigel Lawson, Michael Heseltine and Geoffrey Howe supported, and which Thatcher opposed. The pro-Europeans favoured closer integration, pegging the pound to the German mark, in order to help overcome the destabilising factors introduced into the economy through financialisation. Thatcher argued that this would be too deflationary and would constrain British growth. Howe and Lawson had secretly threatened to resign over Thatcher's intransigence and Eurosceptic speeches in Brussels, with the chancellor operating a de facto ERM policy by pegging the pound to the mark. Thatcher's attack on Delors's plan for economic and monetary union, published in 1989, further exacerbated splits in the Tory leadership, which contributed to a poor showing in the European elections that year. It was Howe's resignation from the cabinet in 1990 over Thatcher's anti-EU speech at a European Council meeting in Rome, signalling that Britain would never join a European single currency, that helped precipitate Michael Heseltine's challenge for the leadership, and Thatcher's downfall.[39]

38: Cliff and Gluckstein, 1996, pp376-378; Crewe, 1983; Heath, Jowell and Curtice, 1985; Harman, 1989; Evans, 1993; Van der Waal, Achterberg & Houtman, 2007; Andersen and Heath, 2002; Evans, 2000.
39: Garry, 1995; Riddell, 1987.

Decline and fall: from Thatcher to Major

On 22 November 1990 Margaret Thatcher announced her resignation from the leadership of the Conservative Party. In effect, she was compelled to leave office because she had clearly lost the confidence of a significant section of her cabinet, illustrated by Michael Heseltine's decision to stand against her. In that year Labour's lead in opinion polls had reached 20 percent. Thatcher's personal popularity ratings were lower than for any prime minister since polling began. The underlying issues were the poll tax, which Tory back-benchers feared would cost them re-election, and Europe, on which a section of the Tory leadership considered her too dogmatically anti-European. John Major was Thatcher's nominated successor, chosen mainly because he was a centrist on Europe, and he was backed by a majority of MPs. Major, though, had already persuaded the cabinet, as chancellor, to join the ERM, a decision that was to weigh heavily on his premiership.

Major was not a Thatcherite. He was explicitly a "One Nation" Tory favouring consensus politics rather than the fights of the 1980s. His first order of business was to conduct a retreat over the issue of the poll tax. Initially he sought to deal with the issue by subsidising it, and thus reducing the burden on those paying it, but—faced with further protests and the possibility of a "no confidence" vote over the issue—he withdrew the tax and replaced it with the less regressive Council Tax.[40] This was an effective move, deflating Labour's lead by removing a polarising issue and allowing centrist voters to return to the Liberals. Following the leadership election, the Tories' poll numbers began to recover somewhat, and the Tories closed ranks around the new leader to stem further losses. Major was also assisted by the fact that his victory was followed by a traditional opportunity to demonstrate the virtues of "strong" leadership through an alliance with Bush the Elder in Operation Desert Storm against Saddam Hussein's Iraq. The Labour opposition weakened their own position by declining to voice any opposition to the war. As a result, throughout the conflict Major enjoyed a majority in the polls.

The scale of Major's subsequent election victory, with the Tories enjoying a 7.6 percent lead over Labour, was a stunning coup. Major had kept the Tory coalition together with 42 percent of the vote. Labour's leadership looked round for people to blame and settled on the unions. However, there is little evidence that the union relationship played any significant role in the outcome of the election. Nor was there much evidence for the widely repeated claim that the *Sun's* attacks on Kinnock "won it" for the Tories. Polling evidence at the time demonstrated that the result represented the continuation of

---

40: Alderman and Carter, 1991; Taylor, 2006, pp49-50.

a historic split in Labourism in the period from 1979 to 1983 which had not been reversed.[41] Arguably, had the Tories continued in a Thatcherite vein, they would have succeeded in reuniting the divided anti-Tory majority.

As it was, the returning Tory administration was weak. After mass disobedience over the poll tax, the Tories were no longer in a position to maintain the bellicose posture of the 1980s. The capitalist class, too, learned that there were limits to the strategy of confrontation with the unions. The last major confrontation that industry and the Tories engaged in with the trade unions was the signal workers' dispute in 1994. There was a concerted class-wide attempt on the part of capital to break the RMT, which was demanding a pay claim well above the government's public service pay limit. The Institute of Directors and the CBI pooled their resources with the management of the recently privatised British Rail, spending hundreds of millions to break the strike. The operation depended on breaking up the cohesion of the railway workers and persuading significant numbers to scab. When that didn't happen, Michael Portillo raised the spectre of further "union reform" including a ban on strikes in key services, a longstanding Tory nostrum which Boris Johnson would like to impose today. In the end, management was defeated and the Portillo never proceeded with his plans. Industrial relations, he argued, were "very good", so confrontation was no longer necessary.[42]

The Tories were also increasingly embroiled in their factiousness. While the poll tax had been a setback for the Tories' ability to fight for business interests, the issue of Europe was an unprecedented crisis at the heart of Conservatism. Ted Heath had infuriated some Tory right wingers by allying with Labour centrists to draw Britain into the EEC, but the majority of Conservatives were resigned to its necessity. Under Thatcher, simmering unease over Europe was partially suppressed by the need for (Western) European unity in the context of the Cold War. But with the collapse of the USSR in 1989, the Tory right was no longer prepared to keep mum.

The outlook of the "sceptics" was not simply narrow and xenophobic, though the propaganda often was. It was just that they were allied with those sectors of capital who either looked further afield for profits than the European markets, or who still looked for Britain to punch above its weight in the world, or who resented new labour protections and restrictions that might come with monetary union, or who didn't fancy their chances of competing effectively with French and German capital in an enlarged single market. Small businesses in particular, the Tory backbone throughout

---

41: See Heath, Jowell and Curtice, 1994.
42: Cliff, 1995; Undy, 1996, p148; Dorey, 1995, p124.

the Thatcher era, were repelled by the idea that "Eurocrats" might set rules on wages, safety laws, or even taxation, that they could ill afford. Lending spurious coherence to these diverse gripes and grievances was the Tory fetish of the nation-state, whose organic evolution over centuries seemed to set it in far better standing than a bureaucratic, rationalist imposition like the EU (dubbed, in some reactionary polemic, the EUSSR).[43]

Major demonstrated his commitment to Atlanticists by joining with George Bush senior in mauling Iraq during Desert Storm, but also wanted to take his party into the Maastricht Treaty, which would draw Britain into a unified European political and economic structure. To make it more palatable to the sceptics, he negotiated opt-outs from the single currency and from the provisions of the "social chapter". But this wasn't enough, and the party whips had to work overtime to avoid embarrassing defeats, some of which nevertheless came. The fact that the rebels were able to repeatedly bloody the government's nose, with a Labour opposition opportunistically backing them up, showed that the MPs were unafraid for their careers because they knew themselves to be far from isolated either in the parliamentary party or among the constituency party members, or among the base.

Not only that, but they blamed the Europhiles for leading Britain into the disastrous Exchange Rate Mechanism, with the resulting losses of "Black Wednesday" destroying the Tories for at least the next election. On 16 September 1992 the Tories were forced to withdraw the pound from the ERM. Under the terms of the ERM, the government pegged the pound to the value of the Deutsche Mark, and was obliged to intervene if the value of the currency fluctuated too widely. In the middle of a recession the British currency was weak and had to be sustained through high interest rates. Currency speculators began to sell off the pound, forcing the government to spend billions buying it up—but this could not stop the currency plummeting. Chancellor Norman Lamont was finally forced to withdraw from the ERM at a cost of £3.3 billion. Following this debacle, and despite the fact that Labour had supported participation in the ERM, the next election was settled, "pushing Conservative support into a new long-term equilibrium".[44]

43: A survey of Tory MP's opinions carried out in 1991 for the Economic and Social Research Council can help explain why this issue can be so crippling for the Conservatives. It found that while the overwhelming majority, some 95 percent, favoured further privatisation in some form, the parliamentary party divided almost evenly into pro-EC and anti-EC camps. There was a strong correlation between social and economic conservatism, and hostility to the EC. The most virulently free market hyperglobalisers, such as Peter Lilley, Michael Howard and Michael Portillo, were the most hostile to Europe—Baker, Gamble and Seawright, 2002.

44: Garry, 1995; Sowemimo, 1996; Baker, Gamble and Seawright, 2002; Whiteley, 1997.

The issue of Europe for the Tory right also tied into a wider set of dissatisfactions, such as over immigration, crime, the cautious pace of privatisation under Major, and Britain's defence posture in the post Cold War world. Even after Labour's 1997 landslide, they were confident that it would fall to them to save the Tories from electoral oblivion. Yet they were deluded. Research showed that the breakdown of the Tory base had been taking place beneath the surface throughout the Thatcher era, that the party apparatus was eroding throughout the 1980s with membership declining and new members less and less active. The Thatcherites' long domination of the parliamentary party had not been based on the conversion of a majority of Tory supporters or MPs to doctrinaire Thatcherism, but on the latter's ability to win elections. That ability had long since been ceded.[45]

The 1997 election wipe-out saw the Tories reduced to 30 percent of the popular vote, with cabinet ministers and senior MPs losing formerly secure seats. Their share was even smaller among workers. Only a quarter of skilled workers and "white collar" workers supported the Tories, while approximately a fifth of "unskilled" and unemployed workers, and 13 percent of council tenants, did so. Only among managers and professionals (the "AB" vote) did the Tories retain a plurality (41 percent). Polling conducted for the BBC indicates that had the economy not been in a relatively strong state at that point, the Tories' annihilation would have been more complete.[46] Following the 1992 election the Tories' popular base had resumed its fragmentation, more rapidly than before. But because Thatcherism had seemingly saved the party once before, the party's right remained convinced that it would do so again. It took the Tories three successive defeats, in which they barely exceeded 30 percent of the vote, and almost a decade of pound-saving to disabuse themselves of that idea.

Cameron's solution

Part of the problem for the Conservatives under Blair was of how to distinguish themselves from the government. On many of New Labour's key policies, such as privatisation and participation in the "war on terror", the Tories did not fundamentally disagree with Blair. Indeed, a layer of Thatcherite "mods" began to admire Blair for his willingness to defy the unions, and the majority of Labour voters, over such issues. Under

---

45: Cox, 1995; Norton, 1990.
46: Kellner, 1997. A more granulated breakdown shows that non-unionised, non-manual workers in the private sector also voted slightly more for the Tories (32.4 percent) than for Labour (31 percent): Johnston, Pattie, Dorling, MacAllister, Tunstall and Rossiter, 2001.

successive leaders—William Hague, Ian Duncan-Smith, and Michael Howard, they differentiated themselves by adopting and espousing hard right social policies, bound to a standard Tory appeal to nationalism. This was the path pursued until David Cameron became party leader in 2005, and it never mustered more than 33 percent of the vote.

Cameron took the leadership with a promise to "modernise" the party, heeding the advice of Tory donor Lord Ashcroft to "wake up and smell the coffee". Though he himself had a standard Thatcherite voting record, he understood that this was no longer a saleable electoral formula. Since 1992 the Tories had lost votes among two key groups: the professional middle class and skilled workers. These voters were "secular" in motivation, having no attachment to the nationalist and socially authoritarian politics of Conservatism. They voted with their wallet, and on that front there had been nothing the Tories could offer that New Labour couldn't do better. Therefore, with the assistance of Ian Duncan-Smith's Centre for Social Justice, Cameron set about trying to expunge the Tory brand of the toxic Thatcherite associations.

In contrast to the provincial, lower middle class base of Thatcherism, with its emphasis on "moral economy" and social authority, Cameron espoused social liberalism. Cosmopolitanism and multiculturalism predominated over nationalism. The new Tory leader was mocked for the "aristocratic" trappings in his background, notably his Eton education and his royal connections. For the first time since 1965, when the Etonian Alec Douglas-Home was replaced by Ted Heath, the son of a small businessman, the Tories had chosen a member of the ruling class to lead them. But Cameron is the son of a successful finance-capitalist, and made his living for a time as an average salaried businessman in a PR firm. His shadow cabinet was similarly integrated with private capital, with William Hague, Ken Clarke, Oliver Letwin, Frances Maude, Eric Pickles and Andrew Lansley all earning tidy sums from various non-executive directorships and advisory roles. In 2008, of 29 shadow cabinet members, 19 were millionaires.[47] What was distinctive about the Cameron leadership, then, was not that it was a clique of "toffs" but that the big business leadership had wrested decisive control from the lower middle class base.

Yet the base could not be completely ignored, and Cameron was forced to triangulate on a number of controversial issues such as the EU and immigration. While the Federation of Small Businesses, the Institute of Directors, and lobbies such as "Business for Sterling" were among the leading campaigners against the single currency, the pro-euro "Britain in Europe" group, backed by Ken Clarke, Michael Heseltine, Tony Blair,

---

47: Peev, 2009; Kirby and Clarke, 2008

Gordon Brown, and Charles Kennedy, has enjoyed the support of such major firms as BA, Nestle, BAe, Dyson, Ford, BT, Kellogs, Reuters, Unilever and others. Polls showed that the CBI overwhelmingly favoured EU expansion and—at least in the past—single currency membership, with only 15 percent of members disagreeing. Cameron had to find a way to unite small businesses and the lower middle classes hostile to the EU with more pro-European big capital, while seeing off the rising threat of the UKIP. Thus he allied with the hard right in Europe and promised a "cast iron guarantee" of a referendum on the EU Treaty, before capitulating on the treaty as soon as it was signed. On immigration, he could not promise to stop EU migration, but did instead offer a cap on migration from non-EU states.[48]

Yet the Tories were determined not to appear too right wing, and began to search for a new ideological articulation for their policies. Beginning with the idea of a "broken society", which recycled age-old moral panics about the feckless poor and dressed them up in compassionate language, they came to develop an idea of the "Big Society". Philip Blond, purveyor of "Red Toryism"—in truth, nothing but reheated "distributism" taken over from the inter-war radical right—also provided some alarmingly opaque soundbites to convey this message.[49] In practice, little was changed at the level of policy. The Tories simply laundered policies from past manifestos—policies which, in fact, differed little in substance from those of New Labour. But the new ideological keywords of the Conservative were, remarkably, poverty, inequality, compassion and society. And in a number of election campaigns the Tories outflanked Labour to the left on key issues such as immigration and Post Office closures.[50]

As regards public spending, until the recession beginning in 2008, Cameron's policy was to match the government's spending totals and then hit them on their priorities within that framework. This commitment was partially responsible for the Tories' recovery in the polls. At the time of the pre-budget report in 2008, however, the Tories performed a volte-face,

---

48: See "Britain in Europe" website: www.britainineurope.org.uk; *BBC News*, 1999; Grice, 2002; Lynch, 2009, pp187-207.

49: Distributism is the doctrine that capital should be distributed as widely as possible in society in order to maintain traditional, small-scale social relationships typical of pre-capitalist societies. As the Catholic writer G K Chesterton put it, "Too much capitalism does not mean too many capitalists, but too few capitalists."

50: Driver, 2009, pp80-96; Bentley, 2007; Coates, 2005, pp116-117. For a comparison of the 2010 Tory manifesto with its predecessors, see Morris, 2010; for the Tories wafer-thin critique of New Labour's handling of the civil service, see Maude, 2010; Editorial, 2008.

declaring that public spending would have to fall.[51] This was a well-timed turn. Prior to 2008 the Tories could not have expected to make any headway with attacking high government spending, but they successfully utilised the crisis and the leveraging of the state in the context of bailing out the banks, to support such an attack afterwards.

Importantly, however, this reversion to form did not come with an aggressive spiel about the value of market discipline, an idea that has been in acute crisis since 2007 and which would jar with the Big Society panacea. It was pitched almost purely in terms of crisis management—a stance enabled by the complicity of the Labour leadership, which also argued for cuts within its working class base. Indeed, only after the recession did Cameron admit that he was seeking to make permanent cuts rather than temporary adjustments to pay off creditors. The same can be said for the reforms of the NHS. Rather than attack the underlying popular common sense about the NHS, Cameron has claimed that market-driven reforms are necessary for efficiency savings in order to protect the core service from cutbacks.[52] While Thatcher was able to come to office with a coherent and distinctive ideology that tapped into aspects of deep-seated discontent with social democracy, Cameron has attempted to be every bit as ill-defined, slippery and impossible to pin down as the condom-sheathed caricature of him that appears in Steve Bell's cartoons.

The Coalition

Cameron's extensive PR efforts were insufficient for the Tories to win in 2010. That they could only muster just over a third of the popular vote with millions of Labour voters in semi-permanent abstention and a fatally weakened opponent, is indicative of just how bad things have become for the Tories, and how urgently they need to repair them. Cameron, failing to command a sufficient plurality of the vote to take office, has instead been the beneficiary of a civil service fix to ensure that a coalition government would be quickly lashed up in the event of a hung parliament. This produced a government which no one voted for, based on a programme that no one was canvassed about. It is, as David Marquand put it, "the least legitimate peacetime British government of modern times".[53]

This is not to say that Cameron did not enjoy any successes. First of all, the alliance with the Liberals gave Cameron a degree of independence from the petty bourgeois base of the Conservative Party. His embrace of

---

51: Lee and Beech, 2009, pp13 & 21-22.
52: Watt, 2011.
53: Marquand, 2011.

a degree of social liberalism in opposition had proved deeply controversial with these elements, whose concerns were vocalised by their traditional Thatcherite tribunes such as Lord Tebbit. Writing in the right wing *Spectator* magazine, Tebbit claimed the "present Conservative strategy is eroding its ultra-loyalist bedrock vote" and giving the strong impression that "respectable working and lower middle class supporters in the suburbs, country towns and villages are not quite good enough for the new 'A' list, Notting Hill party". He was joined in this chorus by other Tory grandees such as Lord Saatchi, who urged him to embrace a more "ideological" approach.[54] In coalition, Cameron was at greater liberty to ignore such voices. A certain pro-business liberalism could dominate, uniting the financial and business elites concentrated in the Tory leadership with the progressive middle classes that make up the Liberal bedrock. The millionaires continued to dominate as, in addition to well-padded Tory capitalists, the Liberal entrants to the new cabinet included millionaire property owners Nick Clegg and Chris Huhne. Of 29 cabinet members, only six were not millionaires.[55]

The shaky alliance with the Liberals reinforced the Cameronites and temporarily detoxified the Tory brand, and partially enabled the Tories to carry the argument on some aspects of their austerity agenda, at least as far as the polls were concerned. One of the aspects of austerity that resonated with a majority of people after 13 years of New Labour was the view that welfare recipients were a drain on the public purse. As a consequence, when Osborne swung the axe heavily in the direction of welfare, polls found that a majority supported the policy. But even here they found it necessary to frame their cuts in terms of an attack on "middle class" benefits, and to pretend that their overall cuts package was "progressive".[56] This makes the coalition highly unstable and fragile.

Further, the Tories are not merely engaging in cuts, but in a risky project of radical social engineering. The cuts in public spending will be coupled with "free schools" and the *de facto* privatisation of the NHS—policies that will inescapably produce deep social polarisation and conflict. Already one plank of the government's reforms, raising tuition fees and scrapping the Education Maintenance Allowance, has produced a stunning student revolt, notable above all for its militancy. Why, having so assiduously courted a reputation for "niceness", which had previously included a promise to match Labour spending totals, has the Tory leader "turned nasty"?

54: Dorey, 2007.
55: Politics.co.uk, 2010.
56: Hennessy and Kite, 2010; O'Grady, 2010.

The Tory leadership appears to be gambling on its ability to ride out and police the crisis, just as the Thatcher administration did, reaping the reward for subsequent growth that picks up in the private sector. Conservative austerity would then be, much like the Thatcher reforms, an attempt to reorganise British capitalism and the Tories' role within it, creating another round of neoliberal growth and engineering a more conservative electorate. But this administration lacks many of the advantages that the Thatcherites benefited from. The latter came to battle far more prepared. Policing the crisis entails, at a minimum, preparing the state to cope with deep and protracted social conflicts. Yet, as in the Comprehensive Spending Review, the Tories planned to severely reduce spending on police. Further, the last time the Conservative Party was engaged in a concerted fight with the unions was during the 1994 signal workers' strike, which they did not win. This is partly why they have attempted to secure the consent of the trade union bureaucracy rather than being ready for outright conflict. Thatcher could rely on a robust Tory majority in the House of Commons to push her measures through, while Cameron depends upon a Liberal ally that is under incredible pressure because its appeal has in the past been based on the moderately social democratic liberalism defended by Jeremy Thorpe and Charles Kennedy. His ally could collapse or split under the application of serious pressure, leaving him isolated and facing a sudden general election. And lastly, there is no guarantee that a global recovery and a new phase of capital accumulation of the kind that began in 1982 will save Cameron.

The beginnings of resistance have manifested themselves not only in the student movement, but in the trade union "March for the Alternative" which drew half a million workers. The social depth of the turn-out, representing the potential power of organised labour, demonstrated what could be achieved in strike action. A poll taken by Yougov on the eve of the march showed that a majority of people agreed with its aims—proving that if workers fight back, they can carry opinion with them.[57] However, the Tories are in this for the long haul. It is prudent to assume that if they're embarking on a project this ambitious, they are prepared for prolonged confrontations which can only be defeated with superior organisation and combativity on the part of the organised working class.

57: TUC, 2011.

References

Alderman, RK, and Neil Carter, 1991, "A Very Tory Coup: The Ousting Of Mrs Thatcher", *Parliamentary Affairs*.

Andersen, Robert, and Anthony Heath, 2002, "Class Matters: The Persisting Effects of Contextual Social Class on Individual Voting in Britain, 1964–97", *European Sociological Review*, volume 18, number 2.

Asthana, Anushka, 2010, "New Labour pushed Britain's beliefs to the right, says academic", *Observer* (24 January).

Atkinson, Hugh Parker, and Stuart Wilks-Heeg, 2000, *Local Government From Thatcher to Blair: the Politics of Creative Autonomy* (Polity).

Bale, Tim, 2010, *The Conservative Party: From Thatcher to Cameron* (Polity).

Baker, David, Andrew Gamble and David Seawright, 2002, "Sovereign Nations And Global Markets: Modern British Conservatism And Hyperglobalism", *British Journal of Politics and International Relations*, volume 4, number 3.

BBC News, 1999, "The Euro Battle for Britain" (1 March).

Beckett, Francis, and David Hencke, 2009, *Marching to the Fault Line: The Miners' Strike and the Battle for Industrial Britain*, (Constable).

Bentley, Tom, 2007, "Can the Centre Hold? British Politics After Tony Blair", *British Politics*, volume 2.

Beynon, Huw, and Peter McNylor, 1985, "Decisive Power: The New Tory State Against the Miners", in Huw Beynon (ed), *Digging Deeper, Issues in the Miners' Strike*, (Verso).

Birchall, Ian H and Norah Carlin, 1983, "Kinnock's Favourite Marxist: Eric Hobsbawm and the Working Class", *International Socialism* 21, (autumn), www.marxists.de/workmvmt/birchcarl/hobsbawm.htm

Blackburn, Robin, 1971, "The Heath Government: A New Course for British Capitalism", *New Left Review* I/70 (November-December).

Blackledge, Paul, 2002, "The *Eighteenth Brumaire* and Thatcherism", in Mark Cowling and James Martin, *Marx's* Eighteenth Brumaire *(Post)modern Interpretations* (Pluto Press).

Callinicos, Alex, 1985, "The Politics of Marxism Today", *International Socialism* 29 (summer).

Cliff, Tony, 1995, "In the Balance", *Socialist Review* (February), www.marxists.org/archive/cliff/works/1995/02/balance.htm

Cliff, Tony, and Donny Gluckstein, 1996, *The Labour Party: A Marxist History* (Bookmarks).

Coates, David, 2003, "The Failure of the Socialist Promise", in David Coates (ed), *Paving The Third Way: The Critique of Parliamentary Socialism* (Merlin Press).

Coates, David, 2005, *Prolonged Labour: The Slow Birth of Labour Britain* (Palgrave Macmillan).

Cornford, James, 1963, "The Transformation Of Conservatism In The Late Nineteenth Century", *Victorian Studies*, volume 7, number 1.

Cowling, Maurice, 2005, *1867 Disraeli, Gladstone and Revolution: The Passing of the Second Reform Bill* (Cambridge University Press).

Cox, Judy, 1995, "How to make the Tories disappear", *International Socialism* 66 (spring), http://pubs.socialistreviewindex.org.uk/isj66/cox.htm

Crewe, Ivor, 1983, "The Electorate: Partisan Dealignment Ten Years On", *West European Politics*, volume 6, number 4.

Dale, Ian (ed), 2000, *Liberal Party General Election Manifestos, 1900-1997* (Routledge).

Darlington, Ralph, and Dave Lyddon, 2001, *Glorious Summer: Class struggle in Britain in 1972* (Bookmarks).

Denham, Andrew, and Mark Garnett, 2001, "From 'Guru' to 'Godfather': Keith Joseph, 'New' Labour, and the British Conservative Tradition", *Political Quarterly*, volume 72, number 1.

Dorey, Peter, 1995, *The Conservative Party and the Trade Unions* (Routledge).

Dorey, Peter, 2007, "A New Direction or Another False Dawn? David Cameron and the Crisis of British Conservatism", *British Politics* 2.

Driver, Stephen, 2009, "'Fixing Our Broken Society': David Cameron's Post-Thatcherite Social Policy", in Simon Lee, and Matt Beech (eds), *The Conservatives under David Cameron: Built to Last?* (Palgrave Macmillan).

Editorial, 2008, "Britain's Resurgent Tories", *International Socialism Journal*, 119 (summer), www.isj.org.uk?id=451

Evans, Eric J, 1991, *Sir Robert Peel: Statesmanship, Power and Party* (Routledge).

Evans, Eric J, 2004, *Thatcher and Thatcherism* (Routledge).

Evans, Geoffrey, 1993, "The Decline of Class Divisions in Britain? Class and Ideological Preferences in the 1960s and the 1980s", *The British Journal of Sociology*, volume 44, number 3.

Evans, Geoffrey, 2000, "The Continued Significance of Class Voting", *Annual Review of Political Science*, volume 3.

Gamble, Andrew, 1979, "The Free Economy and the Strong State", *Socialist Register*, volume 16, http://socialistregister.com/index.php/srv/article/view/5431/2330

Gamble, Andrew, 1994, *The Free Economy and the Strong State: The Politics of Thatcherism* (Palgrave Macmillan).

Garry, John, 1995, "The British Conservative Party: Divisions Over European Policy", *West European Politics*, volume 18, number 4.

Gramsci, Antonio, 1971, "State and Civil Society", in Quintin Hoare and Geoffrey Nowell Smith (eds), *Selections from the Prison Notebooks of Antonio Gramsci* (Lawrence & Wishart).

Grant, Wyn, 1980, "Business Interests and the British Conservative Party", *Government and Opposition*, volume 15, number 2.

Green, E H H, 2004, *Ideologies of Conservatism: Conservative Political Ideas in the Twentieth Century* (Oxford University Press).

Grice, Andrew, 2002, "CBI chief plans autumn euro 'vote' after sterling weakens", *Independent*, (2 July).

Hall, Stuart, Chas Critcher, Tony Jefferson, John Clarke and Brian Roberts, 1978, *Policing The Crisis: Mugging, The State, and Law and Order* (Macmillan).

Hall, Stuart, 1983, "The Great Moving Right Show", in Stuart Hall and Martin Jacques (eds), *The Politics of Thatcherism* (Lawrence & Wishart).

Hall, Stuart, 1985, "Authoritarian Populism: A Reply to Jessop et al", *New Left Review* I/151 (May-June).

Hall, Stuart, 1987, "Gramsci And Us", *Marxism Today* (June), www.scribd.com/doc/18010709/Gramsci-and-Us-Stuart-Hall

Harman, Chris, 1989, "How the Working Class Votes", in Alex Callinicos and Chris Harman, *The Changing Working Class: Essays on Class Structure Today* (Bookmarks), www.marxists.org/archive/harman/1985/11/wcvotes.html

Harris, Nigel, 1972, *Competition and the Corporate Society: British Conservatives, The State and Industry, 1945-1964* (Methuen & Co Ltd).

Heath, Anthony, Roger Jowell and John Curtice, 1985, *How Britain Votes* (Pergamon Press).

Heath, Anthony, Roger Jowell and John Curtice, 1994, "How did Labour lose in '92?", *Independent*, 29 May), www.independent.co.uk/news/uk/1439286.html

Hennessy, Patrick, and Melissa Kite, 2010, "Voters back drive for new welfare cuts", *Daily Telegraph* (9 October).

Hobsbawm, Eric, 1989, *Politics for a Rational Left: Political Writings 1977-1988* (Verso).

Jessop, Bob, Tom Bonnet, Simon Bromley, and Tom Ling, 1984, "Authoritarian Populism, Two Nations, and Thatcherism", *New Left Review* I/147, September-October

Johnston, RJ, CJ Pattie, DFL Dorling, I MacAllister, H Tunstall and DJ Rossiter, 2001, "Social Locations, Spatial Locations And Voting At The 1997 British General Election: Evaluating The Sources Of Conservative Support", *Political Geography* 20.

Joseph, Keith, 1974, "Speech at Edgbaston ('Our human stock is threatened')", www.margaretthatcher.org/document/101830

Kavanagh, Dennis, 1987, *Thatcherism and British Politics: The End of the Consensus?* (Oxford University Press).

Kellner, Peter, 1997, "Why the Tories were Trounced", *Parliamentary Affairs*, volume 50, number 4.

Kirby, Ian, and Alex Clarke, 2008, "WestMINTster: 19 of the 29 Shadow Cabinet members are MILLIONAIRES", *News of the World* (29 July).

Lee, Alan J, 1979, "Conservatism, Traditionalism and the British Working Class, 1880-1918", in David E Martin and David Rubinstein, *Ideology and the Labour Movement: essays presented to John Saville* (Routledge).

Lee, Simon, and Matt Beech, 2009, *The Conservatives Under David Cameron: Built to Last?* (Palgrave Macmillan).

Lynch, Philip, 2009, "The Conservatives and the European Union: The Lull Before the Storm?", in Simon Lee and Matt Beech, *The Conservatives Under David Cameron: Built to Last?* (Palgrave Macmillan).

Marquand, David, 2011, "The Coalition and the Constitution by Vernon Bogdanor—review", *Guardian*, (14 May), www.guardian.co.uk/books/2011/may/15/coalition-constitution-vernon-bogdanor-review

Maude, Francis, 2010, "Labour has tainted the civil service", *Guardian* (8 February).

Mayston, David, 1996, "Healthcare Reform: A Study in Imperfect Information", in Neil Lunt and Douglas Coyle (eds), *Welfare and Policy: Research Agendas and Issues* (Taylor & Francis).

Morris, Nigel, 2010, "Tory manifesto: The case for the big society", *Independent* (14 February).

Mullard, Maurice, 1993, *The Politics of Public Expenditure* (Routledge).

Nairn, Tom, 1983, "Britain's Living Legacy", in Stuart Hall and Martin Jacques (eds), *The Politics of Thatcherism* (Lawrence & Wishart).

Norton, Philip, 1990, "Choosing A Leader: Margaret Thatcher And The Parliamentary Conservative Party 1989-1990", *Parliamentary Affairs*, volume 43, number 1.

O'Gorman, Frank (ed), 1986, *British Conservatism: Conservative Thought from Burke to Thatcher* (Longman).

O'Grady, Sean, 2010, "Budget is not progressive, declares IFS", *Independent* (24 June).

Peev, Gerry, 2009, "Cameron forces his shadow cabinet to give up 'millionaires' row' jobs", *Scotsman* (30 June).

Politics.co.uk, 2010, "Cameron's 'millionaire Cabinet'" (23 May).

Poulantzas, Nicos, 2000, *State, Power, Socialism* (Verso).

Pugh, Martin, 1988, "Popular Conservatism in Britain: Continuity and Change, 1880-1987", *The Journal of British Studies*, volume 27, number 3.

Ramsden, John, 1998, *An Appetite for Power: A History of the Conservative Party Since 1830* (HarperCollins).

Riddell, Peter, 1987, "Thatcher stands firm against full EMS role", *Financial Times* (23 November).

Ross, John, 1983, *Thatcher and Friends: Anatomy of the Tory Party* (Pluto Press).

Sanders, David, Hugh Ward, David Marsh and Tony Fletcher, 1987, "Government Popularity and the Falklands War: A Reassessment", *British Journal of Political Science*, volume 17, number 3.

Saville, John, 1985, "An Open Conspiracy: Conservative Politics And The Miners' Strike 1984-5", *Socialist Register*, www.marxists.org/archive/saville/1985/08/miners.htm

Scott, John, 1979, *Corporations, Classes and Capitalism* (Hutchinson).

Scott, John, 1982, *The Upper Class: Property and Privilege in Britain* (Macmillan).

Seawright, David, 2005, "One Nation", in Kevin Hickson (ed), *The Political Thought of the Conservative Party Since 1945* (Palgrave Macmillan).

Seldon, Anthony, 1994, "Conservative Century", in Anthony Seldon and Stuart Ball (eds), *Conservative Century: The Conservative Party Since 1900* (Oxford University Press).

Seldon, Anthony, and Kevin Hickson, 2004, *New Labour, old Labour: the Wilson and Callaghan governments*, 1974-79 (Routledge).

Seymour, Richard, 2010, "The Changing Face of Racism", *International Socialism* 126, www.isj.org.uk/?id=638

Sofer, Reba N, 2009, *History, Historians, and Conservatism in Britain and America: The Great War to Thatcher and Reagan* (Oxford University Press).

Sowemimo, Matthew, 1996, "The Conservative Party and European Integration 1988-95", *Party Politics*, volume 2, number 7.

Taylor, Robert, 2006, *Major* (Haus Publishing).

Therborn, Goran, 2008, *What Does the Ruling Class Do When It Rules?* (Verso).

Thomas, Peter D, 2009, *The Gramscian Moment: Philosophy, Hegemony and Marxism* (Brill).

Thompson, Graham, 1986, *The Conservatives' Economic Policy* (Croom Helm Ltd).

TUC, 2011, "Majority back aims of TUC March for the Alternative" (25 March) www.tuc.org.uk/industrial/tuc-19397-f0.cfm

Undy, Roger, 1996, *Managing The Unions: The Impact Of Legislation On Trade Unions' Behaviour* (Oxford University Press).

Useem, Michael, 1984, *The Inner Circle: Large Corporations and the Rise of Business Political Activity in the US and UK* (Oxford University Press).

Van der Waal, Jeroen, Peter Achterberg and Dick Houtman, 2007, "Class Is Not Dead—It Has Been Buried Alive: Class Voting and Cultural: Voting in Postwar Western Societies (1956 -1990)", *Politics & Society* 35.

Wallop, Harry, 2010, "Individual share ownership falls to all-time low", *Daily Telegraph* (27 January).

Watt, Nicholas, 2011, "NHS faces funding crisis unless reforms introduced, says David Cameron", *Guardian* (16 May).

Whiteley, Paul, 1997, "The Conservative Campaign", *Parliamentary Affairs*, volume 50, number 4.

Wilenius, Paul, 2004, "Enemies Within: Thatcher and the Unions", *BBC News* (5 March).

Zweiniger-Bargielowska, Ina, 1994, "Rationing, Austerity and the Conservative Party Recovery after 1945", *The Historical Journal*, volume 37, number 1.

The growing social soul of Egypt's democratic revolution

Anne Alexander

This article is a preliminary and incomplete account of an unfinished revolution.[1] It represents a first attempt to explore the implications of the great wave of strikes and social protests which preceded Mubarak's fall from power and dominated the first months of the revolution. Taking Rosa Luxemburg's writings on the 1905 Revolution as a starting point, it argues that a powerful dynamic of reciprocal action between the social and political aspects of the class struggle is deepening the revolution and starting to create the potential for the revolution to "grow over", in Trotsky's words, from a political struggle *within* capitalism to a social and political revolution *against* capitalism.[2]

1:     Three visits to Egypt between February and May 2011 gave me opportunities to witness the Egyptian revolution first hand and interview leading independent trade unionists. I benefited from discussing some of the ideas here with other friends and comrades. I would like to thank in particular Mustafa Bassiouny, Dina Samak, Hisham Fouad, Haitham Muhammadain, Sameh Naguib, Ibrahim al-Sahary, Dave Renton, Joseph Choonara, Charlie Kimber, Unjum Mirza, John Molyneux, Phil Marfleet, Alex Callinicos, John Rose and John Chalcraft.
2:     It does not deal with other crucial aspects of Trotsky's theory of permanent revolution, such as the role of uneven and combined development in producing the conditions for the revolution, with the internationalisation of the revolution which he believed was crucially necessary for its success. It also treats the revolution as a purely Egyptian affair, rather than a phenomenon which had already leapt borders to reach Egypt from Tunisia following the fall of Ben Ali. This is clearly problematic and I hope to deal with the regional and international aspects of the revolution in future articles.

"Potential" has to be understood carefully here: I am not attempting to present a comprehensive assessment of the current balance of forces in the Egyptian Revolution, or to make judgements about how widespread the processes described here are. The current phase of the revolution is characterised by the complexity and unevenness of its political organisations, forms of struggle and the consciousness of its participants. In Egypt one hundred days after the fall of Mubarak, it was possible to simultaneously live under a military dictatorship which was increasingly inclined to use forms of repression even beyond those deployed by the old regime, and work in a workplace run by a democratically-elected union committee, where the boss had been deposed by a popular insurrection and forced to flee.

The point, however, about the examples discussed in this article is that they allow us to think in a new way about the potential for revolution to realise the vision of human emancipation that the uprising against Mubarak illuminated. And the fact that the people whose struggles are offering us the possibility of thinking differently are the bus drivers and mechanics of the Cairo Public Transport Authority, the nurses, porters and doctors at Manshiyet al-Bakri General Hospital, train drivers from Beni Sueif and Fayyum, textile workers from Shibin al-Kom and low-paid civil servants in Egypt's Ministry of Finance, is in itself profound confirmation of the continued relevance of the revolutionary socialist tradition in which Luxemburg and Trotsky stood.

Beyond stages and compartments

Luxemburg and Trotsky's writings on the 1905 Revolution in Russia both convey the same compulsion to tear down the walls which sought to trap the energy of the revolution in a series of neatly-ordered stages and compartments. The target of Luxemburg's polemic was the bureaucratic leaders of Germany's massive trade union and social democratic movements, whose mechanistic formulation of the trajectory of class struggle through "economic" and "political" stages exposed their rejection of revolution and embrace of reformism. For Luxemburg, the idea that workers' struggles would automatically progress from an economic stage to a political stage, accompanied by a corresponding growth of trade union and social democratic organisations was fundamentally mistaken. Her analysis shows how the 1905 Revolution overturned the assumption that workers' economic struggles were necessarily at a lower level or an earlier stage in the revolutionary process than political struggles:

> Every great political mass action, after it has attained its political highest point, breaks up into a mass of economic strikes. And that applies not only to each of the great mass strikes, but also to the revolution as a whole. With the spreading,

clarifying and involution of the political struggle, the economic struggle not only does not recede, but extends, organises and becomes involved in equal measure. *Between the two there is the most complete reciprocal action.*

In the following passage, Luxemburg does not only break the linear progression of economic and political stages, but also breaks down the compartmentalisation of what are different aspects of the same class struggle:

In a word: the economic struggle is the transmitter from one political centre to another; the political struggle is the periodic fertilisation of the soil for the economic struggle. Cause and effect here continually change places; and thus the economic and the political factor in the period of the mass strike, now widely removed, completely separated or even mutually exclusive, as the theoretical plan would have them, merely form the *two interlacing sides of the proletarian class struggle in Russia.* And *their unity* is precisely the mass strike. If the sophisticated theory proposes to make a clever logical dissection of the mass strike for the purpose of getting at the "purely political mass strike", it will by this dissection, as with any other, not perceive the phenomenon in its living essence, but will kill it altogether.[3]

Trotsky likewise, in his theory of permanent revolution, which first saw light in his writings on 1905, and was later elaborated in his *History of the Russian Revolution* and other writings of the 1930s, breaks down a different set of stages and compartments within which many of his contemporaries attempted to constrain the revolutionary energies of the working class.[4] His crucial insight was to see that the peculiarities of Russia's uneven and combined economic development made it necessary for the organised working class to lead the revolutionary movement against the Tsarist dictatorship, and possible for workers therefore to move beyond the goals of bourgeois democratic transformation into a struggle for socialism. Trotsky was equally insistent in his attack on the idea that a workers' revolution against a global system like capitalism could remain compartmentalised within the bounds of the nation state. As Joseph Choonara notes elsewhere in this journal, these insights are contained already in *Results and Prospects* and *1905*, although they were developed and attained even greater resonance and importance in the context of Trotsky's struggle against Stalinism.[5]

3: Luxemburg, 1906.
4: Trotsky, 1907, 1931, 1932.
5: Choonara, 2011.

Trotsky's theory is at many levels more developed than Luxemburg's, as it explains how Russia's uneven and combined economic development— the "enabling conditions" in Neil Davidson's phrase[6]—made permanent revolution possible (although Luxemburg came to relatively similar conclusions of her own accord in *The Mass Strike*), and Trotsky's arguments are more radical than Luxemburg's on the question of the end of the process, drawing the conclusion that it fell to Russian workers to conquer state power in advance of their comrades in Germany.

Upwards and inwards

The reciprocal action between the economic and political aspects of the class struggle which Luxemburg describes as taking place in the context of revolution is woven into the fabric of capitalist society itself, as it is an expression of capital's simultaneous political and economic domination of the working class. Every strike contains within it something more profound, a temporary usurpation of the power of capital by the power of labour. Every strike also has a political dimension, even if a latent one. The disruption of the boss's domination in the workplace is, by logical extension, a potential political challenge to the bosses' domination of government.

Reciprocal action is the process by which these "interlaced" aspects of class struggle during a revolution interact. In one sense it is a sideways movement, with the relative weight of the economic and political aspects of the class struggle constantly shifting in pendulum-like motion. But it has to have overall a movement forwards, penetrating simultaneously further into the heart of the capitalist labour process, and upwards towards the apex of state power. Forms of workers' organisation such as the Russian soviets can be seen therefore as the fusion of the economic and political aspects of the struggle in a form which simultaneously organises workers' power at the point of production and encroaches on the political prerogatives of the capitalist state to a degree at which it becomes possible to speak of a situation of what Trotsky called "dual power".[7]

The exact name and form of these kinds of workers' organisations is not as important as what they do. The large inter-enterprise strike committees which emerged to lead the strikes in Poland during the emergence of Solidarność are one example of organisations of this type.[8] If the workplace-based workers' councils of the Iranian Revolution had been able to

---

6:   Davidson, 2010.
7:   Trotsky, 1932, chapter 11.
8:   Barker, 2002.

coordinate nationally or even at a local level between different enterprises they might have begun to take on some of the same attributes of simultaneous challenge to the capitalist order both at the point of production and in direct confrontation with the state.

And in order to turn the temporary rupture of capitalist relations of production and political domination into permanent system-change, something else is required: the seizure of state power by the working class and the internationalisation of the revolution.

However, if the situation of dual power is one moment of juncture between reciprocal action and permanent revolution, it can be also argued that the relationship between the struggle for bourgeois political reforms led by the working class, and the simultaneous creation of organs of alternative working class power in the soviets, implies a kind of "growing over" which has to take place in workers' consciousness and organisation before the conquest of state power.

As Trotsky explained in his analysis of the 1905 Revolution in Russia:

Already in 1905, the Petersburg workers called their soviet a proletariat government. This designation passed into the everyday language of that time and was completely embodied in the programme of the struggle of the working class for power. At the same time, however, *we set up against Tsarism an elaborated programme of political democracy* (universal suffrage, republic, militia, etc). We could act in no other way. Political *democracy is a necessary stage in the development of the working masses*—with the highly important reservation that in one case this stage lasts for decades, while in another, the revolutionary situation permits the masses to emancipate themselves from the prejudices of political democracy even before its institutions have been converted into reality.[9]

More specifically, we could say that it is the dynamic of reciprocal action between the political and economic aspects of the class struggle in a revolutionary situation which develops workers' organisations and their consciousness to the point which allows them to make the necessary leap beyond the bourgeois state to workers' power. Of course, revolutions do not follow a simple arithmetic progression, so there are always leaps forward and steps back. Nor is there any inevitability about this process. If the dynamic of reciprocal action falters on one side, it can be pulled up or down by the other. Nevertheless, it is the overall trajectory of enlarging the political dimensions of workers' actions in the economic plane, and the deepening of

---

9:    Trotsky, 1907, Foreword.

the economic consequences of workers' political struggles, which is important in opening up the possibility of permanent revolution.

The masses enter history

It is far too soon to assess the real impact of the 25 January uprising. The awesome scale of the popular mobilisation from below did not only leave its traces in grainy YouTube videos, or clouds of tweets, but was written into the lives of millions of people who, after decades of humiliation and marginalisation, forced their way back to the centre stage of history. The sheer numbers of Egyptians who fought the police, braved tear gas, organised strikes, and saw their friends and neighbours shot down in the streets gives the revolution its elemental force, its ability to enter every pore of the skin, to saturate daily life and transform its makers in the process. And, of course, it is not just about the arithmetic of the crowds, but who these millions are. Some are from Egypt's middle classes, to be sure: students, professionals, English-speaking executives employed by Google, liberal politicians. Their quarrel with the old regime lay primarily in their political marginalisation: the common experience of police-state brutality which united so many sections of Egyptian society. But for the vast majority who joined the uprising, political exclusion and poverty are two sides of the same coin. They are the workers, small business people, artisans, the unemployed and underemployed whose families can't support them, those who toil in the shadow economy of petty street-trading and hustling. As Mustafa Bassiouny puts it:

> The most important of the gains of the revolution has been the unleashing of powerful struggles by wide sections of society which were oppressed and marginalised by the old regime and who have discovered their presence as a fantastic power in the revolution.[10]

As I have argued in more detail elsewhere, a crucial feature of the uprising was the explosion of workers' struggles in the final week before Mubarak fell. Beginning with strategic and symbolic workplaces where, in many cases, underground networks of independent union activists already had a track record of organising strikes, such as the Post Office, the Cairo Public Transport Authority bus garages, the Suez Canal service companies, the strike wave quickly broadened out into other workplaces, bringing at least 300,000 workers out on strike by 9 February.[11]

10: Bassiouny, 2011.
11: Alexander, 2011a.

From Tahrir to tathir: cleansing the nation

On February 11, the uprising finally forced one part of the state—its senior military commanders—to act against another part—Mubarak and his immediate entourage—in a desperate attempt to preserve the integrity of the whole. The removal of the dictator opened space for a wave of struggles similar to those of the *saneamento* (cleansing) of the Portuguese Revolution of 1974 which sought to purge the supporters of the old regime from their positions of authority in the state and wider society. In Arabic the process is often described as *tathir* (purification).

At one level the struggle to remove corrupt bosses and officials from power can be seen as playing out the drama of the uprising itself on a more intimate scale: within a workplace, local neighbourhood, hospital or school. Seen in this way, it is easier to understand the revolution as a process actively involving millions of people, rather than a series of spectacular events. However, as Tony Cliff noted in relation to the Portuguese Revolution:

> *Saneamento*…meant much more than simply locking up the secret policemen. Effectively and thoroughly carried out, it means to virtually destroy the structure of the bourgeois state. Because the corporate state meant control over every level of social life, banks, churches, schools, universities, offices and factory managements, a complete *saneamento* would mean the destruction of the entire social hierarchy from board of directors right down to foremen.[12]

The process of *tathir* has already begun to demonstrate the mutually reinforcing dynamic of reciprocal action between political and economic struggles which Luxemburg identified. In particular, the removal of managers and state officials, by popular protests and strikes, has at least temporarily shifted the "frontier of control".[13] More importantly, in a small, but growing number of cases workers have succeeded in imposing formal democratic control over their managers by choosing replacements to the purged officials of the old regime through elections.

Two aspects of the process of *tathir* are important here. On the one hand, *tathir* is literally a repeat of the narrative of the uprising in miniature, impelled by both the scale of the popular mobilisation and the ferocity of the battle with the state. In Mansoura, for example, on 13 February, the first working day after Mubarak's removal on the 11th, one newspaper report alone details strikes and protests demanding the removal of senior officials

---

12: Cliff, 1975.
13: Bayat, 1987.

by employees in two of the city's local authorities, the First Criminal Court, the Mansoura International Hospital, the Mansoura General Hospital, and a demonstration by workers in the province's central administration demanding the sacking of the provincial governor for corruption.[14] A wave of struggles also engulfed the university campuses, with students and staff seizing control of the offices of the hated secret police and organising massive protests against the heads of universities appointed by Mubarak.[15] Government ministries, hospitals, the postal service, and the big public sector workplaces such as the massive spinning and weaving plant in Mahalla al-Kubra went through similar protests and strikes.[16]

However, the "cleansing" of corrupt officials, even when framed in terms which are squarely within a narrative of political reform, if it is carried out by pressure from below, has potentially profound implications in the social dimension. At the very least, the removal of the director through collective action from below overturns normal relations between workers and bosses. In the context of revolution, "cleansing" has much greater potential to grow over from being a largely political campaign (and one which can be taken up by a variety of political forces, not always those on the left), into a deep social process. In Egypt *tathir* has so far been woven about with social demands, often for improved pay and working conditions, since the beginning of the strike wave which exploded in the week before the fall of Mubarak. At one level, "cleansing" can provide a model for social struggles, and *vice versa*, since both are often carried out by the same means. At another level the success of strikes and protests to remove corrupt bosses can encourage workers to raise new, social demands (and a similar feedback loop can be established in reverse where collective action for social goals emboldens workers to demand changes in management).

The politics of the struggle for social justice

Just as the explicitly "political" struggle to remove elements of the old regime in the workplaces and state institutions has had profound implications in the social dimension, so too has the revolution deepened the political impact of the fight for social justice. The raising of social demands was in itself a dramatic political statement. It punctured the complacency of the liberals, who begged the poor to return to their slums and wait for elections. Moreover, for a minority of worker activists, the political nature of the demands outlined by

---

14:   Salih and Al-Dib, 2011.
15:   Ahmad, 2011.
16:   AFP, 2011; Fouad 2011a

independent trade unionists, such as the 40 or so strike leaders who signed "The social demands of the workers in the revolution" was clear from the start, as it articulated a general manifesto of radical social change.[17]

At another level, the needs of the struggle itself are deepening the political impact of workers' battles for social justice. The need to win allies and support among wider sections of the population pushes strikers to formulate general demands which show the broader social benefit of their struggle. The demand for an increased national minimum wage in addition to the specific wage demands advanced by particular workplaces has been raised increasingly widely. Other generalised demands included the issue of maximum wages in different sectors of the economy. The call for a maximum wage dramatically raises the political content of the struggle for better wages by focusing demands on the inequality which lies at the heart of the capitalist system.

By far the most powerful objective factor which is driving the social struggle forward and deepening its impact is the economic crisis. There are two key points here: firstly the legacy of the pre-revolutionary economic situation, characterised by extreme inequality and rampant poverty, and secondly the post-revolutionary economic crisis. From the perspective of the poor, the post-revolutionary crisis has been experienced through rising food prices (after several years in which food price inflation had already reached historically high levels, and was a key motor of discontent), and the impact of loss of wages during the uprising (for people living on the margins of survival already there is no slack in their finances to cover any gap in pay). Food prices in April 2011 were up 20 percent on the same month the previous year.[18] For some of the best organised sections of the Egyptian working class, strikes have won temporary gains to offset some of these pressures in the short term, by forcing concessions on pay and payment of bonuses. From the perspective of the ruling class, the post-revolutionary crisis has involved not only the economic costs of the uprising and the strike wave, measured in terms of lost industrial output, but also the dramatic fall in foreign currency earning following the temporary collapse of tourism.[19]

Finally, there is the state's response: both repression and accommodation to workers' demands in the context of the revolution have an enhanced political impact. Where employers or the state make concessions to workers' demands, in the ferment of self-organisation from below, the likelihood of

17: *Socialist Worker*, 26 February 2011. See www.socialistworker.co.uk/art.php?id=23984
18: AP Cairo, 11 May 2011.
19: Khalaf, 2011.

limiting social demands by these means is much less. Rather the opposite process takes place, with victories by one group of workers being seized on as encouragement by other groups of workers to raise their own demands. This process could already be seen strongly at work in the pre-revolutionary period during the post-2006 strike wave. Since the revolution began, workers' self-confidence and organisation have increased dramatically, significantly increasingly the possibilities of the generalisation of demands across industries and geographical areas.

On the other hand, state repression can have a politically radicalising effect. The uprising stripped away layers of masks from the face of the state, revealing more of its inner structure to the masses. The army has a new role in direct repression, including the crushing of strikes and social protests, which has the potential to push workers towards radical political conclusions. The rash of court cases against prominent strike leaders at the beginning of May gave a sense of what is at stake in this conflict. The intervention of the state in an attempt to discipline the Cairo bus workers, by prosecuting Ali Fattouh, a leader of the independent union, for incitement to strike, had the immediate effect of producing a political strike against his prosecution in the days before the court case.[20] Yet the rapid concessions on the economic demands raised by the bus workers during the strike, without conceding the central demand of dropping the prosecution, were also clearly an attempt to divide and rule.

The state and the counter-revolution

The intoxicating glimpses of liberation opened by the Egyptian Revolution in its first four months are all the more mesmerising because so little has yet changed at the core of the state. The army hierarchy, the iron backbone of Mubarak's state, remains intact under the leadership of Marshal Tantawi, a man who, in the words of Shashank Joshi "embodies the reactionary forces still embedded at the heart of a regime that may have shed its figurehead but not its essence".[21]

Mubarak's old generals preside over the trials of their former civilian colleagues from the ruling party, but few have dared to call them to account. They deploy the same techniques of repression which made the old regime so hated: torture, military tribunals, the silencing of dissent and criminalisation of protest. Moreover, at the time of writing, central democratic demands of the uprising itself remained wholly or partially unmet.[22] A referendum

---

20: Interview with Haitham Muhammadain, Cairo, in Arabic, 2 May 2011.
21: Quoted in Knell, 2011.
22: Key goals included the removal of Hosni Mubarak from power and the neutralisation of

on 19 March endorsed a number of amendments to the constitution, which included limits to the number of presidential terms, a dilution of the president's executive power, the restoration of judicial supervision of elections, and an easing of the restrictions on the eligibility of presidential candidates, but these relatively limited *potential* gains at the level of formal democracy had to be set against the *actuality* of military rule. Independent unions finally gained legal recognition, but a new law announced on 23 March promptly removed the right to organise collective action by criminalising strikes and protests.[23]

The dynamic of reciprocal action outlined above is taking place in a context which is shaped by the balance of forces between the popular movement and the state. However, this balance is never static, not least because the mass institutions of the state, including the army itself, are under intensifying pressure from below precisely because of the dynamic of reciprocal action which the uprising set in motion.

As far as the repressive apparatus of the old regime is concerned, it was Interior Ministry forces which bore the brunt of popular rage during the uprising. The Central Security Forces riot police were defeated in pitched street battles between 25 and 28 January, during which hundreds of police stations were destroyed by protesters. Moreover the leadership of the Interior Ministry, in particular Habib al-Adly, the minister himself, was an early casualty of the regime's attempt to purge itself of its most unpopular figures in order to appease popular anger. However, the regime was able to stage a tactical withdrawal and remove most CSF troops from the streets on 28 January before their internal discipline broke down. Over the following week the regime made selective but extremely violent attempts to break the morale of the protesters by a different strategy: mobilising the *baltagiyya*, probably a mixture of State Security officers and hired thugs, rather than the mass of CSF conscripts, in an attempt to break the protest camps in Tahrir Square and elsewhere. The withdrawal of the regular police from the streets was also seen by many as a deliberate attempt to create a sense of chaos, and prompted the creation of neighbourhood popular committees in at attempt to restore security. In Tahrir itself the *baltagiyya* were repulsed by activists, including many from the Muslim Brotherhood's youth wing. Swelling numbers on the

---

his vice-president, Omar Suleiman, the dissolution of the fraudulently-elected upper and lower houses of parliament, the dissolution of the State Security apparatus, the annulment of the Emergency Law, the drafting of a new constitution, legal rights to form political parties and independent trade unions, the release of those detained during the uprising, the prosecution of those responsible for violent repression and the enactment of the law raising the national minimum wage to £E1200 a month. See Khalil, 2011.

23: El-Wardani, 2011a.

demonstrations, and finally the strike wave after 8 February, paved the way for Mubarak's removal, which then led rapidly to the dissolution of the State Security police on 4 and 5 March. From that high point, however, there have been numerous attempts to reintroduce the police to the streets, beginning with the return of the regular police for traffic control during March, to the reappearance of the CSF in their old role of suppressing protests during demonstrations outside the Israeli embassy on 15 May.

In contrast to the Interior Ministry forces, which were temporarily defeated, the uprising first neutralised the army and then forced its leaders to act on *behalf* of the revolution against their will. Unwilling to break the demonstrations by force, probably out of fear (or knowledge) that orders to shoot would not be obeyed, the army leadership found itself forced not only to remove Mubarak from power, but also to carry out a purge of the civilian leadership of the old regime. Over the months following the fall of Mubarak, the dynamic of pressure from below, in particular periodic "million-man" marches in Tahrir Square on Fridays, forcing concessions from above in relation to the purge of old regime figures, continued. Meanwhile, the army's increasingly open role in repression has begun to undermine the Supreme Military Council's self-proclaimed role as guardian of the revolution and weaken the appeal of the slogans celebrating the army and people as "one hand" against Mubarak. Nevertheless, the army leadership was still presiding over an institution which largely retained its cohesion and internal discipline (with the notable exception of the protest by junior officers on 8 April) and had yet to face a mass mobilisation by civilian challengers, although there were rising calls for a "second revolution of anger" emerging towards the end of May.[24]

The political landscape of the period after Mubarak's fall has been fundamentally shaped therefore by the contradiction that the army's role expresses: the Supreme Military Council was forced by the popular uprising to act for the revolution and remove Mubarak while at the same time the generals are the principal force attempting to lead a counter-revolution. The sheer scale of the mobilisation from below, followed by the enormous wave of social and political protest in an intensifying dynamic of reciprocal action, is what has enlarged the democratic space and held them at bay.

This balance between the popular movement and the state also structures the counter-revolution. As Alaa' Awad reminds us, the counter-revolution is a process which "begins from the first moment of revolution, and its tactics and trajectory are determined by the balance of political

---

24: For example Thawra al-Ghadab, 2011

forces on the ground".[25] Awad argues that there are three principal axes to the counter-revolution: firstly the concerted attempt by the military leadership and its civilian allies to limit the revolution to the narrow set of constitutional changes enshrined in the 19 March referendum, secondly the deliberate escalation of sectarian conflict, and thirdly consolidating a stable post-revolutionary political order based on the creation of a democratic façade for a non-democratic regime.[26]

The first round of struggles to limit the revolution was fought over the constitutional referendum of 19 March, and pitted the Supreme Military Council, the leadership of the Brotherhood and the remnants of the former ruling party against a fairly diverse coalition of liberals and the left. The continuing social protests and the growth of new forms of independent workers' organisations both shifted the terrain of struggle and reconfigured the social and political forces engaged in the battle. The Supreme Military Council and the leadership of the Brotherhood were joined by liberals, businessmen, and even some of the revolutionary youth activists who had leapt to prominence during the uprising, in condemning strikes for expressing "sectional" interests and demanding that workers restart "the wheel of production". Pitted against them was the awakening social force of the working class and urban poor, still weakly organised, but conscious for the first time of their role as a power in the revolution, together with the small organisations of the left and the independent unions.

In relation to the second axis of the counter-revolution, Sameh Naguib argues that the entry of the Salafi movement, Islamist activists who lay strong emphasis on correct personal behaviour according to their strict interpretation of Islam, into the political scene is an expression of the military leadership's attempts to foment sectarian conflict as a means of creating a climate of chaos.[27]

Thus there were a number of incidents in May where Salafis mobilised in force over the alleged kidnapping by Coptic churches of Christian women who had apparently converted to Islam, creating an atmosphere of tension which spilled over into attacks on churches and Christian property in Imbaba on 8 May that left 12 dead and hundreds injured.[28] The trajectory from moral panic over a supposed "threat to Islam" to attacks on Coptic Christians was already set by the tone of the debates over the constitutional

---

25: Awad, 2011.
26: Awad, 2011.
27: Naguib, 2011.
28: El-Elyan, 2011.

referendum in March, where some Islamists posed the question of accepting or rejecting the amendments in terms of a struggle to preserve Article Two of the constitution, which guarantees Islam as the religion of the state. Moreover, as Awad notes, the question of sectarianism overshadowed and diverted the popular struggle against the appointment of the new governor of Qena province in April.[29] The appointment of a Christian governor triggered large popular protests calling for his removal, and although the initial impetus behind the demonstrations was a rejection of the whole principle of centrally-appointed governors (especially those simply replacing the most corrupt and brutal with their second or third in command), the intervention of the Salafis shifted the focus of the protests onto a rejection of the new governor on the grounds of his religion.

There is not space here to explore the question of how far the military leadership and some configuration of its civilian allies will work to consolidate a façade of bourgeois democracy and to what extent this will be an enlarged democratic space in comparison with the pre-revolutionary situation. Certainly, if the principal architects of this new political order are the generals of the Supreme Military Council then it is likely that the bounds of this stabilised "democratic" system will be very precisely determined by the degree to which the masses are prepared and organised to fight to keep it open.

From one perspective then, the resilience of the core of the old regime, its capacity to mobilise for counter-revolution and its ability to build alliances with mass civilian organisations such as the Brotherhood, to limit and even turn back the revolution, presents a bleak picture. Yet it is crucially important to understand that the same dynamics of reciprocal action at work in wider society are also increasing the pressures within both the mass institutions of the state and those political organisations with a mass base, particularly the Brotherhood, holding up the prospect of them fracturing. As Naguib argues in relation to the Brotherhood:

> Permanent vacillation between opposition and compromise, between escalation and calm, is a result of the nature of the Brotherhood as a popular religious group which comprises sections of the urban bourgeoisie side by side with sections of the traditional and modern petty bourgeoisie (students and university graduates), the unemployed and large sections of the poor. This structure remains stable at times of political and social calm, but turns into a time bomb at moments of great transformation, when it becomes almost

---

29: Awad, 2011.

impossible to reconcile the various contradictory social interests under a broad and vague religious message .[30]

At the time of writing, only the briefest glimpses of tensions within the base of the army and the security forces were visible, but these included significant incidents such as a reported strike by Central Security Forces in the Gabal al-Ahmar camp over conditions in their barracks on 1 May. According to newspaper reports the policemen threw out their officers, took over the camp, and elected a strike committee to negotiate with the Ministry of the Interior.[31] More significant were the signs of collective dissidence appearing among the group of junior officers who took part in the massive demonstration in Tahrir Square on 8 April and called openly for the dissolution of the Supreme Military Council.[32]

Organisations to deepen the struggle

One of the crucial roles that revolutionary socialists play lies in building and seeking to win political hegemony over those organisations which are capable of deepening the process of reciprocal action between the political and economic aspects of the class struggle. However, as outlined above, the pendulum motion from politics to economics and back again needs to be combined with movement upwards, towards the apex of the state, and inwards, towards the heart of the organisation of capitalist production. At its highest point, then, the dynamic of reciprocal action produces a fusion between the political and economic aspects of the class struggle: a challenge to the existing state based on workers' collective social power to disrupt the functioning of capitalism in the workplace in the formation of a counterpower capable of overthrowing the existing bourgeois state and replacing it with a workers' state.

The dynamic of reciprocal action is not set in motion by some act of will on the part of a revolutionary minority: it is one of the inbuilt logics of the revolutionary crisis itself, as it is also an expression of the fusion of capital's economic and political domination over the working class. However, at crucial moments in the struggle the actions of revolutionaries do make an important difference to how events unfold. They make a difference to how arguments are put, and what tactics workers adopt to achieve their goals. The sequence and timing of events plays a crucial role in shaping the revolutionary process. Moreover, organisation is not only necessary to act

---

30: Naguib, 2011.
31: Al-Marsaqawi, 2011.
32: Alexander, 2011b.

on the positive dynamic of reciprocal action, but also on its inverse, to stop the virus of sectarianism from infecting the workers' movement and undermining the unity they need to defeat the boss, for example.

Nor is it only important to build organisations that are to some extent initiatives of the left. On the contrary, finding the mechanisms with which to act on the dynamics of reciprocal action means above all being where the masses are. Thus, as will be explored below, socialists are both building independent unions among health workers and leading struggles from below in the existing doctors' union.

Independent unions

The independent unions are currently a mechanism for transforming workers' spontaneous social protests into organised collective action which can be coordinated across sections, between workplaces and even at a national level. They are spreading and popularising workers' general demands such as the rise in the national minimum wage, which, if implemented, will benefit the working class as a whole. As they grow in size and strength, the independent unions show the potential to become mechanisms for forcing the state and the bosses to concede these demands. The emergence and consolidation of a trade union movement which is genuinely independent of the state furthermore set down a significant challenge to the Egyptian ruling class, which has for more than 50 years striven to subsume all mass political and social movements under its own banner (it of course failed to do this with the Muslim Brotherhood, but has not since the 1940s faced the challenge of a mass movement organised for secular goals). Although Mubarak ostensibly abandoned Nasserism when he signed up to the neoliberal project, his most loyal allies at the bitter end were the leaders of the corrupt state-run trade union federation.

The experience of the railway workers from Beni Sueif illustrates how the new unions are creating an excitement and enthusiasm among workers for independent class organisation on a scale that Egypt has not seen for several generations. Rail workers in the Beni Sueif area of the Egyptian State Railways network began a campaign to organise an independent union uniting all grades of railway staff in the wake of the fall of Mubarak. They put up banners at railway stations and soon had a steady stream of people coming to ask for information about the new union. Hundreds of rail workers signed up to join, and workers from the nearby towns started asking about how they could get organised too. The founding conference of the union took place on 4 May in Beni Sueif and was attended by around 5,000 workers, far more than the 1,200 staff in the Central Section alone, as there were large delegations of workers from elsewhere in the rail network and from the local area.[33]

The experience of the hospital workers' union in Manshiyet al-Bakri hospital in Cairo demonstrates the potential for a fusion of political and social struggles which open up completely new horizons for the working class. It also points very concretely to the difference that the intervention of socialist activists can make in this process. Being a revolutionary socialist necessarily involves the act of imagining the world otherwise, of conceiving at a theoretical level that work could be differently organised, and that ordinary people have both the capacity and the will to transform their own lives. The art of turning theory into reality lies in finding the means by which this idea can be realised by workers themselves, through their own struggles—in other words, finding the methods of struggle, the forms of organisation, and the political arguments which organically connect what exists already to the transformed society we are fighting to build.

The story begins in Tahrir Square, with Mohamed Shafiq, a doctor at the public hospital in Manshiyet al-Bakri in Cairo. Shafiq, a socialist activist, describes how he returned to the hospital a few days before the fall of Mubarak:

> It started on 7 February. I had been in Tahrir Square working in a makeshift hospital. I went back to my hospital and found a revolutionary mood. Even people who supported Mubarak were saying the situation in hospitals couldn't continue. So I did a leaflet with doctors' demands. Unlike previous experiences of petitioning, nearly every doctor signed. It was amazing. A number of nurses asked to sign. At first I said no. There has always been an invisible barrier between doctors and nurses. But so many asked that I thought, "Why not?"

Faced with the question of where to take these demands, Shafiq and his colleagues began to discuss taking the petition a step further, and beginning to organise themselves into an independent union. Again, there was an overwhelming response. Hundreds of staff from all grades wanted to get involved.

> We decided to set up one trade union for our hospital. Within two weeks we held elections. Some were uneasy that doctors, porters and nurses would have an equal say. But we won this argument.

With the vast majority of hospital staff now members of the union,

---

33: Muhammadain, 2011.

and against the backdrop of the wider process of *tathir* unfolding across Egypt, it was not long before a clash came with the hospital director:

> We rearranged the hospital and the budget. Our manager refused to implement these changes. Hospital managers are small dictators—Mubaraks. So we told him to go and not come back.

What distinguished this act of "cleansing" was that the hospital staff were already organised and therefore able to propose and implement a new democratic mechanism for choosing the director's replacement.

> The union council ran the hospital but we knew there would be problems—cheques need to be signed and we have to work with government and local officials. So we elected a manager. The new public transport trade union oversaw the process. The technicians made ballot boxes and we had special forms that couldn't be copied. Some workers are illiterate so we used pictures of candidates. About 500 people voted. We asked the deputy minister for health to appoint our manager before news of the election appeared in the press. He tried to argue—but rang us within two hours to agree.

The first crucial point here is that everything is predicated on the mass movement. The simple, concrete demands for improving doctors' conditions and the state of the hospital became, in the context of the uprising, a lightning rod which gathered anger from below like an electric storm. However, the new union became an instrument for imposing workers' control over management not only because hospital staff had the model of the removal of Mubarak in front of their eyes, but also because within the hospital itself a certain threshold of mass mobilisation had also been crossed. The mass membership of the independent union, in the charged political atmosphere following the fall of Mubarak, concretely raised the question of who should control the workplace.

However, the second point is that, in this case, the form of organisation itself helped to intensify the dynamic of reciprocal action. In particular the fact that the independent union was organised to break down the pre-existing hierarchy in the hospital had important effects: it rapidly tipped the balance of power between management and the workforce because it united almost everyone except the very senior managers. The internal democracy of the union itself was a powerful factor attracting the support of nurses, admin staff and porters, because it offered them a real say in running the hospital.

The experience of the Manshiyet al-Bakri hospital workers raises very concretely the question of leadership. At a number of key points in the story the intervention of socialists played a crucial role, from taking the initial step of organising a petition, to arguing for a general union and helping to win the debates over its internal democracy, to building connections with other workers in struggle and looking beyond the hospital itself to organise health workers on a national level. Yet this was also done in dialogue with the wider layers of workers in the hospital who were drawn into building the union. As Mohamed Shafiq stresses in his account above, it was not he who initially thought of trying to organise jointly with the nurses, but they who demanded it, and they who fought the most fiercely alongside him over the question of democracy. The issues of democratic organisation and leadership therefore go back directly to the question of mass politics. Without an organic connection to the living struggle from below, democratic organisation loses its capacity to intensify the dynamic of reciprocal action. Likewise, socialist leadership which consists of projecting theoretically correct demands and programmes onto workers' struggles from outside is not leadership at all.

The degree to which the independent unions are capable of acting on the dynamics of reciprocal action to deepen the revolutionary process does not depend, therefore, on the nature of their leadership, or on their internal organisational arrangements, but on their connection to workers' struggles *and* the overall balance of forces in revolution. Even undemocratic, bureaucratic trade unions can be a launchpad for struggles for the narrowest of demands which are capable of rapidly bursting the bounds of sectionalism.[34]

The national doctors' strikes in Egypt on 10 and 17 May are illustrations of this point. The organising centre for the strike lay in networks of activists within the old Doctors' Union, the Egyptian equivalent of the British Medical Association. In the wake of the revolution it would have been easy to write off the old union, with its fossilised leadership structures, as incapable of expressing the anger from below, or of providing any kind of organising vehicle for the class struggle. In fact, the idea that doctors could be considered part of a wider working class, let alone organise national strike action, was, until the revolution, just as extraordinary in Egypt as it would be in Britain. Yet the pressure of the mass movement from below, the wave of spontaneous strikes and protests in hospitals demanding the cleansing of hospital management, was also washing into the Doctors' Union. On 25 March 4,000 doctors took part in the Doctors' Union general assembly which discussed how to raise doctors' pay, conditions and professional standing and set out a basic programme of demands. On 1 May another general assembly of

---

34: Cliff, 1985.

around 3,000 doctors voted to call a national strike on 10 May and elected a strike committee. Both meetings were punctuated by stormy, and at times physical confrontations between left wing and secular activists and leading figures in the Brotherhood over whether to call for strike action.

The strike itself was an immensely significant event. Not only was it the first doctors' strike since 1951, but it was also the biggest single instance of coordinated national strike action since the revolution, as it was observed by 65 to 75 percent of hospitals in Cairo and Giza, and 90 percent of hospitals in the provinces.[35] Although the initial motor for the strike was doctors' own demands for better pay and conditions, the activists leading the strike (including Mohamed Shafiq from Manshiyet al-Bakri Hospital Union, who is a key member of the strike committee) argued for and won the position that the strike should articulate wider demands for the improvement of the health system.[36]

The Popular Committees to Defend the Revolution

The Popular Committees to Defend the Revolution are another example of organisations which revolutionary socialists are actively building with the aim of deepening the revolutionary process by transmitting the effects of collective action in the political domain to the social domain and vice versa. The Popular Committees have their origins in the spontaneous eruption of "committees of protection" which were formed during the withdrawal of Interior Ministry forces following the defeat of the police in the great street battles on 28 January. However, in their current form, unlike their precursors, the Popular Committees are shaped by a project of organising some of the wide but rather diffuse layers of the population who have been radicalised by the revolution, in order precisely to have a mechanism for intervening in the social and political struggles in the localities to deepen the revolution. Concretely, this has meant Popular Committees taking up and mobilising around demands for improvements in the distribution of local services, and organising campaigns for the election of local officials or against rising prices. Other initiatives of the Popular Committees have included local "popular conferences", giving people in poor areas their first experience of mass political meetings, and demonstrations over specific local and national issues, such as against sectarianism.[37]

35: Fathi, 2011.

36: Higher Committee of the Doctors' Strike, 2011.

37: Selected articles from the Popular Committees' newspaper, Misr al-Thawriyya, have been translated into English by the Tahrir Documents project, www.tahrirdocuments.org/category/revolutionary-egypt/

The Popular Committees as a project are very specifically focused on turning the political energies unleashed by the uprising against Mubarak from national goals to making social and political gains for ordinary people at a local level, in order to deepen the overall revolutionary process and make further political and social gains at a national level. In their first few months of existence the committees have had a high degree of national coordination, with a national committee of delegates from the local committees meeting regularly in Cairo to coordinate national strategy, and a national newspaper, *Misr al-Thawriyya*. The Popular Committees' founding conference in Tahrir Square on 22 April was attended by four to five thousand people representing around 30 local committees, and agreed on a programme of demands including the election of provincial governors and heads of neighbourhoods, the abolition of the system of appointing officials, and the foundation of a national union of unemployed workers.[38]

Towards a workers' party

Like unions anywhere, the independent unions in Egypt are subject to competing pressures from above and below. The leaders of better established unions, such as the Property Tax Collectors Union and the Health Technicians Union, are already being drawn regularly into direct negotiations with ministers on behalf of their members, and will thus be subject to the same pressures towards compromise and accommodation with the state that trade union leaders as elsewhere. Instead of acting to intensify the dynamic of reciprocal action between the political and economic struggles, it is inevitable that some trade union leaders will attempt to separate the two, and act as transmission belts for the bosses and politicians' message that workers should concern themselves with raising production and not meddle in politics.

This is one reason why the efforts to organise workers into an independent political force are so vitally important. The Democratic Workers Party is an initiative to do just this, and represents an important collaboration between revolutionary socialist activists and leading figures in the workers' movement. In its first few months the party has recruited groups of workers from a number of key economic sectors and workplaces, including the Cairo Public Transport Authority, the railways, the textile factories in Mahalla al-Kubra and Shibin al-Kom, and the post office in Alexandria.[39] Many of these members are leading activists in the emerging independent unions and played a central role in the strike waves before and after Mubarak's fall.

38: Al-Wardani, 2011.
39: Khalil, 2011.

The party's founding statement lists six basic principles:

1. Our party reflects all the producers in society: workers, peasants, professionals, employees and students and all who believe in justice and citizenship and the restoration of national dignity in the face of Zionist-American projects in the region.
2. Re-nationalising the looted companies and land, the development of their administration with popular oversight.
3. Expansion of the public sector through investment of strategic projects to be the locomotive of comprehensive social and independent development.
4. Consolidation of democracy through the creation of a constitution which serves human rights, citizenship and freedom of expression and the establishment of a parliamentary republic recognising the freedom of political parties, trade unions, the media and based on the election of all leadership positions starting from local government (the election of village mayors, town mayors and governors) to all educational and research institutions and public services.
5. Development of the health service, education and housing away from the logic of profit, as these are rights for the community and drive forward the energy of society and its ability to develop.
6. Raise the minimum wage to the level that would meet basic needs (at least 1,500 pounds) with a link to prices.

The full draft programme expands on these points to include support for the struggles of peasants and the unemployed, as well as taking up the question of building a civil state with full rights for all citizens regardless of gender, religion or ethnic origin, and other questions.[40]

The difficulty lies not in articulating a programme, but in winning large numbers of workers to support it. There is intense competition on the Egyptian left, with new parties springing up all the time, and old parties reappearing. Workers attending the celebrations in Tahrir Square on 1 May could have chosen between at least half a dozen parties proclaiming their support for a superficially similar set of principles to those adopted by the Workers Party. One factor distinguishing these competing organisations will lie between those which are capable of persuading large numbers of workers to act in ways which deepen the dynamic of reciprocal action between the political and economic struggles and drive the revolutionary movement forward, and those who are not.

40: Hizb al-Ummal al-Dimuqraty, 2011.

The campaign over the renationalisation of the Ghazl Shibin textile mill provides a concrete illustration of how socialist activists can intervene in precisely this way. The mill, a former public enterprise, was privatised and sold to an Indonesian investor in 2007. It has been the site of a wave of strikes and protests over pay and conditions for several years, with growing support among the workforce for the demand to renationalise. Since the beginning of the revolution the demand for renationalisation has emerged with greater urgency during a two week long strike that workers organised in April, which also raised a number of other demands including the reinstatement of a number of sacked workers.[41]

As Kamal Khalil explains, activists from the Workers Party took a number of initiatives around the strike which were aimed at maximising the political impact of the Shibin workers' struggles, encouraging them to see the wider working class as key allies in their fight, and to join the party itself:

> We organised a joint delegation to the factory of workers from the Workers Party from Shibin and Mahalla. We had a big meeting inside the factory, then we went out in a big demonstration to Shibin al-Kom town, which is about 4 kilometres from the factory. We arrived at the Governorate buildings there, and made a delegation of workers to go and negotiate with the provincial governor and the military governor. When the Mahalla workers went in with the Shibin workers to negotiate, the military governor asked, "What are you doing here? We're only negotiating with Ghazl Shibin." But the Mahalla workers replied, "Whatever concerns Shibin, concerns us too".[42]

It speaks volumes both about Egyptian workers' rising self-confidence and the continuing pressure from below on the state, that the Mahalla workers could successfully face down the military governor over this issue, even as a couple of armoured cars menaced the continuing demonstration outside the Menoufiyya Governorate buildings. As Khalil explains:

> The negotiations [over the return of 95 sacked workers] were successful, and it came to making an agreement; the provincial governor and the military governor said "OK, we've agreed then." But the Mahalla workers had experience of these things, and said, "This is just a verbal agreement. A proper agreement needs to be written down and the governors should sign it." One

---

41: Barthe, 2011.
42: A video of the demonstration is available on YouTube here: www.youtube.com/watch?v=ixxixLVfzwO

of the results of the agreement was the return to work of those who had been sacked. Then we went out again into the street to complete the demonstration.

For the Workers Party activists, there was another crucial step to come: asking the Shibin workers to join the party itself:

> Then we went and sat with the Shibin workers and asked them to join the Workers Party. And they said, "Yes, we'll join." And we said, "Fine, now we need to discuss the programme." They said, "No, we can see what the programme means. It's the demonstration we just were on." We're following this model in other areas.

The struggle over Ghazl Shibin has a wider resonance on many levels. It is becoming a symbol of workers' resistance to the whole programme of privatisation that was driven through by the government of Ahmad Nazif in the last years of Mubarak's rule. The demand to renationalise is one which has emerged out of workers' struggles on the ground and has not been taken up by any of the mainstream political forces, as it directly challenges the entire neoliberal programme. Even the inclusion of Mahalla workers in the negotiating delegation is itself of immense political significance at two levels. It is an important step towards re-establishing a culture of solidarity within the Egyptian working class which has been weakened by long years of dictatorship. The strikes and workers' protests that have taken place since 2006 have seldom resulted in concrete expressions of solidarity between workers in different workplaces, and even more rarely been translated into solidarity strike action. It has been common for workers to take up demands raised by colleagues in other workplaces in their own struggles, and to see other strikes as a model for their own, but in the absence of independent unions connecting workers within industries or across geographical areas, it has been hard so far to give workers the sense that their strikes are significant for the class as a whole, beyond the walls of their individual workplace.

It is in relation to the struggle against sectarianism and counter-revolution that the need for workers' organisation beyond trade unions shows itself most clearly in the current situation, however. In the wake of attacks on churches in Imbaba on 8 May thousands of Coptic Christians organised a sit-in outside the Radio and Television buildings in Maspero, just south of Tahrir Square, in protest at the state's failure to protect churches from sectarian attacks. A delegation from the Workers Party joined the protest in solidarity with the Coptic demands, raising a new slogan which was taken up by thousands of the demonstrators: "Muslim and Christian, hand in hand—together we will make a new dawn".[43]

The significance of building workers' solidarity against the oppression of the Copts goes beyond the reflex action of opposition to sectarianism, important though this is. In the wake of the Imbaba clashes there were a number of initiatives by liberal political figures to rebuild a sense of national unity, including a march led by prominent liberal personalities including Wael Ghoneim.[44] What the Workers Party potentially offers which is different to these kind of initiatives is the project of building revolutionary unity of the Muslim and Christian masses from below, united in a common struggle for social justice. The cross-fertilisation of the social and the political struggles here is vitally important in a context where some of the left have already been sucked into a series of abstract debates about the defence of secularism. As Sameh Naguib rightly concludes:

> Secularism itself, as an abstract principle with no connection to the interests of the working class and poor, is meaningless, and in fact defence of secularism on such a basis only serves the Islamists.[45]

The two souls of Egypt's democratic revolution

The struggles of the poor, with organised workers at their heart, are the fundamental force shaping the present phase of the Egyptian Revolution, and they will write its future. The great wave of strikes and protests which began before the fall of Mubarak (and played a crucial role in his overthrow), demonstrated the impossibility of separating the liberal democratic revolution against dictatorship from its "social soul" of rage against economic injustice. The liberal politicians who thought that the masses would return to their slums on 12 February and tell their hungry children to wait gratefully for the next election have so far been disappointed.

Moreover, the ferment of organising from below that accompanied the rising tide of social struggles between February and May showed that a different kind of democracy is stirring. It is too soon to say whether the promise embodied in the process of cleansing the workplaces by the independent unions will be realised, and whether the initiatives of the left will gain enough traction among the wider working class to provide a pole of

---

43: Fouad, 2011b.
44: El-Wardani, 2011b.
45: Naguib, 2011.

political leadership opposed to the state, the Islamists and the liberals. Yet even the small examples discussed in this article demonstrate that the question of the revolution "growing over" from a revolt against dictatorship to a revolution against capitalism is no longer simply a matter of theoretical speculation. The question is not whether Egyptian workers are capable of creating, through their own struggles, the seeds of a more advanced and complete form of democracy which extends into the workplaces rather than being restricted to the rotation of bourgeois parties through parliament. The question is whether these experiences will be generalised or remain at the level of inspiring, but temporary, shifts in the "frontier of control" in the workplace. The success of the revolutionary left in building organisations of sufficient weight which are capable of deepening the dynamics of reciprocal action beyond and between individual workplaces will be a crucial test which will shape the future course of the revolution.

However, the most compelling reason why the struggle for democracy and the struggle for social justice can be neither separated nor counterposed is the unfinished nature of February's revolution. The uprising rocked the state to its core, and shattered some of its outer layers, but the heart of the regime remained intact. More than that, the generals have shown absolutely no compunction about deploying new instruments of repression, such as the legislation criminalising strikes and demonstrations. The principal force that prevents them from applying these more widely is the continuing wave of protest from below. The resilience of the core of the state can only be broken by new processes of reciprocal action which will interlace the coming battles for social reforms, such as raising the national minimum wage, with the struggle to build democracy from below, through the workplaces and neighbourhoods, and with the battle to protect and extend the gains in political democracy made during the uprising.

References

AFP, 2011, "Mahalla's Misr Spinning and Weaving workers strike" (16 February), http://english.ahram.org.eg/News/5695.aspx

Ahmad, Osama, "Tulab masr yu'akidun...al-thawra mustamira", *Masr al-Thawriyya*, (15 March) www.e-socialists.net/node/6655

Al-Marsaqawi, Mustafa, 2011, "Idrab lilamn al-markazi fi muaskar al-jabal al-ahmar... wa al-junud yadrabun al-dubat", *Al-Masry al-Yawm*, (1 May) www.almasryalyoum.com/node/420018

Al-Wardani, Salma, 2011, "Tatawir al-ligan al-sha'abiyya...fin wa siyasa wa adab", *Al-Shorouk* (5 May), www.shorouknews.com/ContentData.aspx?id=447394

Alexander, Anne, 2011a, "The Gravedigger of Dictatorship", *Socialist Review* (March), www.socialistreview.org.uk/article.php?articlenumber=11580

Alexander, Anne, 2011b, "Officers join Egypt's fight for deeper change", *Socialist Worker* (16 April), www.socialistworker.co.uk/art.php?id=24514

AP Cairo, 2011, "Egypt's Inflation Climbs on Surging Food Prices" (5 May).

Awad, Alaa', 2011, "Al-Masarat al-siyasiyya lil thawra al-mudada", (17 May), www.e-socialists.net/node/6913

Barker, Colin, 2002, *Revolutionary Rehearsals* (Haymarket).

Barthe, Benjamin, 2011, "Revolutionary spirit spreads to Egyptian industry", *Guardian* (12 April), www.guardian.co.uk/world/2011/apr/12/egypt-industry-workers-protest-barthe

Bassiouny, Mustafa, 2011, "Mustaqbal al-thawra yaktabuhu al-fuqara", *Awraq Ishtrakiyya* (May).

Bayat, Assef, 1987, *Workers and Revolution in Iran*, (Zed).

Choonara, Joseph, 2011, "The Relevance of Permanent Revolution", *International Socialism* 131 (summer).

Cliff, Tony, 1975, *Portugal at the Crossroads*, www.marxists.org/archive/cliff/works/1975/portugal/3-masses.htm

Cliff, Tony, 1985, "Patterns of Mass Strike", *International Socialism* 29 (summer), www.marxists.org/archive/cliff/works/1985/patterns/index.htm

Davidson, Neil, 2010, "From Deflected Permanent Revolution to the Law of Uneven and Combined Development", *International Socialism* 128 (autumn), www.isj.org.uk/?id=686

El-Elyan, Tamim, 2011, "12 dead, 232 injured, 190 arrested in Imbaba violence", *Daily News Egypt* (8 May), www.thedailynewsegypt.com/crime-a-accidents/12-dead-232-injured-and-190-arrested-in-imbaba-violence-dp1.html

El-Wardani, Lina, 2011a, "Egypt protests anti-protest law", *Al-Ahram Online* (24 March), http://english.ahram.org.eg/NewsContent/1/0/8484/Egypt/0/Egypt-protests-against-antiprotest-law-.aspx

El-Wardani, Lina, 2011b, "National unity march in Imbaba", *Al-Ahram Online*, (9 May) http://english.ahram.org.eg/NewsContent/1/64/11768/Egypt/Politics-/National-unity-march-in-Imbaba-.aspx

Fathi, Yasmine, 2011, "Egyptian doctors hold first nationwide strike", *Al-Ahram Online*, (11 May) http://english.ahram.org.eg/NewsContent/1/64/11842/Egypt/Politics-/Egyptian-doctors-hold-first-

Fouad, Hisham, 2011a,"Al-shurta al-askariyya tuhasir muwadhafi mudiriyyat al-quwa al-amla wa tathahirat bil alaf fi qina and al-daqhiliyya" (16 February), www.e-socialists.net/node/6492,

Fouad, Hisham, 2011b, "Muslim qubty al-yid fil yid...lajl ma nakhalq fajr jadid", (18 May), www.e-socialists.net/node/6917

Higher Committee of the Doctors' Strike, 2011, "Communiqué Number One" (1 May), www.e-socialists.net/node/6843

Hizb al-Ummal al-Dimuqraty, 2011, "Bayan ta'sisi", (1 May).

Luxemburg, Rosa, 1906, *The Mass Strike, the Political Party and the Trade Unions*, www.marxists.org/archive/luxemburg/1906/mass-strike/index.htm

Muhammadain, Haitham, Interview, Cairo, in Arabic, 2 May 2011.

Khalaf, Roula, 2011, "Political Turmoil Need not Presage Economic Disaster", *Financial Times* (9 May).

Khalil, Kamal, Interview, Cairo, 1 May 2011

Khalil, Wael, 2011 "Mutalib al-thawra al-misriyya", *WaELK* (10 February) http://waelk.net/node/33

Knell, Yolande, 2011, "Egypt after Mubarak: Mohamad Hussain Tantawi profile", BBC News website (12 February), www.bbc.co.uk/news/world-middle-east-12441512

Muhammadain, Haitham, 2011, "Al-Yawm, al-i'lan 'an niqaba mustaqila bimustashfa al-du'aa wa ukhra fi sikkak al-hadid", (4 May) www.e-socialists.net/node/6848

Naguib, Sameh, 2011, "Al-Islamiyun wal thawra", Awraq Ishtarakiyya (16 May), www.e-socialists.net/node/6911

Salih, Muhammad and Sharaf Al-Dib, 2011, "Bil suwar: 'itisamat tatawasil bi addad min qita'yat dahaqillia" *Al-Yawm al-Saba'a* (13 February), www.youm7.com/News.asp?NewsID=351252

Thawra al-Ghadab al-Misriyya al-Thaniyya, 2011, Facebook page, www.facebook.com/THAWRA.MASRYA

Trotsky, Leon, 1907, *1905*, www.marxists.org/archive/trotsky/1907/1905/index.htm

Trotsky, Leon, 1931, *The Permanent Revolution and Results and Prospects*, www.marxists.org/archive/trotsky/1931/tpr/index.htm

Trotsky, Leon, 1932, *The History of the Russian Revolution*, www.marxists.org/archive/trotsky/1930/hrr/index.htm

Culture and multiculturalism

Gareth Jenkins

M ulticulturalism is once more under attack. David Cameron's speech, delivered in Germany on 5 February 2011 at a European governmental conference on security, repeated many familiar criticisms of multiculturalism. It was delivered on the same day as the viciously anti-Muslim English Defence League (EDL) attempted to march in Luton. Fortuitous though this may have been, one might see in this coincidence Cameron playing soft cop to the EDL's hard cop. Cameron took pains to surround his message with caveats designed to distance himself from the far-right. But these were barely reported. The central message was that multiculturalism is responsible for the growth of Islamist extremism, terrorist violence, "the weakening of our collective identity" and toleration of behaviour by "segregated communities...in ways that run completely counter to our values".[1] So much did this play to the idea that "Muslims are the problem" that the leader of the BNP was able to claim that Cameron was catching up with what he had been saying for years.[2] Thus Cameron's speech reinforced the refrain that far from strengthening social cohesion in the interests of tolerance and racial harmony multiculturalism has weakened the fabric of British society by undermining its core values. Instead of the common purpose that comes from shared goals, there is division, disunity and lack of integration.

1: Cameron, 2011.
2: Griffin, 2011.

This underlying theme of permitting alien cultural values to rot "our way of life" is concentrated in the notion of the danger of tolerating "segregated communities". There is, of course, no evidence for this—Danny Dorling and Ludi Simpson demolished the myth more than five years ago by showing that there was more, not less, racial mixing across the country—but it nourishes the idea of "an enemy within".[3] Muslims allegedly practise "*self*-segregation"—they are not the victims of discrimination that might exclude them, but rather they deliberately choose not to integrate with non-Muslims by living in separate communities, by insisting on markers of difference (like Muslim women covering their faces) or by not learning English. This indicates a deliberate refusal to become part of the community, prioritising a culture of seclusion over a culture of inclusion, theirs over ours.

If that is the problem with Muslims (a problem that slides responsibility for anti-Muslim discrimination onto the shoulders of the victims themselves) the other problem is the way in which multiculturalism has operated apparently to reinforce this process of self-exclusion and entrenchment of an alien culture. In the name of tolerance of diversity, of openness to communities from other backgrounds, it has, so we are told, "condoned" minority values at the expense of alienating the values of the majority (whose feelings of hostility towards minority communities are thereby legitimated). It is in this peculiar sense that multiculturalism has "failed": only by abolishing multiculturalism as a state policy can the majority accept the minority and the minority appreciate *for their own good* the necessity to fit in. Thus multiculturalism must end not only because it runs counter to the interests of the long-suffering majority but because people from different cultures have themselves been made the victims of official toleration. If we are being "aggressively liberal", in Cameron's terms, then it is for the benefit of Muslims themselves. What this leads to is the notion that Muslims have to stop being responsible for their own discrimination by "proving" that they are "innocent" of the "bad" culture attached to them (a trial, of course, they can never really win).

3: Dorling, 2005; Simpson 2005. Dorling draws a distinction between "segregation" and "isolation": "segregation" measures "the proportion of people would have to move home for a group to be evenly spread across the country", which is "falling for all minorities". "Isolation", on the other hand, measures "how often individuals from a particular group are likely to meet other individuals from their group". On this basis, the most isolated group are Christians, followed by people of no religion, and the most segregated religious groups are Jews and Sikhs—not Muslims. His conclusion is that the data show that "no neighbourhood ghettos are being formed in Britain". See also Mahamdallie, 2005.

Cultural racism

Cameron's anti-multiculturalism can be traced back to the way in which Thatcher pointed to "culture" rather than "race" as the problem raised by immigration and the presence of minority communities. In a *World in Action* interview in 1978 she asserted that British people were "really rather afraid that this country might be rather swamped by people of a different culture".[4] This became part of a new racism, which as Martin Barker and Anne Beezer wrote in 1983, "has tended to take the form of appeals to "British culture" and the "national community". Immigrants threaten to "swamp" us with their alien cultures; and if they are allowed in large numbers, they will destroy the "homogeneity of the nation". At the heart of this "new racism" is the notion of culture and tradition. A community *is* its culture, its way of life and its traditions. To break these is to shatter the community".[5] With the rise of terrorism following imperialist intervention in the Middle East, the image of a shattered community took on ever greater urgency in the minds of the rabid right, particularly following the bombings in London in 2005. Thus Melanie Phillips ranted that multiculturalism was part of the disembowelling of the nation by "mass immigration…and the onslaught mounted by the secular nihilists against the country's Judeo-Christian values";[6] and William Pfaff hysterically claimed that the British bombers of 7/7 were the product of "a half century of a well-intentioned but catastrophically mistaken policy of multiculturalism".[7]

But Cameron has also taken on board much of the New Labour thinking about multiculturalism. This can be seen in how close he is to Trevor Phillips, former chair of the now defunct Commission for Racial Equality, who argued in 2005 that the emphasis on multiculturalism was dividing rather than uniting us, making us more, rather than less, unequal. We were, he said, "sleepwalking our way to segregation":

> In recent years we've focused far too much on the "multi" and not enough on the common culture… We have allowed tolerance of diversity to harden into the effective isolation of communities, in which some people think special separate values ought to apply.[8]

For Trevor Phillips, British society was being weakened because an

---

4:   Thatcher, 1978. As noted by the Margaret Thatcher Foundation, the Granada transcript has "rather swamped by people with a different culture".
5:   Barker and Beezer, 1983, p125.
6:   In Ashley, 2006.
7:   Pfaff, 2005. See also Modood, 2007, pp10-14, for further discussion on this point.
8:   Phillips, 2005.

indiscriminate tolerance of diversity stopped us challenging those "special separate values" that some cultural communities outside the mainstream believed they have a right to. This is pretty much the argument Cameron put forward in February. What Phillips and Cameron, New Labour and Cameronian conservatism, all reflect is a shift away from the racism of traditional Toryism, with its harking back to the fantasy of an all-white Britain. The new anti-multiculturalism can be just as racist (scapegoating Muslims) yet be grafted onto acceptance that today's Britain is multiethnic, and onto endorsement of socially liberal views (women's and gay rights).

Anti-multiculturalism meshes with Islamophobia while at the same time claiming to be anti-racist. Cameron, for example, went out of his way to distinguish between the faith practised by Muslims and Islamist extremism—conscious, no doubt, of the need to preserve the appeal of the Tory party as a "modern" party committed to inclusiveness (the Tory party chair, Baroness Warsi, no less, complained in a speech shortly before Cameron's about dinner table acceptability of anti-Muslim prejudice).[9] In practice, however, the distinction is not made: Islam appears as the problem rather than some "bad" aspect of it. Islamophobia is condoned as being about a "culture" only, and not as a racial prejudice on a par, say, with anti-Semitism. The writer Martin Amis, for example, defended his musings about Muslims on the grounds that he was concerned with a belief system and not a racial group (an argument brilliantly demolished by the Marxist critic Terry Eagleton and the novelist Ronan Bennett).[10] It is true that outside the fantasies of the far-right "race" is no longer an acceptable marker of difference between peoples in terms of "inferiority" or "superiority". Culture, on the other hand, is.

Culture, change and capitalism

There is a deeply flawed assumption that a culture can be defined monolithically, as a single, uniform and undifferentiated "way of life". It might be possible to talk, as anthropologists sometimes do, in such terms about societies where there is little by way of class differentiation or conflict and whose structures are relatively fixed. But it is impossible to view modern societies in this light. The dynamism of capitalism, its constant dissolving of all that is solid into air, means that every attempt to define a culture as fixed and unchanging founders.

9: Warsi, 2011. Cameron thus distanced himself from the kind of hard right claim that Muslim terrorists "are fuelled by an ideology that itself is non-negotiable and forms a continuum that links peaceful, law-abiding but nevertheless intensely ideological Muslims at one end and murderous jihadists at the other", to quote Melanie Phillips again—Ashley, 2006.
10: Eagleton, 2007; Bennett, 2007.

Yet anti-multiculturalists assume that cultures are essentially different one from another and that they are internally homogeneous. Thus there is "our" way of life, a British monoculture, which is distinct from "their" way of life, the monoculture of a minority. The two are not really compatible. Either "our" way of life is diluted or "their" way of life has to give way to ours.

The idea that there is a British monoculture is patently false, for a number of reasons.[11] In the first place, it is clear that there has never been some "pure" British culture just as there has never been some original "British" people. Whatever the culture of the emigrants who first settled here (and it would have been one shared across a much wider geographical area than these islands), that culture itself would have been the product of earlier cultures that would themselves have developed and changed in response to new advances in the modes of production. Each subsequent migration and invasion—Celt, Roman, Anglo-Saxon, Scandinavian, Norman-French—would have added new elements. (These cultures themselves borrowed from other cultures, as the Romans did from Greece.) Thus to point back to some "foundational" culture is impossible: culture is always already "impure".

In more recent historical times, interaction with other societies through trade or conquest has played its part and foreign products (like tea and the potato) have been "nativised" as part of the culture. Further "imports" have displaced what passes for traditional British food culture, with the dethronement of fish and chips as the national dish by chicken tikka masala (Robin Cook's example).

It would be more accurate to say that a culture (in the modern world) constantly changes as it absorbs new elements and discards old ones because of broader economic transformations, including shifts in population. That it appears not to change, to stand above history, is only an ideological expression of the assumption that existing (capitalist) social relations are "natural". It suits ruling class opinion (as politicians from Margaret Thatcher to Tony Blair demonstrate) to argue that any challenge to society runs counter to "our" culture—and to try to deflect any challenge into fear of some "alien culture". The right's wish to appeal to a common British culture is like the appeal to "national unity", an attempt to divide and rule.

So, wherever one looks, it is impossible to pin down "our way of life" as some "essence" of what it means to be British. Any attempt to sum up a culture as "all the characteristic activities and interests of a people" (as the right wing modernist poet and critic TS Eliot put it in 1948) is going to run into

---

11: Michael Rosen's excellent riposte to Cameron's notion of culture can be found at Rosen, 2011.

the problem of giving a purely arbitrary definition: who now, 63 years later, would see English culture, as he did, as "Derby Day, Henley Regatta, Cowes, the twelfth of August, a cup final, the dog races, the pin table, the dart board, Wensleydale cheese, boiled cabbage cut into sections, beetroot in vinegar, 19th century Gothic churches, and the music of Elgar"?[12] Even George Orwell did not escape the same problem. However much he argued in 1941 in *The Lion and the Unicorn* that "there is something distinctively and recognisable in English civilisation", no one would now see this in the "*characteristic* fragments" he selects, the "clatter of clogs in the Lancashire mill towns, the to and fro of lorries on the Great North Road, the queues outside the Labour Exchanges, the rattle of pin-tables in the Soho pubs, the old maids biking to Holy Communion through the mists of the autumn mornings".[13] This supposedly "distinctive" culture is as dead as a dodo. And a similarly arbitrary selection we could make today is just as likely to be unrecognisable in another 70 years time. The reality is that what might appear typical of the British way of life at one point is only momentary.

Yet, it is possible to recognise that such historically contingent definitions are limited because they mostly focus on secondary aspects of dress, leisure, social codes or consumption and still insist there remains some "core" of Britishness—Orwell, for example, though harshly critical of British hypocrisy, barbarities and anachronisms, talked about "the gentleness of English civilisation" and "respect for constitutionalism and legality" as central.[14] This "core" is seen as tied to certain values said to be central to "our collective identity"—belief in "freedom of speech, freedom of worship, democracy, the rule of law, equal rights regardless of race, sex or sexuality", to refer back to Cameron's speech. Thus "forward-looking" anti-multiculturalists (of the New Labour, or Cameronian variety) might welcome a modern diversity of consumption, reflecting the diverse ethnic mix of the British population, while coming down hard on the idea of abiding by the values that have made Britain what it is.

This brings us to the second point. Such values are not some inherent quality of "our collective identity"—they are the product of a struggle

---

12: Eliot, 1948, p31. Significantly, Eliot had argued in the early 1930s for the desirability of a monoculture and warned of the threat posed by the presence of an "alien" culture (in his days, it was not the presence of Muslims but of Jews): "The population should be homogeneous: where two or more cultures exist in the same place they are likely either to be fiercely self-conscious or both to become adulterate…reasons of race and religion combine to make any large number of free-thinking Jews undesirable"—Eliot, 1934, pp19-20.
13: Orwell, 1971, p75.
14: Orwell, 1971, p81.

in which the rulers of society have been forced progressively to concede freedoms and rights to the vast majority, starting with the 17th century English Revolution. Furthermore, it is utter hypocrisy for our rulers to claim that they are defending such values when they are engaged in both supporting dictatorial regimes abroad and restrictions on the right to protest at home. And of course, these values are not even uniquely "British". Revolutionary struggle in 18th century America and France were key to further democratic advances in equal rights and freedoms.

Thus, the question to be asked of any supposedly unified culture, over and beyond any hybridity, is, whose culture? Culture as a "common way of life" (the anthropological definition) can only apply strictly to societies in which classes have not emerged: in class societies culture is fundamentally marked by conflict between the different values of the dominant and the subordinate classes. To the extent that there is a "shared" culture, it reflects the degree to which the dominant class has been able to impose its hegemony on the classes below it. Culture, then, is ideological in that talk about "our way of life" is not a description of the characteristic mode of a people (the anthropological sense) but a process of selection of cultural traits designed to play on the perception of difference from some feared "other" and reinforce the illusion of commonality beyond the unwelcome divisiveness of class.

Demonising other cultures

The mirror image of this way of examining "our way of life" is the way in which Islam is reduced to an equally essential monoculture. If the right homogenises British culture, stressing its seamless unity, it does the same to the cultures it demonises. Thus Muslims are assumed, by virtue of religious affiliation, to possess a common culture whatever their country of origin or social background, and so are assumed to have one political identity, often "Islamist" in some vague, but threatening, "clash of civilisations" sense. Nothing could be further from the truth than this image of Islam. Other factors—country of origin, class, even personal choice—play an enormously important role in modifying what it means to be Muslim. The Marxist critic Aijaz Ahmad indicates just how complex this process is:

> For most, being a Muslim mainly signifies the fact of birth in a Muslim family, at best a Muslim subculture within a wider national culture (Egyptian, Nigerian, Lebanese or whatever); while religion, even when observed, is lived as one of the many ingredients in one's complex social identity, which is always specific, and hence deeply tied to language, region, custom, class, and so on; religious observance, if any, remains largely local and personal. This subcultural

Muslimness itself is contextual, deeply shaped by history, geography, politics, the larger multi-religious milieu, myriad rhythms of material life.[15]

To which one could add that to be a Muslim in a Punjabi village is very different from being a Muslim in rural Albania—and even more different from being a Muslim (even an observant one) in the great cities of the Muslim world, like Istanbul, Cairo or Lahore. It would be a bit like assuming that you can talk about a common, uniform Christian culture which covers rural southern Africa, Protestant Belfast, Catholic Rome or the millions of English people who at best could be described as coming from a vaguely Anglican background. Other factors—levels of economic development, differences between town and country, impact of globalisation—clearly play a more important role in shaping a culture than purely religious ones.

Ahmad's focus is on the Indian subcontinent. Even here, where hundreds of millions of Muslims live, the picture is far from straightforward. There are more Muslims in India itself than in Pakistan, supposedly a Muslim state (though officially as secular a country as its majority Hindu neighbour). And though a Bengali-speaking Muslim in India may share the same language and religion as someone from the neighbouring state of Bangladesh, their experience is a very different one. Within India itself, which has the second largest population of Muslims in the world (Indonesia has the biggest), "Muslims living in any particular region of the country...share well over 80 percent of their daily cultural practices with their Hindu neighbours in the same region, and very little with Muslims of distant regions within the country". Even in Indonesia, "for the vast majority the culture of daily life bears notable imprints of Hinduism, in particular, and, in some places, even Buddhism".[16]

This differentiation within the Muslim world, yet simultaneous blurring with non-Muslim ways of life, makes talk about some single Muslim/Islamic "culture" meaningless—and this is to say nothing about the role played by other religious (Sunni, Shia, Sufi, etc) or ideological divisions, let alone the complex and contradictory modernising role of secularism:

> The ecumenical popular Islam of Indonesia; the varieties of the lived Muslim subcultures in secular, multi-religious India; the vagaries of the "Muslim nationalism" which provided the ideological justification for the creation of Pakistan; the incoherence of the linguistic nationalism of the East Pakistanis, which led to the creation of Bangladesh as a secular nation—all these indicate

---

15: Ahmad, 2007, p1.
16: Ahmad, 2007, p2.

how misleading it is to ascribe to some inherent Islamic-ness of the polity or the culture as such. To refer to all these people as "Islamic" is to occlude the specificity and novelty of Islamism in general, to posit hyper-Islamicity of Muslim peoples, and to succumb to the idea propagated by the religious right as well as the Orientalists, that religion is the constitutive element of a culture, and hence also of its social existence and political destiny.[17]

It is important to take on board the significance of what Ahmad has to say here. Once we understand there is no single Muslim cultural identity even in the countries that can be termed Muslim, it is clear that it makes no sense to impose any such identity on Muslims living in Britain, as racists in general, and opponents of multiculturalism in particular, do. The net effect is not only to project a selectively false Muslim identity—it is also to project it as "other", as radically different and hostile to British identity. This reinforces notions of the superiority of British (and more generally Western) culture and the inferiority of Muslim culture. This is most evident in the way an opposition is constructed between women in Islamic culture and women in Western culture. The former are oppressed, the latter liberated, with the presence or absence of head covering acting as a marker of difference. This has become a dominant symbolic discourse throughout Western Europe, pushed to extremes in countries like France where the banning of the burka (affecting a tiny minority, thus confirming how much this is a symbolic question) stands, for all its coercive and illiberal nature, as an assertion of the liberal freedoms of our advanced society. Such discourse simply ignores the complex reality of the lives of women with a Muslim background whether in Muslim or non-Muslim countries. Large numbers of Muslims in urban societies do not dress any differently from their Western sisters; and covering the head is to some extent the norm (or certainly has been till recently) for non-Muslim women in many predominantly agrarian societies as it was for European middle class and upper class women in public a hundred years ago or so. Similarly, it makes no sense to assume that what Western women wear is somehow a sign of their liberated status in opposition to what Muslim women wear.

This is not the only example where complex reality is reduced to a cultural stereotype. Female genital cutting[18] is often held up as an example of the barbarity of Islamic culture. Yet, as Frances Althaus has noted, this practice

---

17: Ahmad, 2007, p2.
18: I have chosen to use this term rather than female circumcision or female genital mutilation. Female circumcision implies a cultural analogy with male circumcision, while female genital mutilation implies that the practice has no cultural dimension. Both terms have been contested.

is virtually unknown outside a very small part of the Islamic world (the central belt of Africa, chiefly the Horn of Africa and Egypt) and has no Koranic basis. It predates the arrival of Islam in Africa and where it is practised is not confined to Muslims—it also occurs among Christians, animists (worshippers of natural spirits) and some Ethiopian Jews.[19] To emphasise the point that it is false to leave "civilised" assumptions out of the picture, Althaus also asked whether female genital cutting is more culturally regressive than the medically unnecessary cosmetic surgery that Western women undergo.[20]

Though Muslims suffer most from such assumptions about their "culture", the same homogenising (and distorting) process applies to other peoples. To talk of "African culture", for example, is to ignore the fact that a continent bigger in size than Europe possessed a wide range of different societies before falling prey to conquest by Europeans. These went from societies with no class divisions (hunter-gather societies), through horticulturalist societies to plough-based farming (with incipient class divisions), to societies with cities, states and deep class divisions.[21]

The nature of capitalist culture

We return, then, to the way in which capitalism constantly revolutionises not just the instruments and relations of production (in the words of the *Communist Manifesto*) but to its constant revolutionising of the whole relations of society, including its culture. This means that capitalism is constantly remaking what appears to be a fixed "way of life" and constantly breaking down cultural differences between settled, established populations and newly arrived groups from other areas of the world. Thus whatever people's background the tendency is for virtually everyone to share with everyone else working and living in Britain the same assumptions about how life should be lived—assumptions that are radically different from those of feudal society or earlier modes of production.

What all this means is that attempts to define different ethnic groups as living according to radically different and opposed "cultures" are mistaken. Capitalism has continuously drawn people from different backgrounds into working in the same way and in the process tends to homogenise the way they live. This was true of the Irish peasantry pulled into the factories of Manchester in the early 19th century. The same is true of the great influx in the post-war period of people drawn from the West Indies and the Indian

---

19: Althaus, 1997, pp130-131.
20: Althaus, 1997, p132.
21: I owe this point to Chris Harman.

subcontinent (among them Muslims) to work in factories and offices across Britain. People coming from countries not yet transformed by modern capitalism (although already capitalist) saw their cultural habits transformed within a couple of generations. The young came to speak and behave like the young of the established population, alongside whom they were educated or worked, whose own culture absorbed elements of linguistic usage and music from the newcomers. The tendency of capitalism, insofar as it submits new populations to the same rhythms of work as the established population, acts therefore to break down differences and continuously resynthesise a culture in its image.

This breaking down of cultural differences between older and newer communities can be seen in the way changes in capitalism also transform the cultural norms of the older communities themselves. So what is sometimes seen as peculiarly the product of Muslim culture—an attitude towards women which confines them to a particular role, with prescribed ways of behaving and appearance in public—is not so different from what would have been considered the norm of Victorian Britain (indeed, some elements of this norm persisted well into the 20th century). The dynamic of capitalism itself broke down these distinctions (without, of course, abolishing oppression) within British culture. It is clear that as new communities from parts of the world not yet absorbed by capitalism find themselves more and more integrated, particularly because of participation in the workforce, their culture will change.

However, it would be mistaken to assume that capitalism simply wears away difference. It also acts in other ways, forcing people to compete with one another over jobs and resources, like housing and access to welfare. Residual cultural differences—differences most clearly visible in matters of religion (dress code, eating habits, family arrangements)—then take on a disproportionate significance. People are invited to see them in terms of identities of belonging or not belonging. Out of real or imagined differences, which have ceased to be of importance, racists and anti-multiculturalists create a "Muslim identity", which they claim is essentially incompatible with a "British identity". Conversely, and understandably, people from a Muslim background may themselves reach for an Islamic identity as a way of asserting self-confidence—in the same way that a generation ago black people sought to articulate Black Pride as a counter to the racism they encountered. For the "new" communities, the shock of discovering that acceptance is going into reverse may lead some to reach for the supposed security of traditional cultural practices. These can become the heart of a heartless world, offering support and recognition because the promise of "integration" is illusory. If you are going to be attacked as a Muslim, even if you are not a particularly observant one, then you might as well be a "proper" one: at least then you have something of your own to be proud of—a mode of self-assertion to counter the falseness of the society that asks you to belong but that in practice bars the door to you. It goes without saying that this reaching out for a "Muslim identity" cannot be viewed in the same light as white people clinging to a "British identity"; one is a reaction against racism, however inadequate and locked within a polarity of assumed fixed cultures, the other a concession to, if not a wholesale embrace of, racism.

Defending multiculturalism

Because anti-multiculturalism reinforces racist stereotypes of Muslims (and other minority groups), socialists defend multiculturalism and vigorously contest the notion that it has "failed". But *how* should it be defended?

Clearly, the starting point has to be the right of immigrant communities to live their lives without pressure to conform to some supposedly superior culture. Quite correctly, therefore, the fight against racism involves defending cultural diversity and refusing the idea that there is only one good culture, British culture. Not surprisingly, given that inner-city schools demonstrate most vividly the cultural and ethnic diversity of the British population, multiculturalism has been a central feature in primary and secondary education. Schools have done their utmost to be inclusive, not to assume that all pupils adhere (or should adhere) to one British, white or Christian culture. Hence space has been made to recognise the religious festivals of other faiths, to respect the beliefs, languages and cultural traditions of immigrant communities. This inclusivity is reflected elsewhere in public sector institutions, local councils primarily, who find themselves operating within mixed communities. Thus forms and notices are printed in a variety of languages and town halls, particularly in inner city areas, make a point of reaching out to community organisations, sometimes with funds.

Opposition to the idea of Britain as a monoculture has led to more ambitious attempts to assert the validity of alternative cultures. Hence the celebration of Black History Month in schools and local authorities becomes a way of countering myths about slavery and about how it was ended—or the celebration of Muslim culture (particularly in the realms of philosophy, science and architecture) as a way of countering the perception that it is inferior to Western European civilisation or that its achievements are derivative.

Much of this is valuable insofar as it challenges racist dismissals of other cultures as inferior. But this multiculturalism often falls short because it doesn't always move beyond the same assumptions about cultures as relatively fixed "ways of life". The danger is of falling into the same essentialising trap as the opponents of multiculturalism and not understanding how cultures continuously mix and cross-fertilise, though many supporters do recognise this—indeed for them, multiculturalism is all about intercultural connections and the benefit to society of this process. However, there remains a real problem if the contradictory role of capitalism itself is not understood, its simultaneous homogenising and resurrection of cultural difference.

Theorising multiculturalism

This is largely absent from the work of multiculturalist theorists from the 1990s onwards.[22] The question they raised was whether culturally defined groups in society had rights that needed recognition, either legally or in terms of public policy, over and beyond the rights of individuals not to be discriminated against because of their ethnic background. The shift from ethnicity to culture as the defining term was seen as indicative of the need for a shift from individual rights to group rights. The state had a duty not just to ensure a level playing field in terms of jobs or housing, for example, but to give public recognition to the plurality of cultures in British life (a minor example of this would be the printing of forms in languages other than English). The right of the citizen to be treated equally under the law, to vote, to have the same economic opportunity as everyone else (through eliminating economic disadvantage) presupposed an economic and political framework neutral between the different cultures to which citizens belonged. Modern society was, as Bhikhu Parekh, one of the foremost British theorists of multiculturalism, put it, now not just "a community of citizens" but "a community of communities".[23]

With the advent of the plurality of cultures in British society, the presupposition about the neutrality of public space and the assumption that everyone shared a common idea of what the good life was could no longer be taken for granted. Different cultures had different concepts of the good life—and it was wrong to deny minority cultures their right to pursue the good life in ways they saw fit, even if it failed to conform to majority expectations. There can be no single concept of "the good life", to which

---

22: In what follows I have ignored the work of Will Kymlicka, the Canadian political philosopher. Pioneering though his work is, it is more directed towards the rights of already long established communities (eg French Canadians), rather than those of newly arrived immigrant communities (the context of multiculturalism in Europe). For further discussion of this point, see Modood, 2007, pp3-9.

23: The Parekh Report, 2000, p ix. The Parekh Report was the collective product of contributors to a commission on the future of multi-ethnic Britain, established by the Runnymede Trust and chaired by Bhikhu Parekh. The quotation is taken from the preface, which appeared under his name. The report as a whole reflects Parekh's thinking. See also Modood, 2007, whose analysis of multiculturalism closely follows Parekh's.

all conform, because all such concepts are themselves culturally determined. Thus tolerance is not tolerance within some supposedly universal concept of the good life (what Parekh elsewhere calls a moral monist view of the world).[24] Tolerance has to be tolerance of different cultures' understanding of the good life and respect for the right of people to live by their culture's view of the good life. A new set of rights, therefore, was needed—over and beyond the legal, political and economic rights that had been won at different points over the last three centuries. These were group rights—the right of a cultural group to have its cultural needs recognised—in addition to the individual's legal, political and economic rights. Recognising group rights would promote equality between cultures and prevent discrimination against minority groups in the name of the supposedly incontestable values of the dominant culture.

An objection often raised is how society should adjudicate in the event of a clash between group and individual rights. Can a community, whose right to conduct its affairs according to its own cultural views has been recognised, compel an individual within that group to abide by that right? Or do her rights as an individual not to be defined by that culture but to adopt the cultural norms of the dominant group in society outweigh those of her community? On the one hand, individual rights seem universal. On the other, they seem inapplicable in the context of other cultures that emphasise collective values, rather than in individual rights, which are alien to them.

It is this contradiction that leads to accusations that multiculturalism lands us in a relativist swamp, a moral confusion, where we are invited to accept (even champion) reactionary, inegalitarian and undemocratic practices—all in the name of equal respect for all cultures that comes from rejecting a monist view of the world. On the other hand, acting on the basis of egalitarian or "progressive" rights, particularly when it comes to women's or gay rights, often involves the opposite shift: liberals backing repressive governmental action (as, for example, in France) in the name of universal values.

Parekh's answer to this contradiction was a pragmatic one. We don't need to lose our moral compass—it is still possible to criticise particular cultural practices, on condition that we recognise the *cultural* element determining our own viewpoints. Since cultures for Parekh are neither closed nor

---

24: Parekh, 2000. Parekh devotes a long chapter to the monist tradition, going back to the Greeks, and argues that even John Stuart Mill, the great 19th century liberal champion of the right to act as one chooses (provided no one else is harmed), and so of diversity, nevertheless assumed that only liberalism held the key to the good life. He concludes the chapter by arguing that since all forms of monism (in which he includes Marxism) "cannot see any good outside its favoured way of life, it either avoids all but minimum contact with them or seeks to assimilate them by peaceful or violent means"—p49.

lack internal dynamic, dialogue can open up a space for evaluating culture clashes. Through a shared discourse of mutual recognition, we can escape the twin traps of either dismissing cultures as failing to conform to a supposedly supracultural set of standards or of never being able to evaluate them on the grounds that they are incommensurate. Multiculturalism does not have to be a morally indifferent celebration of pure difference that only a stiff dose of transcendental universal values can cure. You can a respect a person's right to their own culture while engaging in critical evaluation of contested cultural practices—whether from minority or majority cultures.[25] Through intercultural dialogue, common ground over contested values can be established.

But arguably this view still leaves us with a problem—which is that it appears to ground universals in a kind of will to agreement between reasonable people, no matter what their cultural belief-systems. Useful though this might be as a challenge to cultural arrogance (particularly the arrogance of the dominant culture), it does imply a certain ambivalence about whether reasoning can rise above cultural subjectivity, or intersubjectivity.

This ambivalence reflects another limitation: nearly all multiculturalists tend to think of the politics of multiculturalism in terms of citizenship, that is, they accept the theoretical framework of liberal parliamentary democracy as the only possible structure in which political choices can be played out. So the overwhelming preoccupation is with how to replace a monocultural concept of citizenship with a multicultural one, one kind of Britishness by another—not to question why Britishness is needed in the first place. It is one thing to want there to be recognition of the diversity of cultures in British life—and of course, when a black athlete drapes herself in the union jack, socialists understand that this is an assertion of a black person's right to be included. But the search for a new Britishness is no protection against politicians who simultaneously use pride in supposed British virtues of tolerance, diversity and democracy as the pretext for the demonisation of Muslims and the pursuit of ever more reactionary policies over immigration. And it can disarm the fight for real equality.[26]

25: Parekh discusses, among other things, female circumcision and polygamy. He also debates whether the right to free speech is an adequate response to Muslim objections to *The Satanic Verses*.
26: Something of this can be seen in Modood, 2007. His understanding of how culture must neither be essentialised (assumed to be some single, monolithic entity) or made so internally heterogeneous that it ceases to have any meaning is very useful, as is his discussion of secularism and religion (though Parekh's analysis of France and the Muslim headscarf is much fuller and more complex). But his concentration on the policy implications for multiculturalism amount to little more than an attempt to build on the interest shown by politicians of the left (among whom he counts Gordon Brown!) to create a more inclusive national identity.

Critiques of multiculturalism

This criticism is at the root of two different kinds of critique of multiculturalism. One, going back to the 1980s, is that offered by A Sivanandan of the Institute of Race Relations.[27] His argument was that it was only the joint fight in the 1960s and 1970s by Asians, Afro-Caribbeans and whites against racism and the discrimination affecting employment, housing and social services that allowed cultural diversity to flourish. This unified struggle was instrumental in forcing the introduction of anti-discrimination legislation in the late 1960s. However, this success brought its own problems as multiculturalism became institutionalised: "Multiculturalism was stripped of its anti-racist roots and remit. It ceased to be an outcome of the struggle from below, and became government policy imposed from above".[28] This shift came, as Sivanandan argued elsewhere, in the wake of Labour home secretary Roy Jenkins's celebrated speech in 1966 defining integration not as a "flattening process of assimilation, but as equal opportunity accompanied by cultural diversity, in an atmosphere of mutual tolerance". With equal opportunity being a dead letter, in the context of further racist immigration law, "the emphasis was on "cultural diversity"—and the integration of those cultures into a "cultural" pluralist set-up. Racism was not a matter of racial oppression and exploitation, of race and class, but of cultural differences and their acceptability".[29]

The further shift for Sivanandan and his co-thinkers in the institutionalisation of multiculturalism came in the wake of the 1981 riots in Brixton, Toxteth and Bristol. The Scarman inquiry did not, as it should have done, see the problem as police "institutionalised racism". The issue became a matter of "ethnic disadvantage" faced by the Afro-Caribbean community. The answer therefore lay in targeting "problem groups" within society rather than targeting the racism of British society. One aspect of problematising these groups was to see them in cultural terms. Thus "West Indian families" have been at a disadvantage because of their culture—a culture of absent fathers and lack of role models, linked to educational underachievement and criminality. This served to shift the blame away from the racist use of stop and search police powers and the racist bias in school exclusions. It was made to seem that "African-Caribbean families had a cultural propensity to failure... If it was their 'alien' culture that was the primary cause of African-Caribbean poverty, then British society could absolve itself of responsibility".[30]

27: See in particular Sivanandan, 1990. This collection of articles, *Communities of Resistance*, mostly appeared first in *Race and Class*, of which he was the founding editor.
28: Sivanandan, 2006.
29: Sivanandan, 1990, p80, which also contains the quotation from Jenkins's speech.
30: Kundnani, 2007, p45.

Culturalism became the basis of targeting resources. "Meeting cultural needs would somehow stave off protests about inequality and injustice", as Sivanandan put it in his analysis of government response to the anti-police riots of the 1980s. Money was channelled towards groups said to represent particular cultures. Anti-racism was replaced by what Sivanandan called "culturalism or ethnicism" as different groups become "part and parcel of a competitive fight for central and local government favours".[31] This clientelism could only deepen divisions (by culturally ghettoising immigrant groups) and invite resentment as some groups were seen as favoured over others:

> The ensuing scramble for government favours and government grants (channelled through local authorities) on the basis of specific ethnic needs and problems served, on the one hand, to deepen ethnic differences and foster ethnic rivalry and, on the other, to widen the definition of ethnicity to include a variety of national and religious groups—Chinese, Cypriots, Greeks, Turks, Irish, Italians, Jews, Moslems, Sikhs—till the term became meaningless (except as a means of getting funds).[32]

There is much to be said for this critique of a multiculturalism that was turned into an instrument of state policy, one whose formal anti-racism did nothing to contest institutionalised racism, though at times it has a limited view of the broader involvement of white people in the anti-racist struggle.[33]

Another critique of a much deeper recuperation of multiculturalism by capitalism comes from the cultural critic Slavoj Žižek. Žižek argues that multiculturalism, far from being a radical challenge to the status quo, is the logic of capitalism in the age of globalisation. Where once capitalism, located in the nation state, had as its corollary a colonising (subordinating and exploiting) relationship with the countries it was colonising, we have now reached the final moment of the process of capital's movement beyond national boundaries: "the paradox of colonisation in which there are only colonies, no colonising countries—the colonising power is no longer a nation-state but directly the global company". Consequently, Žižek concludes, global capitalism generates a new ideal form of ideology, multiculturalism. Multiculturalism is:

31: Sivanandan, 2006.

32: Sivanandan, 1990, p94.

33: See, for example, the comments on the Anti Nazi League (Sivanandan, 1990, pp88-89); and the suggestion that (by implication, "white") trade unionists took over the Grunwick 1976-77 strike "to meet their own preoccupations" (whatever those were) and therefore killed it—Sivanandan 2006.

the attitude which, from a kind of empty global position, treats *each* local culture the way the coloniser treats colonised people—as "natives" whose mores are to be carefully studied and "respected". That is to say, the relationship between traditional imperialist colonialism and global capitalist self-colonisation is exactly the same as the relationship between Western cultural imperialism and multiculturalism: in the same way that global capitalism involves the paradox of colonising without the colonising nation-state metropole, multiculturalism involves patronising Eurocentrist distance and/or respect for local culture without roots in one's particular culture. In other words, multiculturalism is a disavowed, inverted, self-referential form of racism, a "racism with a distance"—it "respects" the Other's identity, conceiving the Other as a self-enclosed "authentic" community towards which he, the multiculturalist, maintains a distance rendered possible by his privileged universal position. Multiculturalism is a racism which empties its own position of all positive content (the multiculturalist is not a direct racist, he doesn't oppose to the Other the *particular* values of his own culture), but nevertheless retains this position as the privileged *empty point of universality* from which one is able to appreciate (and depreciate) properly other particular cultures—the multiculturalist respect for the Other's specificity is the very form of asserting one's own superiority.[34]

Multiculturalism, then, far from offering resistance to the system, is complicit with it. Far from coming out of opposition to racism, it is the new racism. Respect for another's culture is not a counter to a false universality claimed by the dominant culture; it proves on inspection to be the false neutrality by which cultures are appropriated by capital and subordinated to it. If Sivanandan criticised multiculturalism because it could become the tool of government policy, Žižek goes a step further and makes it the necessary accomplice of the latest phase of post-national capitalism. Evidence for this might be Sky Televison's "respect" for local culture in China, the better to dominate the market; evidence for the indirect racism of the multiculturalist might be the Hitler-worshipping Leni Riefenstahl's "respect" for the Nuba people (her photos stress their pure "otherness", the better to reinforce their "distance" from us); and Nick Griffin in his more playful musings says that just as non-white people have a right to their own culture so too do the British people—which is a kind of twisted multiculturalism. But Žižek's claim seems altogether too sweeping. It is difficult to see how a teacher fostering multicultural approaches to learning that challenge racist notions of cultural superiority is an "indirect" racist acting as an accomplice of global capitalism.

34: Žižek, 1997, p44.

Egalitarianism and multiculturalism

The problem of culturalism appears in different guises in the egalitarian critique of multiculturalism, of which Brian Barry's is the most powerful.[35] Is, for example, the idea of equality one that is culturally determined (a Western idea) and therefore not necessarily applicable to (non-Western) cultures? Clearly, it is right to be sceptical of Eurocentric claims about the superiority of Western culture. But the problem with equality is not that its applicability outside Western liberal societies is suspect but that Western liberal societies are very far from having real equality within them. A multiculturalist approach can miss this point and in the interests of dialogue between cultures reach some dubious conclusions. Barry makes the point that if "each culture constitutes a self-contained moral universe" then there can be "no room for any approach to cultural conflict that aspires to transcend the limits of any one culture". Not only does this involve rejecting a doctrine of "universal human rights", but it also involves (among other things) a slide into pragmatics: if the culture works, its values are valid (a "kind of justification by results"). Thus:

> The argument...is deployed to show that a concern for human rights must be a local prejudice, because some countries in Asia have had high rates of economic growth while trampling on human rights.[36]

Though no doubt, while most multiculturalists would reject the conclusion Barry draws, even Parekh gets close to making some dubious concessions. Parekh says of East Asian societies, for example, when discussing "Asian values" and culture, that they:

> wish to pursue such collective goals as social harmony and cohesion, moral consensus, integrity of the family and economic development, and that these involve different kinds of rights and greater restrictions on individual freedoms than is common in liberal societies. Although some of these goals and the restrictions they entail do not find much favour among liberals, *that is not an argument against them.*[37]

What Parekh fails to distinguish between here is culture and ideology: if he had said that rulers in these countries make ideological use of cultural

---

35: Barry, 2001a; see also his article written as an immediate rejoinder to the Parekh Report—Barry, 2001b.
36: Barry, 2001a, p281.
37: Parekh, 2000, p139—my emphasis.

traditions he could have avoided falling into the trap of seeing something positive in the politics of local ruling classes.

Barry's general argument is that a robust liberalism, which argues for social and economic justice, is a sufficient guarantee against discrimination. As far as group rights are concerned, Barry asserts that the classic liberal position "that individuals should be free to associate together in any way they like, as long as they do not in doing so break laws designed to protect the rights and interests of those outside the group" is sufficient—with two provisos, one of which is individuals participate voluntarily in the group and so are free to leave when they want.[38] He rejects the idea that there is something different between a group and a culture, whereas a multiculturalist would argue that a culture is something you are, so to speak, born into and is therefore not the same as a group, which you choose to join. There is clearly an element of truth about this difference between a culture and a group—but does that mean that a culture can have some kind of collective right as opposed to the individuals in that culture having the right to abide by it if they wish (and therefore the right not to abide by it if they do not)? For Barry the idea of group rights may even be harmful, if used to stifle dissent by members of a cultural group to dissent and to protect reactionary practices. Multiculturalist policy can also work against redistributive policies aimed at improving the lives of the poor in general by targeting resources at cultural groups, some of whose members are not necessarily more deserving than other members of society: "multiculturalism may very well destroy the conditions for putting together a coalition in favour of across the board equalisation of opportunities and resources".[39]

Barry scores some telling points in his critique but we can point to two problems. One is the liberal position of freedom of association as long as the interests of others are unharmed. Apply that to trade unionism and the possibility of effective action is severely curtailed: the point of collective militancy (and the "right" to pursue it) is precisely to hurt the bosses' interests. Liberalism is defective when it comes to the collective rights of workers' struggle—or indeed to those of any group resisting oppression.

The second has to do with universals—and problematic though multiculturalist theory may be in this respect it does not follow that Barry has an answer. The argument about universals needs to take on board the fact in a society divided by class the state cannot lay claim to universal values or claim to act on their behalf against backward cultural practices. However liberal the modern parliamentary-democratic state may be in championing individual

---

38: Barry, 2001a, p148.
39: Barry, 2001a, p325.

rights and equality, it remains a state ensuring that the ruling class can maintain the rule of capital over the exploited and oppressed of whatever culture.

Multiculturalism and struggle

So appeals to the state are worse than useless. This is clear in respect of difficult cultural questions referred to earlier. No genuine multiculturalist, *pace* those who accuse multiculturalism of relativism, condones oppressive practices as acceptable because they are part of a "culture". But they don't always see what the alternative is to falling in behind top-down initiatives by governments despite the fact that these governments may be implicated in barbarous imperialist intervention or stoking up racist oppression at home. Socialists are clear, however, that any such initiatives are likely to be counterproductive because they will be resisted as coming from the oppressor.

This is evident in the struggle against female genital cutting. Colonial African governments which tried to outlaw the practice were met with resistance—particularly when, in post-war Sudan, midwives were arrested for infibulating girls whose parents attempted to beat the ban. More recently, western feminists calling for action provoked this reaction from an infibulated Somali woman: "If Somali women change, it will be change done by us, among us. When they order us to stop, tell us what we must do, it is offensive to the black person or the Muslim person who believes in circumcision. To advise is good, but not to order." Where there has been success it is because of what local activist groups have done: the challenge to tradition has come from within, not imposed from outside.[40] Support for enforcing change from above will undermine the possibility for unity from below between people from different backgrounds. It also reinforces the authority of conservative elements in the oppressed community (the elders) as defenders of a culture under attack.

Much the same can be said about conflicts in European societies around oppression, which pit liberal defenders of gay rights against "backward" Muslims. Žižek makes an interesting comment in his discussion of what happened in Holland with the gay community increasingly turning to anti-immigrant nationalist parties in response to vociferous homophobia coming from the Muslim community. He pointed to the inadequacy of the "pure liberal-multiculturalist line of tolerance". Of course, everyone, including Muslims, should be asked to accept a multiplicity of religious and sexual ways of life. Nonetheless, what "complicates the simplicity of this position is the underlying gap in economic and political power":

40: Althaus, 1997, pp130-132.

The tension is ultimately between upper middle class Dutch gays and the poor exploited Muslim immigrants. In other words what effectively fuels the Muslims' animosity is their perception of gays as part of a privileged elite which exploits and treats them as outcasts.

Žižek draws the conclusion as far as what needs to be done—who is going to resolve the problem and how:

> Our question to the gays should thus be: what did you do to help the immigrants socially? Why not go there, act like a Communist, organise a struggle with them, work together? The solution of the tension is thus not to be found in multicultural tolerance and understanding but in the shared struggle on behalf of a universality which cuts diagonally across both communities, dividing each of them against itself, but uniting the marginalised in both camps.[41]

We can broaden this insight to say that class is the key. To think in terms of society as a community of cultures is to miss the shaping power of capitalism in driving those it exploits from whatever background to play a central role in combating the other tendency of capitalism to seize on difference as a means to divide. Where Žižek talks of shared struggle uniting the marginalised in each camp in the name of a universality, we can rephrase that as an argument about the centrality of the working class, the only truly universal class.

Why should this be? Capitalism absorbs new communites and submits them to sharing the common fate of exploitation alongside older ones. This produces an enormous overlap in the way in which working people, whatever their cultural background, experience the world. But exploitation in itself shows only part of the picture. The degree to which there is a struggle against exploitation defines the degree to which there is recognition of common working class interests, irrespective of cultural background. In the absence of struggle, however, culture can be turned into a significant marker of division. The current assault on multiculturalism is an attempt to blame one section of the population for the failures of capitalist society to deliver on its promises.

In this process there is a struggle between an active, conscious rejection of the dominant ideology and a passive, unconscious acceptance of it. That can be seen most sharply in the fight against racism, as older communities experience the impact of the arrival of new ones: the tradition of resistance to racism built up through trade union struggle and the influence of left wing politics lines up against the tradition of passivity and deference produced by

---

41: Žižek, 2011, p138.

the hegemony of ruling class ideas. The same applies to the culture of immigrant groups as they relate to older communities. One tendency is to look outwards, and another is to retreat into the security of what passes as the "traditional" culture. The degree to which one tendency wins out over the other depends crucially on whether the tradition of resistance to racism encourages the breaking down of cultural barriers or their reinforcement.

Socialists should not be caught between fighting backward cultural practices in collusion with "enlightened" ruling classes and condoning them in the name of respect for cultural autonomy. There can be both defence of the right to cultural self-determination and commitment to struggle against what is backward within a culture. This does not involve recommending a "superior" culture over an "inferior" one. It is based on how the shared factor of class—mixing people from different cultural backgrounds—creates the potential for a common struggle from below against all reactionary practices. Socialists need not feel shy about tackling "difficult" cultural issues, provided we remember that our starting point is class, not culture. Thus, with the oppressor never (however "superior" his culture); and critically with the oppressed always (however "backward" their culture).

Lenin, culture and nationalism

Lenin's discussion of the national rights of oppressed peoples has some bearing on the question of the freedom of minorities to practise their cultures. His hostility to Russian nationalism, which went hand in hand with implacable hostility to the idea of the superiority of Russian culture, coexisted with his defence of the right of oppressed nations to self-determination and of their right to their culture (for example, education of non-Russian school students in their language). This did not mean, however, that he was uncritical of the nationalism of the oppressed—quite the contrary. Lenin fulminated against not just crude manifestations of bourgeois nationalism (Great Russian chauvinism, for example) but against "refined" versions—by which he meant the demand for "national-cultural autonomy" for oppressed nations. This, he argued, crucially ignored the class dimension in the struggle by the oppressed for self-determination, inviting workers in the oppressed nation to believe they have more in common with their "own" ruling class than with the workers of the oppressor nation: "it joins the proletarians and bourgeoisie of one nation and keeps the proletarians of different nations apart". Lenin reinforced the argument about how even the culture of the oppressed, is split along class lines:

> We do not support "*national culture*" but *international* culture, which includes only part of each national culture—only the consistently democratic and

socialist content of each national culture. The slogan of "national-cultural autonomy" deceives the workers with the phantom of cultural unity of nations, whereas in every nation today a landowners', bourgeois or petty bourgeois "culture" predominates. We are against national culture as one of the slogans of bourgeois nationalism. *We are in favour of the international culture of a fully democratic and socialist proletariat.*[42]

Lenin applied this thinking to the status of the Jews in Tsarist Russia—whom he defined as "the most oppressed and persecuted nation" (he was using nation here in the modern sense of "community"). The right of Jews to their culture did not stop Lenin damning the Jewish leaders and businessmen's slogan of Jewish national culture and praising Jewish internationalism. The first was a reflection of the backwardness in which Jews as a caste were kept in non-advanced parts of the world; the other a reflection of the entry of Jews into the modern world. As he remarked, "There the great world-progressive features of Jewish culture stand revealed; its internationalism, its identification with the advanced movements of the epoch".[43]

We can apply the same argument to Muslims today. Lenin's forcible criticism of "national-cultural autonomy" is a useful way of looking at the limitations of the non-class ways in which multiculturalism in conceptualised.

Culture and universalism

There is one final consideration in respect of culture. Trotsky makes the point that culture is contradictory. The progressive accumulation of all those skills and mental attributes that enable humanity to liberate itself from dependence on nature comes up against their appropriation by the exploiters in any epoch. Culture, in other words, is both a universal benefit and the particular property of a ruling class. There is progress in culture (or rather the potential for progress) in the sense that the motor of class struggle allows the enlarging of what is universal as opposed to what is particular.

The advent of bourgeois culture was an enormous advance. The notion that all individuals were equal and entitled to self-determination was the basis of its challenge to whatever was dark, backward and superstitious in social life. This "universalism", however, has never effectively challenged the economic basis of bourgeois culture—its roots in ceaseless and ever deepening exploitation. So for all its "enlightenment" superiority, its accompanying shadow is barbarism—the way in which it justifies the eradication, in the name of

---

42: Lenin, 1963, p116.
43: Lenin, 1964, p26.

"rational" values of democracy and equality, of pre-bourgeois cultures. Imperialism has been the clearest expression of that ideological drive—one that has returned with the latest phase of conquest and the demonising of peoples and cultures it deems as "failing" to share "enlightened" values.

The defence of multiculturalism is part of the resistance to this process and the notion that "our" values are better because they stem from the universalism of enlightenment thought must be fought. That involves much more than defending the right of different peoples to their cultures (itself an aspect of enlightenment thought, though itself capable of irrationalist distortion because it can become the basis of backward cultural practices). It has to look beyond to the question of tackling the "irrationality" of capitalist exploitation itself. And in that context only the final destruction of class society by working class revolution will permit the emergence of a truly universal human culture, to which every progressive element within particular cultures will contribute. It is the struggle for this, rather than any quest for a new multicultural Britishness, which offers a perspective on how we most effectively counter the attacks on multiculturalism.

References

Ahmad, Aijaz, 2007, "Islam, Islamisms and the West", *Socialist Register 2008: Global Flashpoints, Reactions to Imperialism and Neoliberalism* (London), http://socialistregister.com/index.php/srv/article/view/5872/2768

Althaus, Frances, 1997, "Female Circumcision: Rite of Passage Or Violation of Rights?", *International Family Planning Perspectives*, volume 23, number 3, www.guttmacher.org/pubs/journals/2313097.html

Ashley, Jackie, 2006, "The Multicultural Menace, anti-Semitism and Me: Interview with Melanie Phillips", *Guardian* (16 June), www.guardian.co.uk/politics/2006/jun/16/media.politicsphilosophyandsociety

Barker, Martin and Anne Beezer, 1983, "The Language of Racism—an Examination of Lord Scarman's Report on the Brixton Riots", *International Socialism* 18 (Winter).

Barry, Brian, 2001a, *Culture and Equality* (Polity).

Barry, Brian, 2001b, "The Muddle of Multiculturalism", *New Left Review* II/8 (March-April).

Bennett, Ronan, 2007, "Shame on Us", *Guardian* (19 November), www.guardian.co.uk/uk/2007/nov/19/race.bookscomment

Cameron, David, 2011, "PM's speech at Munich Security Conference" (5 February), www.number10.gov.uk/news/speeches-and-transcripts/2011/02/pms-speech-at-munich-security-conference-60293

Dorling, Danny, 2005, "New study shows racial mixing, not segregation, in the UK", *Observer* (25 September), www.guardian.co.uk/uk/2005/sep/25/communities.politics

Eagleton, Terry, 2007, *Ideology* [new edition with new introduction] (Verso).

Eliot, T S, 1934, *After Strange Gods* (Faber and Faber), www.archive.org/details/afterstrangegods00eliouoft

Eliot, T S, 1948, *Notes Towards a Definition of Culture* (Faber and Faber).

Griffin, Nick, 2011, "Cameron's 'War on Multiculturalism' Speech—Another Milestone in the 'Griffinisation' of British Politics", BNP website (5 Feburary).

Kundnani, Arun, 2007, *The End of Tolerance* (Pluto).

Lenin, V I, 1963 [1913], "Draft Platform for the Fourth Congress of Social Democrats of the Latvian area", *Collected Works, volume 19* (Progress), www.marxists.org/archive/lenin/works/1913/may/31.htm

Lenin, V I, 1964 [1913], "Critical Remarks on the National Question", *Collected Works, volume 20* (Progress), www.marxists.org/archive/lenin/works/1913/crnq/index.htm

Mahamdallie, Hassan, 2005, "Racism: A Boost for the Bigots", *Socialist Review* (November 2005), www.socialistreview.org.uk/article.php?articlenumber=9579

Modood, Tariq, 2007, *Multiculturalism* (Polity).

Orwell, George, 1971, *The Collected Essays, Journalism and Letters of George Orwell, Volume 2, My Country Right or Left*, 1940-1943 (Penguin).

Parekh, Bhikhu, 2000, *Rethinking Multiculturalism* (Palgrave Macmillan).

Pfaff, William, 2005, "A monster of our own making", *Guardian* (21 August), www.guardian.co.uk/uk/2005/aug/21/july7.terrorism

Phillips, Trevor, 2005, "After 7/7: Sleepwalking to Segregation", Speech to Manchester Council for Community Relations, 22 September, www.humanities.manchester.ac.uk/socialchange/research/social-change/summer-workshops/documents/sleepwalking.pdf

Rosen, Michael, 2011, "'Interculturalism'—a response to David Cameron's speech on multiculturalism" (31 March).

Simpson, Ludi, 2005, "Measuring Residential Segregation", *The Cathie Marsh Centre for Census and Survey Research* (16 November), www.ccsr.ac.uk/research/migseg.htm

Sivanandan, A, 1990, *Communities of Resistance: Writings on Black Struggles for Socialism*, (Verso).

Sivanandan, A, 2006, "Attacks on multicultural Britain pave the way for enforced assimilation", *Guardian* (13 September), www.almendron.com/tribuna/11547/attacks-on-multicultural-britain-pave-the-way-for-enforced-assimilation/

Thatcher, Margaret, 1978, "TV interview for Granada *World in Action* ('rather swamped')" (27 January), www.margaretthatcher.org/document/103485

The Parekh Report, 2000, *The Future of Multi-Ethnic Britain* (Profile).

Warsi, Baroness, 2011, "Tory chief Baroness Warsi attacks 'bigotry' against Muslims", *Daily Telegraph* (19 January), www.telegraph.co.uk/news/religion/8270294/Tory-chief-Baroness-Warsi-attacks-bigotry-against-Muslims.html

Žižek, Slavoj, 1997, "Multiculturalism, Or, the Cultural Logic of Multinational Capitalism", *New Left Review* I/225 (September-October).

Žižek, Slavoj, 2011, *Living in the End Times* (Verso).

Geert Wilders and the rise of the new radical right

Maina van der Zwan

If someone in England stands up and establishes a party which positions itself between the racist BNP and the conservatives, it would also get 20 percent of the vote. I would very much like to establish parties in other countries. The people want it. An anti-Islam wave that is unstoppable.[1]

A week before this comment by the leading Dutch far-right politician Geert Wilders, the English Defence League announced it was considering standing candidates in national and council elections. EDL leader Tommy Robinson said, "I think this country needs a party that is not afraid to say things some would consider unpopular".[2] Undoubtedly, the sort of party he has in mind is Wilders's anti-Islamic Party for Freedom (PVV). Just a few months earlier Robinson and his violent gang had organised a demonstration in Amsterdam in his support. The demonstration, meant as a show of strength and launchpad for a "European Defence League", failed miserably.[3] But the intention of the EDL is clear: it is searching for ways to force a political breakthrough. And it sees Wilders's party as a model to follow.

1: Kuiper and Benschop, 2011. Thanks to Pepijn Brandon, Alex Callinicos, Martin Smith and Peyman Jafari for their comments on an earlier draft.
2: Hughes, 2011.
3: Thomas, 2010.

Robinson is not the only far-right figure who wants to draw lessons from Wilders's success. Marine Le Pen, while struggling for control and political direction of the French Front National, announced she wants to strengthen the ties with the PVV.[4] At around the same time a new party called "Die Freiheit" (Freedom) was launched in Germany, modelled explicitly on the PVV and endorsed by Wilders.

These examples of mutual attraction among Europe's far-right are part of a wider trend. Nazi parties, street movements like the EDL and populist racist electoral parties are cross-pollinating and making political breakthroughs. The fascist Jobik has doubled its vote and has become the third largest party in Hungary; the extreme right Sweden Democrats have entered parliament for the first time; the Northern League won regional elections in 2010 in Italy; and the nationalist "True Finns" became the third largest party in the Finnish elections in April 2011.

Concurrently with these advances, racist policies are gaining ground—deportation of Roma, denaturalisations of convicted migrants, banning of the hijab and the building of mosques, and pogroms against immigrants. Wilders, junior partner of the current Dutch minority government, is one of the figureheads of this trend. His party has become the third largest in Dutch politics, and his viciously racist politics play a central role in Dutch political life.

In just five years Wilders has gone from an isolated radical rogue who split away from the mainstream right to one of the most powerful politicians in the Netherlands and an influential exponent of the far-right internationally. He has started building an international network of like-minded groups and think-tanks.[5] This year he will publish a book with the aim of taking his crusade against "Islamisation" to the United States. Given the fact that Wilders is not just a Dutch peculiarity, an analysis of the driving forces behind his rise to power could be useful for activists battling similar formations elsewhere.

The heritage of Pim Fortuyn

Wilders's rise has been meteoric. He created his own parliamentary faction in 2004, and won nine out of 150 seats in 2006 and 24 in 2010. But his success did not come out of nowhere. It had been prepared by shifts in mainstream politics that took place over a decade and were catalysed by Pim Fortuyn, a flamboyant anti-Islamic columnist turned populist politician.

4:   Gross, Halifa-Legrand and Thierry, 2010.
5:   In July 2010 Wilders announced the International Freedom Alliance, a network of groups and individuals who are "fighting for freedom against Islam"

Fortuyn's entrance into the political arena in 2001 marked a profound shift in the political climate in the Netherlands. Until then all had seemed well in a country famous for its social stability and supposed tolerance. But something had been brewing beneath the surface and erupted with a vengeance when Fortuyn started attacking the political establishment. He hit a weak spot at the right time.

The then reigning "purple government", an alliance between social democrats and liberals, was hugely unpopular. Fortuyn presented himself as a fresh "neither left nor right" outsider on a mission to upset "old politics". This struck a chord with a lot of voters who were sick of the mainstream parties. Their anger was channelled into a typical right wing populist agenda, which raged against "the bureaucracy", immigration, crime and specifically Islam.

Where other far right forces that had attempted to break through in the 1980s and 1990s had been branded as fascists and were consequently isolated, Fortuyn succeeded in shaking off this contaminated baggage. He was openly gay and explicitly pro-Israel, distancing himself from the anti-Semitism and homophobia of traditional Nazi parties like the French Front National and the Dutch Centrum Democrats. This crucially helped him ward off attacks of extreme right affiliations and present himself as a respectable politician.

In March 2002 Fortuyn won the council elections in Rotterdam, winning 35 percent of the vote in the second largest city in the Netherlands. Two months later, just before the national elections, he was shot and killed by an environmental activist. His party, the List Pim Fortuyn (LPF), posthumously got 17 percent of the national vote. It went into government, but without its central figure it succumbed to infighting and imploded after a series of splits.

The years after Fortuyn's murder saw a fight over his political heritage. Survivors of the LPF, breakaways from the free-market liberal VVD and leaders of small Nazi splinters, all tried to fill the space Fortuyn had left behind. One of those was a VVD-parliamentarian by the name of Geert Wilders.

Born in 1963 to a Catholic family in Venlo, Wilders has his roots in the economically depressed south of the Netherlands. As a young adult he travelled to Israel where he volunteered for several years in a *moshav* (Zionist settlement), becoming in his own words "a true friend of Israel".[6] Back in the Netherlands he worked in the health insurance industry before becoming a parliamentary assistant to Frits Bolkestein in 1990. Bolkestein was the party leader of the VVD and the future European Commissioner for Internal

---

6:   Liphshiz, 2008.

Market and Services.[7] It was from him that Wilders learned the tricks of the trade. Bolkestein is a leading neoliberal and provocative xenophobe, who consistently tried to push the boundaries of public debate to the right.

Wilders was elected into parliament in 1998. At first he remained fairly invisible, but this changed when he was appointed VVD spokesperson for foreign affairs in 2002. He used his new position to vent his ideas about the dangers of "Islamic extremism" and "Islamisation", often going further than his party's point of view. Bolkestein had departed to the European Commission in 1999 and since then Wilders had become more and more dissatisfied with the course of the VVD. Confronted with the success of Fortuyn and radical-ised by 9/11, Wilders wanted his party to become a hard right force which could radicalise the political environment and cut off any competition from the right. The leadership however, wanted the party to remain on the centre-right, dedicated to the European Union (EU) and coalition politics.

In 2004 Wilders was expelled after leaking his own internal memo calling for a more right wing course and subsequently refusing to promise to restrain himself.[8] He remained in parliament as an independent, with hate speech against Muslims and migrants as his trademark. From 2005 onwards he headed the parliamentary fraction of the newly established PVV.

The social context within which this occurred was very turbulent. The years following Fortuyn's murder saw massive anti-war demonstrations and union mobilisations against pension reforms. In 2005 62 percent of the Dutch electorate rejected the EU Constitutional Treaty, despite (and partly encour-aged by) a fierce "Yes" campaign by the government, the union bureaucracy, NGOs, the social-democratic Labour Party (PvdA) and the Green Left. Only the anti-neoliberal Socialist Party (SP), the far left and Wilders had cam-paigned against.[9] Consequently, approval rates for the government hovered between 15 and 20 percent, and the next general election showed strong political polarisation.[10] On the right, Wilders had been the most extreme rep-resentative of Fortuyn's politics and won the fight over his heritage. In the 2006 national elections he won nine seats and his far-right competitors none. Meanwhile, on the left the SP obtained a historic victory, gaining 25 seats.

Disillusionment followed the failure of mass demonstrations to change government policies and all eyes turned to the parliamentary scene, with espe-cially high expectations in the SP. But in the following years it was not the left,

---

7: See, for a documentation of the relationship between Bolkestein and Wilders, Fennema, 2010.

8: Fennema, 2010, pp70-88.

9: Brandon, 2005.

10: TNS NIPO, 2005.

the social movements or the unions that set the tone of debate: it was Wilders, often leaving the rest of the political landscape confused and disorientated.

The politics of the PVV

Taking a lead from Fortuyn, Wilders has been pushing for a rightward shift by channelling general discontent towards an agenda of authoritarian neoliberalism and Islamophobia. His politics are a combination of aggressive verbal attacks on "the left elite" (specifically the social democrats, but more generally the whole political establishment, the media and intellectuals), concealed neoliberalism and rampant Islamophobia dressed up in a post-9/11 world view.

Wilders argues that Islam is a monolithic political ideology, inherently opposed to "Enlightenment values", poised at world dominance and about to take over Europe. Here he takes the American political scientist Samuel Huntington's prediction of a developing clash of civilisations to a new level. It is not only that post Cold War international politics is supposedly driven by cultural and religious conflicts: according to Wilders an existential battle between the West and Islam is nearing the end phase. Speaking at the Hudson Institute in New York in 2008, he told an enthusiastic crowd:

> I come to America with a mission. All is not well in the old world. There is a tremendous danger looming, and it is very difficult to be optimistic. We might be in the final stages of the Islamisation of Europe. This not only is a clear and present danger to the future of Europe itself, it is a threat to America and the sheer survival of the West. The United States is the last bastion of Western civilisation, facing an Islamic Europe.[11]

Wilders is an avowed supporter of Israel, which he sees as the crucial external frontier. For him, parties like the PVV form the last line of defence against a fifth column of Muslims. The only way to win would be an Israelification of Europe, treating Muslims as second-rate citizens and a permanent threat to "our way of life". He has argued for a "raghead-tax" (a thousand euro fine for wearing the hijab, described by him in a speech in parliament as "making the polluter pay"),[12] proposed that the Dutch army fight "street terrorists" (ie youth of Moroccan descent) at home instead of in Afghanistan,[13] and wants to abolish the first article of the constitution

---

11: "Geert Wilders spreekt bij het Hudson Institute in New York", PVV website, 29 September 2008—www.pvv.nl/index.php?option=com_content&task=view&id=1310&Itemid=1
12: "Wilders wil 'kopvoddentaks'", *Trouw*, 16 September, 2009.
13: "Wilders: Stuur het leger naar Gouda", *De Telegraaf,* 15 September 2008.

which declares all citizens equal and replace it with one identifying the "Christian-Jewish and humanist" tradition as the dominant culture.

Around these policies Wilders has built an international network, ranging from American neoconservatives and evangelicals to members of the armed settler movement and high officials in Israel, with the more traditional extreme right parties from Europe uncomfortably in between. Most of his funding comes from the United States, where Daniel Pipes of the Middle Eastern Forum boasted of having raised "an amount of six figures" for Wilders.[14] His American speaking tours have functioned as an ideological ice-breaker for a new radical right in the US, going much further with his Islam-bashing than most American politicians and institutions dare to go.

Wilders's social-economic policy is intentionally fuzzy, combining hard liberalism with more social measures, supposedly aimed at defending the "hard-working Dutch". This has caused some commentators to describe Wilders as "culturally right wing, but socio-economically left leaning". This is spectacularly mistaken. Coming from the VVD, Wilders has neoliberalism ingrained in his DNA. In his "Declaration of Independence" of 2004 he wrote that the welfare state, regulation and taxation need to be cut down to create a more corporate friendly environment.[15] He has always stood for economic liberalism with a typical do it yourself, middle class twist to it. By "hard-working Dutch" he does not mean working class; he means the ideal of the self-made entrepreneur. Tellingly, the new candidates for the provincial elections in March were described by one journalist as "tie-types", pro-business and keen on countering any formal obstructions to building projects and entrepreneurial initiative.[16]

The so-called social shifts Wilders has made were intended opportunistically to broaden his electoral base. In the run-up to the 2010 general election he made promises to resist the raising of the pension age and cuts to social security. The first he abandoned just hours after the election results had come in, and the second when he was able to become junior partner to the most right wing government in Dutch history. Put to the choice, Wilders has consistently opted for neoliberalism, from furthering the privatisation of the health sector to dismantling rent control in the social housing system.[17]

This commitment to neoliberalism has only occasionally led to an upset among his voters. In October 2010 bus drivers in The Hague were

---

14: Meeus and Valk, 2010.
15: Wilders, 2004.
16: Versteegh, 2011.
17: Wetenschappelijk Bureau van de SP, 2011.

enraged after the PVV discarded their earlier promises and supported the privatisation of public transport in the political capital.[18]

There is nothing left wing in Wilders's politics. He is a power-politician who is more willing to lie about his real nature than any other representative of the mainstream right. The main reason he has got away with this deceit is his effective use of racism as an electoral battering ram, which he has managed to connect very explicitly to social issues. Since the onset of the economic crisis he has been insisting on the necessity of saving billions of euros by cutting "costs of mass migration". He has pleaded among other things for limiting social security to non-Western migrants, minimising judicial aid to those having lived in the Netherlands for longer than ten years and forcing immigrants to pay for their own integration and language courses.

This racist scapegoating has functioned as a very effective lightning rod for class anger, deflecting it against migrants. The result has been that a large part of the social base of the PVV believe that they stand to benefit from the repressive and racist measures, even if in practice it means a continuation of the ruling class neoliberal onslaught. The elements of racism and neoliberalism are present in all mainstream parties, but the way Wilders takes this to new extremes and combines it with aggressive anti-establishment rhetoric has made him a dynamic political force that differs fundamentally from the rest of the political spectrum.

Characterising Wilders's new radical right
The rise of Wilders is not an exclusively Dutch phenomenon. The last two decades have seen the rise of new, more aggressive right wing political forces, ranging from Forza Italia to UKIP to Jobik. All these formations defend an extreme form of neoliberalism and a return to authoritarian politics and police-state methods, and fully identify with the "war on terror". In most of the cases they use Islamophobia as a way to give their programme a popular base, sometimes also engaging in anti-Roma or even anti-Walloon agitation in the Flemish case. They all harbour authoritarian, racist and anti-democratic politics that call upon forces outside of the established institutions.

But there are also important differences, especially in strategic orientation. Roughly three currents can be distinguished. First of all there are euro Nazi parties like the Front National and the British National Party. They bind together an older cadre hardened by fascist politics with an electoral strategy aimed at creating local strongholds. Second, there are violent

18: "PVV voor privatisering opernbaar vervoer", *Socialisme.nu*, 18 October 2010–
http://socialisme.nu/blog/nieuws/10661/pvv-voor-privatisering-openbaar-vervoer-den-haag/

street movements like the EDL and those we have seen in Russia and other Eastern European countries. Third, there are populist racist parties like the PVV and UKIP, which retain a purely electoral strategy and try politically to distance themselves from the fascist elements within the extreme right.

It is important to note how these currents are cross-fertilising. The rise of Islamophobia and the electoral success of far right forces have given confidence and political space to smaller fascist formations. These in turn have learned from their big brothers and looked for ways to broaden their base by downplaying their racism and joining the electoral process. This seems to be the direction that the EDL is taking, starting out from a position very different from Wilders, but now steering much more closely towards his model. The recent research by the Searchlight Education Trust found that 48 percent of Britons would back an anti-immigration party if it was not linked to fascist imagery, confirming the frightening potential for this strategy.[19]

Other fascists have decided to try their luck joining the existing electoral projects. Despite trying to keep them outside the PVV, research showed that 20 known extreme right activists were involved in the regional elections of the PVV.[20] Fully fledged fascist formations are currently still marginal, but austerity capitalism creates a social dynamic that can push these currents in the direction of fascism. So where does the PVV stand within this spectrum?

For a long time the significance of Wilders's political project has been downplayed. The established parties chose to ignore him as much as possible, whitewashing Wilders as a harmless clown and hoping the storm would blow over. Clearly this perspective has been wrong. Wilders has proven to be a very intelligent political operator, who has gone from success to success, and in the process has succeeded in pushing the whole political landscape to the right.

Wilders stands apart as an extreme racist, an aggressive neoconservative, and according to several commentators and activists, a modern fascist. This last argument is mostly made by comparing the current situation to the 1930s, Islamophobia to anti-Semitism and thus Wilders to Hitler. There is obviously ground for the comparison. The PVV systematically dehumanises Muslims and minorities, rejects universal values, displays a deep-seated hatred towards anything that resembles the left, and its elected officials have a high level of acceptance for violence (with a quarter of its parliamentarians convicted of criminal activities).

But there are also problems with labelling Wilders a fascist, both analytically and in terms of strategy. The PVV maintains a purely electoral

---

19: Townsend, 2011.
20: Kafka, 2011.

strategy and has little street presence. Party organisation has been limited to parliamentary work and volunteers for electoral campaigns. The PVV has no local branches, although there have been a dozen tightly controlled local meetings since its establishment that have been important in securing Wilders's electoral base. The PVV does not have membership, aside from Wilders himself.[21] Only a few of the elected officials of the PVV are allowed to speak to the press without prior consent of Wilders. He is a maniacal control-freak wary of a dynamic he cannot master.

His fear that a more vocal and visible membership would reveal its extreme right tendencies is justified. Numerous party candidates have been removed from lists because of revelations of ties to the extreme right, and the first instance of open dissent over the question of organising a youth wing immediately led to an internal crisis. The only PVV demonstration that has had Wilders's approval brought together a colourful array of fuming, flag-waving loonies and half the cadre of former Nazi clubs.

The rudimentary elements for a development towards fascism are present, but are consciously suppressed in fear of destabilisation. This is mostly a result of Wilders's instrumentalist approach. For him politics is about gaining influence and so far his estimation has been that the best way to do so is by following a controlled electoral approach. Why rock an unsteady boat if it progresses on course? Furthermore, the current material situation is not pushing the party towards fascism. In the Netherlands the effects of the current economic crisis on people's lives, though severe, are still in no way comparable to those of the 1930s. This means there is not yet the kind of desperation in the middle classes to drive them towards more violent solutions, a key characteristic of fascist movements.

Of course this could change. The unfolding economic crisis is already creating the kind of social turbulence and political polarisation in which fascism can grow. Moreover, with his hateful rhetoric against Muslims, Wilders has created a dangerous dynamic that could take on a life of its own by manifesting itself as a movement on the streets. We are already seeing the signs of violent attacks on mosques and Islamic schools and threats against leftist activists and intellectuals. This leaves the future trajectory of the PVV as an open question. Further success or a severe crisis could drive its radicalisation further, but it is also possible that it will be absorbed into the establishment or that increased pressure will cause it to implode like the LPF before it.

It would therefore for the moment be most accurate to characterise the PVV as a populist party of the new radical right. The strategic consequence

21:   A purely legal construction to discourage infighting.

of this is that combating the PVV does not centre on physical confrontation to stop the movement on the streets. But like fighting fascism it does require a broad movement that can counter the racist ideology and unmask Wilders as an enemy of working people, of whatever colour or creed. This is a very urgent task for the left. Furthermore, combating the PVV calls for clarity in ideas, for an understanding of its historical roots, how its ideology functions and what the role of the mainstream parties has been in facilitating its rise.

The roots of bitterness

Where does the support for Wilders come from? The dominant analysis is that a winner must be right and so there must be a general popular anger over multiculturalism, crime and Islam, which Wilders simply recognises and verbalises like any other elected representative.[22] This is a convenient analysis, because it dodges all kinds of difficult questions about the role of the political establishment in paving the way for Wilders—it is also wrong and dangerous.

The motivation to vote for the PVV is as much racist as it is a general expression of protest against the established political parties. In one poll, 38 percent of voters said the main reason for voting PVV was "its programme". Another 38 percent answered "Distrust in government and politics in general". Asked what the most important programmatic points of PVV are, 33 percent answered "Too many foreigners" and 22 percent answered "Tougher on crime". When given the opportunity to put their motivations in their own words, two themes stand out. One is a fear of foreigners and Muslims (government soft on "criminal foreigners", for preservation of Dutch culture and against mosques). The other emphasised anger against the government (self-enrichment of The Hague, not delivering on promises, and "pocket-filling social-democrats").[23] PVV voters see politicians as thieves, are vehemently against rescuing banks and have (very) little trust in "the current government"—95 percent against 71 percent of average eligible voters![24]

Practically all research into the PVV's base stresses the combination of xenophobia and strong distrust in government. All too often these two are causally linked ("Government is softer on immigrants than voters want them to be, so that is why there is a voters' revolt"), but that is just too easy. Both the "No" vote in the EU referendum and the huge win for the SP in the 2006 elections (17 percent of the vote against 6 for the PVV) demonstrate

---

22: This is the rough line of argumentation from left to right. See, for example, Fennema, 2010, Scheffer, 2007, Rossem, 2010, and Wansink, 2010.
23: Synovate, 2009a.
24: Synovate, 2009b, p18.

that the anger is much broader, more diffuse and politically fluid than just straightforwardly anti-immigrant.

Looking more closely at the changes in society sheds light on the question what feeds this general anger. Like elsewhere in Europe the past 30 years have seen a stealthy takeover by neoliberalism and a transformation of Dutch society.[25] The collective tax burden was lowered, state budgets were divided into sectors and capped, government services were privatised and social security became a repressive instead of a supportive institution. The economy was deregulated, even more integrated into the world economy than it already was, and by the end of the 1990s the Netherlands had become one of the world epicentres for financial innovation.[26] With unemployment at a historic low at the turn of the century there was talk of the "Dutch Miracle". The Economist Intelligence Unit wrote in 2001 that the Netherlands was "the best place in the world for investment".[27]

But beneath the surface tensions were building. Most of the 1.4 million newly created jobs in the 1990s were low-skill, low-productivity and low-paid. Moreover, 50 percent of those created between 1994 and 2000 were part-time and 40 percent were flexible.[28] Household debt had exploded and there had been a stark rise in overtime work, way above the European average.[29] The job market had become segmented into an upper echelon that was doing a lot better and the rest experiencing the imposition of greater "flexibility" and a decrease in salaries and secondary benefits.[30] And with taxation for multinationals near zero and a new range of taxation loopholes for the rich, a wealth gap between the haves and have-nots opened quickly. Between 1980 and 2005 the richest 10 percent saw their purchasing power rise by an average of 60 percent, while the poorest saw theirs decline by 10 percent.[31]

There was an astonishing level of political consensus over the neoliberal operation. The ideological counter-revolution after the revolt of the 1960s, which stresses that people are responsible for their own success or failure, had been very effective. All mainstream parties adapted smoothly to the neoliberal consensus, party programmes converged and the economy was depoliticised. A pact between the bosses and the unions to keep wages

25: To my knowledge the best book on the neoliberal takeover of the Netherlands and its effects is Dam, 2009.
26: Meeus, 2008.
27: Economist Intelligence Unit, 2001.
28: Sociaal en Cultureel Planbureau, 2001, p60-73.
29: Storm and Naastepad, 2003, p145-146.
30: Delsen, 2002, p74.
31: Dam, 2009, p214.

low was institutionalised and called "the polder model". As a result, the working class was pushed onto the defensive, with most strikes aimed at retaining employment.[32]

Figure 1: Development of purchasing power for lowest income group and highest 10 percent income (1980=100)
Source: CBS

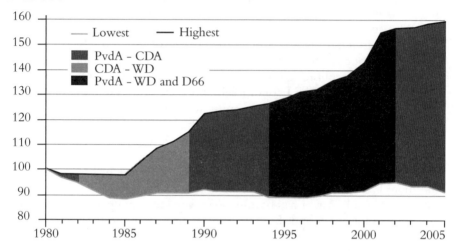

These developments were not without effects. One was a sharp increase in pressure on individuals, both at work and in society more generally. It was established in 2000 that one in five workers struggled with psychological fatigue,[33] and in 2005 that one out of ten workers would suffer a burnout at some point during their lives.[34] By 2008 there was talk of a "depression epidemic", caused by a combination of neoliberal policies, the pharmaceutical industry, marketing companies and clustered health agencies.[35] According to Storm and Naastepad the increasingly anonymous and threatening world environment had the effects of what Erich Fromm once called "mutual human indifference, and relatedly, a loss of self-confidence as the 'sense of self' is determined by market success".[36]

Another effect was a deep-seated distrust of established social institutions,

32: Velden, 2000, p307-308.
33: Nederlandse Organisatie voor Wetenschappelijk Onderzoek, 2000.
34: Hupkens, 2005.
35: Dehue, 2008, p261.
36: Storm and Naastepad, 2003, p147.

politics in general and the government in particular. An opinion poll on democracy and government in 2007, with more than 100,000 participants, revealed a huge gap between what kind of society a large majority wanted (one based on solidarity and equality, with a government taking responsibility for education, childcare, health, public transport and aiding people in financial distress) and the way the present society is perceived (anti-social, stressful, with solidarity undermined and government managed irresponsibly).[37] Less than half of the respondents said they feel politically represented. This is not only a remarkable figure. The poll shows that the roots of the bitterness are much more anchored in social-economic frustration than is generally assumed.

While the whole political establishment bears responsibility for this, the ensuing instability and political crisis was most serious for the social democrats. They had adapted to the new fashion, officially shaking off their "ideological feathers", as they put it themselves, and becoming the favourites of the international Third Way jet set. The career of PvdA leader Wim Kok tells the whole story: labour leader in the 1980s, prime minister in the 1990s and board member of multinationals and banks in the new millennium. His successor, former Royal Shell manager Wouter Bos, confessed to no longer having dreams for the future, and reduced the aim of socialists to "making life just a little bit better".[38]

So the bitterness and distrust caused by decades of neoliberal policies goes very deep. For the new radical right it was a matter of tapping into this general anger and channelling it against "the left elite", who they framed as having naively opened the floodgates of the immigration that is destroying "our way of life". Wilders did not do this on his own. His path was paved by a multitude of intellectuals, journalists and politicians.

Forging the new racism

Looking back, it is easy to see two intertwined ideological trends developing in reaction to the crumbling support and growing resentment towards the political establishment. One is "integrationism", which argues that "metropolitan problems" (crime, unemployment and social deprivation) are caused by an influx of migrants who were unable to integrate into Dutch society because of their cultural baggage. The second trend is a resurgence of nationalism, creating a sense of community based on conservative (often articulated as Christian) values.

The "integration debate" was forced into the mainstream by 9/11,

---

37: 21minuten.nl, 2007.
38: Tegenlicht, 2007.

the "war on terror" and Fortuyn. But the issue had been pioneered in the years prior to this by Frits Bolkestein and social-democratic publicist Paul Scheffer. From the early 1990s onwards Bolkestein regularly published opinion articles in which he blamed "failing integration" on the cultural relativism of the political elite and pleaded among other things for the right of asylum to be restricted to occasional individual cases since the Netherlands were "full".[39] In 2000 Scheffer wrote an essay that would become a landmark in the racist turn of the public debate called "The Multicultural Drama", in which he said that "unemployment, poverty, school abstention and criminality pile up among ethnic minorities... We are talking about an enormous number of stragglers and people without prospect, who will increasingly burden Dutch society".[40]

The arguments of the likes of Bolkestein, Fortuyn and Scheffer rest on three assumptions: there are distinct "ethnic" groups who differ from each other by cultural identity; these groups cannot live alongside each other unproblematically; national or "ethnic" identity is the most important binding factor from which individuals derive a sense of solidarity. Despite all the evidence pointing towards a *social-economic* rather than a multicultural drama, the mainstream, including most of the left, has been won for this reasoning.

The flip-side of scapegoating cultural differences for social problems is a resurgence of Dutch nationalism. With "inferior" culture being framed as the main cause of society's problems, the solution is seen as making "Dutch culture", whatever that may be, hegemonic. As Scheffer formulated it in the same essay, "a lazy multiculturalism is gaining ground because we insufficiently articulate what binds our society together... Let's start by taking the Dutch language, history and culture seriously", which in turn should lead to a new "national consciousness".[41]

What has followed is a trend of forced assimilation, with among other things mandatory Dutch lessons and cultural entrance tests for migrants, and a national awareness programme for moral values run by the state. The latter was the flagship of the Christian-Democratic prime minister Jan-Peter Balkenende, who led four different cabinets between 2002 and 2010. Ranging from advertisements against littering to a plea for citizenship based on "Jewish-Christian values", the programme has been ridiculed as old-fashioned moralising, but its effects should not be underestimated. Based on the theories

---

39: Bolkestein, 1991, and Bolkestein, 1993.
40: Scheffer, 2000.
41: Scheffer, 2000.

of "moral leadership" and communitarianism of the American Third Way sociologist Amitai Etzioni, it has strengthened the right wing assumption that people are responsible for their own social situation. Policy should not be there to support people, but to punish those who do not conform.

These intertwined ideological trends of scapegoating migrants and renewed nationalism have aided the forging of a "new racism", which has shifted racist focus from colour to culture, from body to belief.[42] The social dynamic, however, is the same as with the old racism: static stereotypes about minorities that fuel fear, hatred, discrimination and racist violence.

As a result racist ideas have become more rooted in Dutch society. According to research in 2006 half of the Dutch consider themselves Islamophobic and 66 percent find Islam irreconcilable with "modern European life". A shocking 10 percent consider themselves racists. They find "native Dutch" more intelligent than and superior to migrants. According to 66 percent of the participants, racism is widespread and 80 percent think racism has increased over the past years.[43] Results of research among youth underline the trend: 54 percent of 14 to 16 year olds say they have (very) negative feelings about Muslims. Interestingly the resentment is strongest in rural areas and white schools, where students get most of their opinions about ethnic and religious minorities from the media instead of personal experience.[44] In 2010 the PVV won the mock general elections among school students.[45]

The rise of the new racism has not been confined to the sphere of ideas and opinions. Discrimination against job applicants has risen, especially against young men with "Muslim beards" and Arab features.[46] Attacks on mosques have increased, with incidents of arson, blood smears on walls and even a decapitated swine on the doorsteps of a mosque in the northern town of Groningen.[47] In 2008 researchers observed "a sharp rise in violent incidents against Muslims… Which is all the more striking, since this trend goes against a general decrease in racist violence".[48]

These developments have been picked up and actively pushed by mainstream media outlets, right wing bloggers and a battalion of

---

42: See, for an elaborate analysis of the new racism, Seymour, 2010.
43: Motivaction, 2006.
44: Dekker and van der Noll, 2007.
45: "PVV wint scholierenverkiezingen", Trouw, 18 June 2010.
46: Sociaal en Cultureel Planbureau, 2010, p15.
47: "Groeiend geweld tegen gebedshuizen"—www.radio1.nl/contents/21482-groeiend-geweld-tegen-gebedshuizen
48: Anne Frank Stichting, 2008, p35.

neoconservative intellectuals.[49] Together they have formed a new activist right which has found coherence around the issues of integration, Islam, freedom of speech, security, the phantom of the "left elite" and climate change as a conspiracy of the environmental movement.

Explaining Wilders's success

Wilders's electoral success is thus based on the emergence of a much broader new right playing into a generalised feeling of discontent, actively creating a right wing "common sense", an accepted vision of reality which Wilders only had to refer to and build upon. He differentiates himself from this broader movement by positioning himself on the most extreme wing of it and framing every issue as part of the existential battle against "Islamisation". The question as to how his political project has been so successful, however, remains. It is one thing to *want* to create a new right political force, and another to actually succeed in it.

The first reason for the success of the new radical right is that its racism has been very useful for a neoliberal project in crisis and was thus aided by the establishment. Years of pushing through hugely unpopular policies had reduced the political effectiveness of the mainstream parties. Given the rise of anti-market sentiment the mainstream right could not continue on its old ideological footing that "the market is best for everyone".

In this context the discourse of Dutch society being burdened by mass immigration and calls for a stronger state provided the centre-right parties with both a distraction and an excuse for a more authoritarian form of neoliberalism. That is why the extremist hate speech of Fortuyn and Wilders, which a decade before would have been rather marginal and probably prosecuted, has now found a resonance in the entire political establishment.[50]

In an unusually candid interview former minister of justice Piet-Hein Donner revealed how this interaction between the mainstream and radical right functioned. Looking back at the period right after the murder of Fortuyn he explains that, despite being immensely unpopular,

---

49: *De Telegraaf, Elsevier, HP/de Tijd, GeenStijl,* the Edmund Burke Stichting, Theodor Holman, Max Pam, Leon de Winter, Afsin Ellian, Paul Cliteur and Joshua Livestro, to name just a few of the key players.

50: There is a case pending against Wilders for inciting hatred, brought to the court by anti-racist activists. It has been used to great effect by Wilders for publicity, while deflecting time and resources from building a movement against him. The case does reveal a drastic shift in the political climate. Contrary to the situation in the 1990s, when a far-right parliamentarian was convicted for less extremist remarks, the public prosecutor now demands acquittal for Wilders, this among calls by left and right alike that Wilders's freedom of speech should be safeguarded.

his hard right government was able to use the political polarisation to push through neoliberal reforms: "Against the background of the critique that Fortuyn had formulated there was a feeling that firm decisions had to be made... We thought that in the eyes of the public we could not do the right thing anyway, so we just did what we wanted. That was a very liberating feeling. There was simply less discussion about the why".[51]

The ideological momentum created by the new right and the "war on terror" also opened a space for all kinds of measures that had been unthinkable 20 years ago: a law that allows for pre-emptive arrest of whole groups, area interdictions for youth with some kind of conviction on their record, a biometric database of all citizens, the highest density of phone taps in the world, preventive searches, body-scans at the airport, quotas for poor people settling in certain neighbourhoods, and so on and so forth. The argument is, of course, that these measures are necessary for fighting crime and terrorism, but in practice they are used for social control, from criminalising protesters to disciplining minority and working class communities, very much fitting with the needs of authoritarian neoliberalism.

The second reason for the success of the PVV is the lack of a counter-force. The left parties have ideologically adapted to Wilders's offensive rather than confront it. Moreover, the low level of class struggle means that workers' collective action has not provided an alternative outlet for the discontent at the bottom of society. A united fightback along class lines against neoliberal attacks could have helped overcome prejudices over creed and colour, thereby narrowing the breeding ground for the new radical right. The different trajectories of Fortuyns's LPF and Wilders's PVV are telling. When anti-war and labour mass movements peaked in 2003 and 2004, the LPF was nowhere to be seen and vanished as a political force after internal fights led to several splits.

The PVV rose to electoral success in a period of very low social struggle and with a mainstream left that was traumatised by the experience of Fortuyn. The blame for his murder had been put on them, for supposedly having created "a climate of demonisation". Wilders then cunningly used this to create a taboo on criticising him, resulting in a left that was even weaker on the issue of anti-racism than it already had already been.

Furthermore, the union leadership and the left have not only failed to organise the fightback against austerity measures, but have also moved to the right on the social-economic front, leaving themselves badly positioned to channel class anger. This has been a key reason why Wilders has been able to get away with presenting himself as an anti-establishment force.

51:   Bessems and Nieuwenhuis, 2008.

Revealingly, when the government moved to raise the pension age in 2009 there was a large majority of the country, let alone union members, who were opposed to this. Instead of transforming popular opposition into mass struggle, the union leadership opted for a strategy of lobbying the social democrats in government. When that failed, it was Wilders and not the left parties who denounced the unions for having betrayed the "hard-working Dutch", resulting in another leap for his party in the opinion polls.

The social democrats have been in permanent crisis over how to deal with Wilders and their own unpopularity. They have the largest migrant voting base. This has resulted in sporadic statements of Labour politicians against racism, mostly on a rather soft basis. At the same time they have been part of the same logic that drove the rest of the political establishment to adapt to the new right. The PvdA has been responsible for tightening immigration laws pushing through more repressive measures for social control. Its city councillor for The Hague has mimicked Wilders by warning of a "tsunami of East Europeans" and its parliamentarians have among other things pushed for legislating pre-emptive arrests of "problematic street youth". Party leader Bos famously argued that the party should dare to break with consensus politics and polarise more, not on the economic front, but against the multiculturalists. "We should generalise more. [PvdA Mayor of Rotterdam] Aboutaleb says it is little Moroccan brats who have created Wilders. I think he is right".[52] The social democrats are covering for their own role in the neoliberal onslaught by howling with the wolves.

Green Left and the SP also have an ambiguous track record, firmly criticising Wilders at certain specific moments, while at the same time embracing parts of his agenda. Both parties have gone out of their way to defend Wilders's "freedom of speech" and both have refused to take part in anti-racist activities, with the argument that it is "not done to attack a colleague outside of parliament". Former Green Left leader Femke Halsema has called on Muslim women to throw off the veil and has called on the left to criticise Islam.

The overall position of the SP is possibly worse. As long ago as 1983 it published a notorious pamphlet called *Migrant Labour and Capital*, in which it stated that "the difference in development and culture makes it very difficult for the Dutch to work and live together with their foreign colleagues".[53] Consequently they argued that migrants should be encouraged to return "to their own country". Back then the pamphlet was condemned as racist by the

---

52: Peeperkom and Sommer, 2008.
53: Socialistiese Partij, 1983, p14, quoted in Brandon, 2009, p204.

rest of the left. In the current climate the SP seeks revenge by claiming credit for "having recognised the problem of integration way ahead of the pack".

This has led it to take very dubious positions on migration and integration issues, recently calling for a reduction in "the stream of workers from Eastern Europe" or the "raw invasion of Poles", as one SP parliamentarian put it, instead of attacking bosses and the Bolkestein directive for undermining collective contracts.[54] Not surprisingly, the SP has been soft on Wilders. Its serious attacks have been on the level of Wilders "not keeping his promises", specifically on social-economic policy. Its criticism of Wilders's witch-hunt of Muslims and migrants is either formulated very generally or framed pragmatically along the line that there are more pressing problems than burqas and that Wilders's solutions are "not realistic" and "go too far".

The mainstream right has used the PVV's extremism to push through neoliberal policies while the left has been half-hearted and unprincipled in its opposition, moving so far to the centre that it has been incapable of providing an alternative agenda to the cuts that are creating the anger Wilders builds on. Any effective answer to the far-right should challenge both problems, combining principled resistance to racism and Islamophobia with the building of a new left that goes into the offensive against the establishment, instead of wishing to be part of it.

Lessons from the Netherlands

The trajectory of the PVV corresponds to a more general trend of a far right on the rise in Europe and the US. So what are our lessons for those who are combating similar formations elsewhere? It is clear that the left cannot fight the right from the centre and cannot win by ideological adaptation. All Dutch political parties have reacted to the rise of Wilders by adopting part of his rhetoric and agenda. The idea is that this would take the wind out of his sails. Instead it has given credibility to the PVV and emboldened it to go even further.

Economism is not good enough. The SP has focused on attacking Wilders's neoliberal agenda, but without also combating his racism this will prove to be a futile exercise, precisely because it is racism that binds Wilders's voters to his pro-business programme and undermines the potential of a collective fightback. Similarly, attacking Wilders on the grounds that his ideas cannot practically be implemented does not work—ethnic cleansing *can* be implemented and it is the *story* that matters. People do not vote for Wilders

---

54: SP, 2011, and Zwan, 2011.

because of his practical policies, but because they have been convinced by the totality of the new right "common sense".

So what strategy would work? Fighting the rise of the PVV requires pulling together all forces from the Muslim communities, the left, trade unions and social movements to fight his racist ideas and policies through campaigns, demonstrations and meetings. This also calls for challenging ideological misconceptions that are still widespread on the left, such as the idea that Islamophobia is fundamentally different from traditional racism because it is a "critique of religion". Furthermore, it is of the utmost importance to build opposition to the austerity politics that Wilders supports. Such strong opposition can undermine Wilders's base among sections of the working class that believe he defends their interests, and at the same time lay the basis for creating solidarity among Muslims and non-Muslims by bringing them together for a common cause. Finally, because the growth of the PVV is partly based on the failure of the mainstream left, countering it requires building a new radical left that does not leave attacking the political establishment to Wilders.

Given the developments of the past five years it would be easy to draw pessimistic conclusions about the chances of this strategy materialising. While recognising that there is no doubt that the political climate has become more difficult for socialists, such pessimism would be wholly unjustified.

First, the PVV is an unstable formation. Its ideas have sunk more deeply in working communities and the party has developed somewhat of a core of capable people around Wilders. But its rapid growth has depended on a strong contradiction: a social face of respectability to broaden its base combined with an extremist ideology that conceals its pro-business neoliberalism and stimulates extreme right activism. So far this contradiction has not been exposed, either by events or by its opponents. But this has been in circumstances which have been more than favourable to Wilders. Serious pressure on his fragile apparatus can push this contradiction to the fore and crack his mask of being a respectable representative of "the people".

Secondly, as is true everywhere in Europe, we are witnessing the first signs of a resurgence of combativity. So far these are only hopeful beginnings: a hard won nine week cleaners' strike,[55] a surge of student protests and a first series of one-day protests against austerity measures in public transportation, culture and education. But with an economic crisis that will continue to create shocks, an unstable right wing minority coalition that is pushing through incredibly unpopular cuts, and international examples of people fighting back, it is very unlikely that Dutch workers

---

55: Dekker, 2010.

will remain docile. And a resurgence of class struggle would be the best hope for turning the tide against the new radical right.

References

21minuten.nl, 2007, Democratie en overheid (October), www.21minuten.nl/21minuten/ images/21minuten_2007_rapport.pdf

Anne Frank Stichting, 2008, *Monitor Racisme & Extremisme*.

Bessems, Kustaw, and Marcia Nieuwenhuis, 2008, "Een minister twijfelt niet", *De Pers* (17 February), www.depers.nl/binnenland/176847/Een-minister-twijfelt-niet.html

Bolkestein, Frits, 1991, "Integratie van minderheden moet met lef worden aangepakt", *De Volkskrant* (12 September).

Bolkestein, Frits, 1993, "Asielzoekers", *De Volkskrant* (31 August).

Brandon, Pepijn, 2005, "A note on the Dutch referendum", *International Socialism 108*, (autumn), www.isj.org.uk/?id=133

Brandon, Pepijn, 2009, "Internationalisme en de SP: kritische kanttekeningen", *Kritiek* (Aksant).

Dam, Marcel van, 2009, *Niemandsland* (De Bezige Bij).

Dehue, Trudy, 2008, *De depressie-epidemie* (Augustus).

Dekker, Henk, Jolanda van der Noll, and Tereza Capelos, 2007, *Islamofobie onder jongeren en de achtergronden daarvan*, Universiteit Leiden (12 January).

Dekker, Willem, 2010, "Letter from the Netherlands", *Socialist Review* (June), www.socialistreview.org.uk/article.php?articlenumber=11291

Delsen, Lei, 2002, *Exit poldermodel? Socioeconomic changes in the Netherlands* (Greenwood Press).

Economist Intelligence Unit, 2001, "EIU Ranks Netherlands Best Place to Do Business" (August 14).

Fennema, Meindert, 2010, *Geert Wilders. Tovenaarsleerling* (Bert Bakker).

Gross, Estelle, Sarah Halifa-Legrand and Maël Thierry, 2010, "Marine Le Pen: "Le sursaut vital face au mondialisme", *Le Nouvel Observateur* (13 December).

Hughes, Steve and Emily Hall, 2011, "EDL to go political", *Daily Star* (9 February).

Hupkens, Christianne, 2005, "Burn-out en psychische belasting" *Central Bureau voor de Statistiek* (25 July), www.cbs.nl/nl-NL/menu/themas/gezondheid-welzijn/publicaties/artikelen/ archief/2005/2005-1738-wm.htm

Kafka, 2011, "Rechtsextremisten actief bij de PVV" (16 February), http://kafka.antenna.nl/ ?p=3158

Kanne, Peter en Tim de Beer, 2009, "Nieuwe PVV-aanhang komt van VVD", *De Volkskrant* (28 February).

Kuiper, Martin, and Lucas Benschop, 2011, "De anti-Islam wave is niet meer te stoppen", *Nu.nl* (27 February), www.nu.nl/politiek/2456211/de-anti-Islam-wave-niet meer-stoppen.html

Liphshiz, Cnaan, 2008, "Far-right Dutch politician brings his anti-Islam rhetoric back to Jerusalem", *Haaretz* (11 January), www.haaretz.com/far-right-dutch-politician-brings-his-anti-islam-rhetoric-back-to-jerusalem-1.237038

Meeus, Jan, 2008, 'Een markt van 8,000 miljard', *NRC* (November 14), http://vorige.nrc. nl/nieuwsthema/kredietcrisis/article2060967.ece/Een_markt_van_8.000_miljard.

Meeus, Tom-Jan, and Guus Valk, 2010, "De buitenlandse vrienden van Geert Wilders", *NRC* (5 May).

Motivaction, 2006, "Zo tolerant is Nederland" (3 June), www.motivaction.nl/content/zo-tolerant-nederland

Motivaction, 2009, *De achterban van de PVV* (16 April).

Nederlandse Organisatie voor Wetenschappelijk Onderzoek, 2000, "Psychische vermoeidheid varieert sterk binnen bedrijf", Universiteit van Maastricht, www.nwo.nl/nwohome.nsf/pages/NWOA_7G8TKH

Peeperkorn, Marc, and Martin Sommer, 2008, 'Geen emancipatie zonder confrontatie', *De Volkskrant* (1 March), www.pvda.nl/politici/politici/wouterbos/Interviews/2008/Geen+emancipatie+zonder+confrontatie.html.

Rossem, Maarten van, 2010, *Waarom is de burger boos?* (Nieuw Amsterdam).

Scheffer, Paul, 2000, "Het multiculturele drama", *NRC* (29 January).

Scheffer, Paul, 2007, *Het land van aankomst* (De Bezige Bij).

Seymour, Richard, 2010, "The changing face of racism", *International Socialism 126*, www.isj.org.uk/index.php4?id=638&issue=126

Sociaal en Cultureel Planbureau, 2001, *De sociale staat van Nederland.*

Sociaal en Cultureel Planbureau, 2010, *Discriminatiemonitor niet-westerse migranten op de arbeidsmarkt.*

Socialistiese Partij, 1983, *Gastarbeid en Kapitaal* (Socialistiese Partij).

SP, 2011, "Roemer: 'reguleer de instroom van werknemers uit Oost-Europa'", (16 February), www.sp.nl/nieuwsberichten/8695/tw

Storm, Servaas, and Ro Naastepad, 2003, "The Dutch Distress", *New Left Review* 20.

Synovate, 2009a, Motivaties om op de PVV te stemmen (27 August), www.novatv.nl/data/media/db_download/46_b8d723.pdf

Synovate, 2009b, "De PVV-stemmer: profiel, achtergrond en motieven" (25 September), http://vorige.nrc.nl/multimedia/archive/00251/91221_rap_v_1_01_251044a.pdf

Thomas, Mark L, 2010, "Racists humiliated as Euro-launch flops", *Socialist Worker* (6 November), www.socialistworker.co.uk/art.php?id=22941

TNS NIPO, 2005, "Vertrouwen in Balkenende II op historisch dieptepunt", *Politieke Berichten* (18 May), www.tns-nipo.com/pages/nieuws-pers-politiek.asp?file=persvannipo\vertrouwen_balkenende_II_dieptepunt05.htm

Townsend, Mark, 2011, "Searchlight poll finds huge support for far right 'if they gave up violence'", *Guardian* (26 February), www.guardian.co.uk/uk/2011/feb/27/support-poll-support-far-right

Velden, Sjaak van der, 2000, *Stakingen in Nederland* (Stichting Beheer IISG / NIWI).

Versteegh, Kees, 2011, "De PVV-kandidaat is een stropdastype", *NRC* (7 January).

Wansink, Hans, 2010, *De kiezer heeft altijd gelijk* (Nieuw Amsterdam).

Wetenschappelijk Bureau van de SP, 2011, "De gebroken beloften van Geert Wilders" (February).

Wilders, Geert, 2004, "Onafhankelijkheidsverklaring", www.pvv.nl/index.php/component/content/article/30-publicaties/684-onafhankelijkheidsverklaring.

Tegenlicht, 2007, "De Wouter Tapes", http://tegenlicht.vpro.nl/afleveringen/2006-2007/de-wouter-tapes.html

Zwan, Maina van der, 2011, "De SP en de 'rauwe invasie' van Polen", *Joop* (13 March), www.joop.nl/opinies/detail/artikel/de_sp_en_de_rauwe_invasie_van_polen/

The Great Unrest and a Welsh town
Tim Evans

The trade union leaders, almost to a man, deplored it, the government viewed it with alarm, the Independent Labour Party regretted this untoward disregard for the universal panacea of the ballot box, the Social Democratic Federation asked, "Can anything be more foolish, more harmful, more...unsocial than a strike"; yet disregarding everything, encouraged only by a small minority of syndicalist leaders, the great strike wave rolled on, threatening to sweep everything away before it.[1]

In August 1911...a general strike developed on the railways. During those days a dim spectre of revolution hung over Britain.[2]

The key confrontation of Britain's first national railway strike—for better pay and an end to an unfair arbitration system—occurred on Saturday 19 August 1911 in Llanelli, a tinplate-producing town in south west Wales. The strike was part of one of the longest waves of sustained industrial rebellion in British working class history—the "Great Unrest" of 1910 to 1914. Unofficial rail strikes in Manchester and Liverpool spread elsewhere until the union leaders were forced to call a national stoppage. This hit the whole transport network: south Wales, because of its coal, tinplate and steel production and transport links to an insurgent Ireland, was a crucial area for British

---

1: Kendall, 1969, p26.
2: Trotsky, 1974, p8.

capitalism. In Llanelli mass picketing brought all rail traffic to a halt. Soldiers were drafted in as tinplate and other workers came onto the streets in solidarity, joining crowds of people from the railway and dockside communities. As strikers attempted physically to prevent a train passing through, soldiers of the Worcester regiment opened fire, killing two men and wounding others.

Instead of being cowed by the carnage, the workers' districts rose up in anger. Despite accusations of purposeless rampaging by "the mob", there was a high degree of purpose and direction in the targets attacked. A magistrate who brought in the troops saw his shop looted and arson attacks made on two of his farms. Another magistrate's shop had its windows smashed. A crowd of 500 attacked the police station where a scab engine driver was being held. Strikers and their supporters engaged in pitched battles with soldiers who tried to clear the streets at bayonet point. Many protesters received bayonet and baton wounds, avoiding hospital for fear of arrest. At the height of the disturbances the soldiers stood back and refused to engage, at one point penned in the railway station while crowds attacked it, smashing all the windows. For hours the authorities seemed paralysed, unable or unwilling to intervene as the trucks and sidings of the Great Western Railway Company were assailed, looted and torched, triggering an explosion which killed another four people. One soldier refused to fire on the crowd, was arrested, escaped from military custody and went on the run, raising the authorities' fears of a wider mutiny.

These events occurred in a town not especially noted for militancy. Llanelli was not viewed as a potential flashpoint by the authorities. It was said that in 1911 political violence there had been unknown since Liberal Party supporters had lobbed a brick through the windows of the Conservative Club during the 1885 General Election campaign.[3] Although the miners of nearby Trimsaran had been locked out nine months prior to the strike, with rioting in the village in January, Llanelli itself had not been affected by the wildcat strikes on the railways that had been breaking out elsewhere since the beginning of August. So sanguine had the authorities been that 15 local police officers from Llanelli had been sent to Tonypandy, to police the continuing unrest in the coalfields of the Cambrian Combine. And on Wednesday 9 August another 25 officers left to augment police numbers at Cardiff, where seafarers, dockers and transport workers had been on strike.

In Llanelli politics the Liberal Party was hegemonic, epitomised in the personage of W Llewelyn Williams, chair of the Baptists' Union, barrister, scholar, historian, golf partner of David Lloyd George and the Liberal MP for Llanelli. When the House of Commons debated the shootings, he

---

3:   Griffiths, 2009, p41.

was nowhere to be found, citing illness as an excuse: the local press complained about his complete silence. In fact his first words on the subject were not uttered until 9 October 1911, when he blamed the uprising on "hooligans and casual labourers". For the Llanelli establishment, this would be the pattern for the future. The inappropriately-named *Tarian y Gweithiwr* (*The Worker's Shield*)—a Liberal paper—thundered that "[Llanelli] from now on...will not be known as a peaceful town, but as the abode of rioters, thieves and drunkards".[4] So terrified had the authorities been by events, the military so compromised by its mistakes and inept tactics, that attempts were first made to smear those who had fought back, focusing on the "shameful" rioting and sentencing those found guilty of looting to hard labour. This was followed by a determined campaign to blot out all memories of what had happened. People will have heard of the rioting at Tonypandy in 1910— quite justly seared into Welsh working class consciousness—but not of the arguably more serious battles at Llanelli a year later. The shootings were the subject of an official cover-up. Despite regular calls for a public inquiry and compensation for the families of the dead men, the government stonewalled all appeals. The authorities quite literally got away with murder.

Mass rebellions

In 1911 the continuing industrial insurgency was shaking the British ruling class to its core.[5] The period from 1899 to 1907 had been a period of industrial peace unparalleled between 1891, when statistics started, and 1933. Many commentators believed that in British society the potential for continental-style revolutions had been neutered by the British trade union system and the "traditional common sense of the nation[6]". The great wave of strikes blew all that away. Driven by rank and file workers, it swept aside a horrified union leadership, and was characterised by direct action, widespread industrial solidarity, community involvement and physical confrontation with the forces of the state. Its far-reaching effects went beyond the purely short-term economic: it was identified as a major precipitating factor in the ongoing breakdown of the Liberal consensus. Tony Cliff and Donny Gluckstein, in their history of the Labour Party, point out that, "Labour's final emergence from the cocoon of Liberalism owed nothing to its own efforts, or even to those of the left. It arose from the second, and far more serious alternative to Labourism, the

---

4:   *Tarian y Gweithiwr*, quoted in Griffiths, 2009, p55.
5:   Not just the British ruling class. From 1907 to 1913 many countries, including Spain, Sweden, Argentina, France, Ireland and America, saw industrial rebellions.
6:   A Clay, quoted in Holton, 1976, p73.

'Labour Unrest' of 1910-1914...[in which] the working class returned to the stage of history with a ferocity which terrified the Labour Party as much as the ruling class".[7] These convulsive struggles might have coalesced into a serious challenge to capitalism, had it not been for the outbreak of war. As it was they shaped working class politics for decades to come.

The strike wave was a class response to a nexus of economic, industrial and political pressures and dashed hopes. The Liberal government had been elected in 1906 on the promise of widespread reforms, in what was a land-slide defeat for the Conservatives. It promised a campaign against "landlords, brewers, peers and monopolists", as well as launching schemes for national insurance and old age pensions. At this time Labour was essentially a trade union sponsored appendage to the Liberal Party, having signed a secret elec-toral pact with the Liberals three years earlier. This was how it secured its first substantial representation in parliament. But voters were to be hugely disap-pointed. Wages did not increase, nor did the position of the mass of workers improve. In fact, over the next few years the opposite occurred.

British capitalism was centralising and restructuring itself to meet changing global circumstances. By 1910 a prolonged world economic upswing was drawing to a close. This period represented the peak of British imperialism's power, which was now being challenged by Germany and America. The loss of Britain's privileged position, and its falling rates of growth of industrial productivity, forced its ruling class to rationalise its industrial base and cut back on the concessions that had been won by organised workers. The New Unionism of the late 1880s and early 1890s had been a direct response to these new conditions and the class movement of 1910-14 was a qualitative deepening of the process.

The strikes were also, crucially, a protest against capital's new strategy of incorporating labour and union leaders. Mike Haynes relates the direct and uncompromising nature of the struggles in part to the fact that they were not contained within the existing union organisation.[8] They were a dual revolt, against employers on the one hand, and the established union leaderships and collective bargaining machinery on the other. The new strategies, especially the fundamental innovation of the period, the solidarity strike, were developing as ways of exerting maximum pressure by rank and file workers and excluding the leadership. The rising level of struggle created a sharp polarisation not only between workers in relation to their employers and the state, but also between workers and their official union leaderships.

7:    Cliff and Gluckstein, 1988, p47.

8:    Haynes, 1984, p93.

Bob Holton contrasts the features of earlier periods of working class militancy, such as 1871–73 and 1889–91, with 1910–1914:

> There is...a vivid contrast between the London dock strike of 1889, when dockers marched peacefully through the City of London to gain public sympathy, and the 1910 Welsh miners' strike when miners clashed violently with civil power at Tonypandy and elsewhere... "the evangelistic organising campaigns of the dock strike period" as against the "mass rebellions" of the later explosion... The spirit of compromise fostered within collective bargaining mechanisms was being replaced by direct action.[9]

The strikes represented a militant challenge to the bosses, the mainstream leadership of the trade unions and the political system as a whole.

The culture of direct action was liberating. Sabotage and action against blacklegs, employers and magistrates developed within the context of what Haynes calls "a belligerent working class self-confidence". The slogans and songs used during the course of strikes, free speech campaigns and other public demonstrations clearly express such a mood. In the Black Country strikes of 1913, "strikers marched from factory to factory singing with considerable intimidation what became their theme song 'Hello, hello, here we are again'."[10] At Llanelli pickets battling police and the military sang the warlike Llanelli rugby song "Sosban Fach", as did the crowd which ransacked and trashed the shop of one of the magistrates who had called in the troops.[11] At the all-night mass picket which occupied the town's level crossings, stopping all rail traffic, proceedings became a "carnival of the oppressed", with not only songs and speeches but tap-dancing contests and a mock election.

With the arrival of the military at Llanelli railway station the mood changed to defiance. A soldier of the Worcester regiment said that after a warning shot was fired, "the crowd took no notice...and simply jeered and called out, 'We don't mind your shots'."[12] Strikers not only physically blocked the passage of moving trains or boarded them to argue with or attack scabs but also tore up track to make movement impossible, placing obstacles on the line and damaging telegraph systems. This was characteristic of the railway

9:   Holton, 1976, pp73-74.

10:   *Wolverhampton Express and Star,* 30 June 1913, quoted in Haynes, 1984, p93.

11:   This folk song became the song of the Scarlets, Llanelli's rugby team. *Sosban Fach*—Little Saucepan—refers to the tinplate manufacturing which was the town's main industry. One of the verses, which refers to "Little Dai the soldier, with his shirt-tail hanging out", is a direct reference to the shootings and the riot.

12:   Griffiths, 2009, p48.

strike on a national level, where official recognition of spreading unofficial action was not enough to head off the "explosive" character of rank and file grievances in many strike centres. "The advice of local officials to remain calm was often rejected by the strikers, many of whom had...no experience of union membership and discipline...there developed many instances of industrial aggression and collective violence".[13] These included attacks on scab labour, particularly at signal boxes. At Portishead near Bristol 1,000 people attacked a signal box that was still working, with similar occurrences at Llanelli, where blacklegs were chased out of signal boxes and the windows smashed. Confrontation with soldiers took place at many other key points like Liverpool where another two men were shot dead as they attempted to free imprisoned rioters, and Chesterfield, where the station was set ablaze, and the West Yorkshire Regiment repeatedly attacked the crowd with bayonets.

The revolutionaries

The explosive character of the strike was in part an expression of the way in which in 1911 strike activity itself represented a radical challenge to the existing political system, and to the extremely restrictive limits of what constituted political activity in Edwardian Britain. As Haynes points out, at a time when playing street football was a major "crime" of working class youth[14], the willingness of strikers to engage in street politics, to undertake mass picketing, or to march several miles at a moment's notice to bring out another factory, constituted major defiance in the face of what was regarded as "acceptable" politics. For many workers this developed into a more conscious and coherent critique of the nature of the system itself. The strategy of independent direct action solved the problem of the cowardice of the conservative trade union leadership, and for many the ideological framework which contextualised and supported this was that of revolutionary syndicalism. This can be characterised as a series of distinctive social movements that existed in many parts of Europe, the USA, Latin America and Australia between the 1890s and the 1920s. In broad terms, syndicalism aimed to overthrow capitalism through revolutionary industrial class struggle and to build a new socialistic order free from economic or political oppression, in which workers would be in control. Change would come neither through parliamentary pressure nor political insurrection leading to state socialism, but would be achieved through direct action and the general strike leading

---

13: Holton, 1976, p104.

14: In 1911, 132 out of 605 children in court for non-indictable offences were there for playing street football—Haynes, 1984, p114.

to workers' control. Rank and file trade union bodies would serve both as organisers of class warfare and as the nuclei of the post-revolutionary society.

The organised syndicalist presence in Britain was not negligible: it included internationally known industrial militants like Tom Mann and Guy Bowman, John Maclean in Scotland, In Wales Noah Ablett, Will Hay, Sam Mainwaring and A J Cook, and in Ireland Jim Larkin and James Connolly. In 1912 the arrest, trial and six-month prison sentences handed out to Mann and Bowman under the Incitement to Mutiny Act made syndicalism a household word up and down the country. Sales of the Industrial Syndicalist Education League's paper, the *Syndicalist,* reached 20,000 in 1912 and two conferences organised by the paper claimed to represent 100,000 workers. Syndicalism was rooted in the workplace, the picket line and the streets, tending to an "*ouvrierism*" which stressed an exclusive reliance on mass working class experience and action, rejecting "outside experts" and parliamentary intermediaries. Holton talks of "proto-syndicalist behaviour...forms of social action which lie between vague revolt and clear-cut revolutionary action".[15] Deian Hopkin takes up this idea, arguing that events at Llanelli showed many workers there sharing "the aspirations of syndicalism without articulating, or even being aware of, its theoretical framework".[16] Tens of thousands of workers learned from their own experience that the state was on the side of capital, that their own leaders could not be relied on and that solidarity and mass direct action worked. In Llanelli in 1911 class lines were sharply drawn, and the class role of the state's armed bodies of men was posed particularly starkly. This is not to argue that all or even the majority of workers were somehow syndicalist, but that syndicalist ideas resonated with the daily experience of many.

Syndicalism on the railways

By 1890 south Wales had one of the most densely developed railway networks in the world. But this existed in a context of widespread poverty and hardship for workers. In his account of the Llanelli events, *Remembrance of a Riot,* John Edwards says that:

In 1911...almost a third of all adult males earned less than 25 shillings a week, about the absolute minimum required to keep a family and three children. Most workers worked 12 hours a day for this kind of money and their daily lives, apart from Sunday, consisted of going from bed to work, and from

---

15: Holton, 1976, pp76-77.
16: Hopkin, 1983, p511.

work to bed...even a small measure of income above the minimum made a striking difference to living standards.[17]

Although the railway companies were flourishing and their shareholders receiving very healthy dividends, their employees were less well looked after. Two thirds of the workforce worked for at least 60 hours a week over six days, with most of the others working 72 hours. Rob Griffiths, in his study of the 1911 strike, *Killing No Murder*, estimates that for this,

A porter, platelayer or general labourer at the Great Western Railway's Llanelli station...would have been rewarded with 17s...a shunter would be entitled to 20s. Even the engine driver, upon whom so many lives depended, would earn little more than 28s a week—less than the average coalminer. From these miserable sums a total of 1s 2d would then be deducted for sick pay, pensions and widows' and orphans' funds—all administered by the company...the directors of the railway companies pointed out that employees benefited from such "indirect advantages" as free or cut-rate travel...and tips.[18]

It was dangerous work—between 1897 and 1907 some 5,238 railway employees had been killed and 146,767 injured in industrial accidents.[19]

Yet the amount of capital tied up in Britain's growing railway network had increased from £860 million in 1890 to £1,229 million in 1905: total receipts from freight and passenger traffic had rocketed from £73 million to £250 million a year.[20] In 1907, for example, the companies spent £30 million on wages while making £45 million in profits.[21] In August 1911 the publication of the railway companies' half-yearly financial reports showed that they were making record profits and handing out substantial dividends. On 10 August the Great Western Railway Company raised the dividend rate on its ordinary stock from 4 percent (already up from 3.5 percent in 1910) to 4.5 percent in the light of "buoyant" profits—an increase which on its own could have funded a 5 percent pay increase of one shilling a week for most GWR employees.[22]

The leaders of the rail unions—the Amalgamated Society of Railway

---

17:   Edwards, 1988, p20.

18:   Griffiths, 2009, p10.

19:   Figures on pay, working hours and accidents were collected by the Amalgamated Society of Railway Servants in its *Green Book,* 1907. Quoted in Griffiths, 2009, p10.

20:   Griffiths 2009, p10.

21:   Griffiths, 2009, p10.

22:   *South Wales Daily News,* 11 August 1911—quoted in Griffiths, 2009, pp29-30.

Servants (ASRS), the Associated Society of Locomotive Engineers and Firemen (ASLEF) and the General Railway Workers' Union (GRWU)—had in 1907 accepted a scheme, heavily promoted by the Liberal MP for Caenarfon Boroughs, Lloyd George. The scheme established

> several sectional boards in each [railway] company, each board to consider the wages and hours of the grades within its remit; should the workers' and company's representatives fail to agree, the matter would be referred to the company's central conciliation board and then—if necessary—to outside arbitration. Agreements and arbitration verdicts would be binding for at least 12 months, with the overall scheme to run for an "experimental period" of seven years.[23]

The rail companies in return were not even obliged to accept the principle of trade union recognition. In the years immediately following their introduction, the conciliation boards became hugely unpopular, being recognised by railway workers for what they were, a mechanism intended to tip the balance of power firmly in the direction of the rail companies. So much were they hated that when the first, unofficial, walkouts took place in early August 1911, railway workers were striking not only for higher pay but for an end to the conciliation boards and the whole arbitration system.

Syndicalist railwaymen were present across Britain before the strike, including Sheffield, Manchester, Wakefield and Gateshead, the most prominent being Charles Watkins of Clay Cross and later Sheffield, a strong supporter of the Industrial Syndicalist Education League (ISEL), a national propaganda and activist organisation, and the Plebs League. In ISEL's monthly journal, the *Industrial Syndicalist*, Watkins criticised the 1907 railway settlement for keeping wages down and made an explicitly syndicalist case for revolutionary change—not nationalisation but workers' control, to be achieved by an aggressive policy of offensive industrial action, undermining the passivity of the trade union leaders by direct action and the taking of the union as well as the railway system under the control of rank and file workers.[24] The experience of the 1911 strike boosted syndicalism on the railways. Dockers' leader and quasi-syndicalist Ben Tillett spoke at a rally in Llanelli to protest against the shootings, and in 1913 the platform at the mass rally at Swansea to celebrate the second anniversary of the 1911 strike was dominated by syndicalists, notably Guy Bowman and George Hicks.

23: Griffiths, 2009, p14.
24: Holton, 1976, p107.

The "40 political cowards"

The Labour Party at this time was, as we have seen, a trade union pressure group closely allied with the Liberals. The major gain made by the formation of the Labour Representation Committee (LRC) was organisationally to detach the trade union leaders from the Liberal Party: they now owed political allegiance to their own creation. Although in one sense this represented the direct entry of the trade unions into politics, it was also a retreat from trade unionism and from the belief that collective organisation could defend itself. For many of the trade union leaders who affiliated their organisations to the LRC, parliamentary activity became a substitute for trade unionism.

The turn by many workers to direct action was a response to the problems this posed. A delegate told the 1912 Trades Union Congress: "Let us be clear as to what syndicalism really is...a protest against the inaction of the Labour Party".[25] In Lenin's wonderfully astringent prose, writing in 1907: "In Western Europe revolutionary syndicalism...was a direct and inevitable result of opportunism, reformism, and parliamentary cretinism... Syndicalism cannot help developing...as a reaction against this shameful conduct of 'distinguished' Social-Democrats".[26] Although the 1906 general election had sent 29 Labour MPs to parliament with 346,000 votes behind them,[27] the *Weekly Despatch* of 10 March 1912 could say that the parliamentary Labour Party "has no effect on the matters most important to Labour; wages did not rise, the price of necessities of life increased... It is enough to state that [the Labour Party] has no influence on those vital issues." Furthermore, "The fact is that the Labour representatives, from their own point of view, become demoralised when they enter parliament... Their friends in the constituencies who expect so many things from the Labour Party are disappointed... They realise, though, rather late, the Labour Party is but an appendage of the Liberal Party".[28] As the Liberal chief whip reported in 1910, "Throughout this period I was always able to count on the support of the Labour Party".[29]

This tail-ending of the Liberals created widespread demoralisation among Labour supporters. Whether it was the House of Lords blocking Liberal social reforms, unemployment or the Insurance Act, Labour MPs took positions indistinguishable from or sometimes to the right of the Liberals. The *Weekly Despatch* of 10 March 1912 reported, "The Labour

25: Quoted in Cliff and Gluckstein, 1988, p47.
26: Lenin, 1962, p166.
27: Cliff and Gluckstein, 1988, p37.
28: *Weekly Despatch*, 10 March 1912, quoted in Cliff and Gluckstein, 1988, p48.
29: Quoted in Cliff and Gluckstein, 1988, p43.

members...talk valiantly on platforms about their independence...but in the House itself they are as obedient as trained poodles".[30] A rank and file Labour activist wrote a poignant letter to the radical Labour MP George Lansbury: "We feel the most fearful disappointment, the kind of hopelessness that creeps over us after years of organising to get men into parliament only to be sold at every turn like oxen...if the 40 political cowards [Labour MPs] had the pluck of a mouse all might be different".[31] A syndicalist leaflet called on strikers, "Fight for yourselves... Leaders only want your votes; they will sell you [a reference to the outcome of the 1911 railway dispute]. They lie, parliament lies and will not help you, but is trying to sell you".[32] These sentiments had real resonance, and fed the growth of direct action.

Parliamentary socialists?

On the eve of the Labour Unrest the left consisted of three main organisations: the Social Democratic Federation (SDF), the Independent Labour Party (ILP) and the Labour Representation Committee (LRC) which became the Labour Party. The oldest and most radical was the SDF—a "Marxist" organisation but an extreme form of the arid and dogmatic Marxism of the main parties of the Second International embodied by Karl Kautsky and mediated in Britain by the foibles of its founder H M Hyndman. It was incurably sectarian and ignored the value of trade union activity. Having said this, it had survived a number of breakaways—including that in 1903 of the Socialist Labour Party,[33] which played a significant part in the development of syndicalist ideas among industrial militants, particularly in Scotland, despite its even more profound sectarianism—and in 1909 had a membership of over 10,000. The more moderate ILP had been founded in 1893 and now had some 30,000 members. Although formally socialist, its leaders had always been ready to "subordinate their socialism to the task of winning seats in parliament".[34] They did not regard themselves as a Marxist organisation and contained a wide spread of socialist opinion. George Lansbury, who had an excellent record campaigning for workers' rights, for example, was a Christian Socialist bitterly opposed to Marxism. Their electoralism led them to act as the midwife to the founding of the Labour Representation Committee in

---

30: *Weekly Despatch* 10 March 1912—quoted in Cliff and Gluckstein, 1988, p43.

31: C G Rowe to Lansbury, quoted in Holton, 1976, p184.

32: *Times*, 8 March 1912, quoted in Holton, 1976, p116.

33: What makes the SLP important is the fact that it, alone among the political groups, had a serious industrial orientation. Haynes points out that at the Singer factory on the Clyde in 1911 it briefly held perhaps 1,500 out of 10,000 workers in its trade union organisation.

34: Haynes, 1984, p102.

1901. As we have seen, a parliamentary Labour Party became viable after the 1906 elections in which the LRC won 29 seats.

Although there were important differences between these parties, they were all focused primarily on winning seats in parliamentary and local government elections. Not only were they ideologically committed to parliamentary methods, but their structures had developed to support this. This meant that they were ill equipped to respond to a strike wave which was essentially extra-parliamentary and whose militants denounced parliament as a sham. The parties were "blind to working class actions such as strikes, a politically 'disruptive' activity to which they were either indifferent or opposed".[35] With a largely middle class membership capable of quite anti working class sentiment, they were a part of the labour movement but they did not organise within it. The result was that the left parties entered the strike wave without any organisation capable of capitalising on the revolt. It was out of this failure that dissatisfaction with the lib-Lab policies of the Parliamentary Labour Party (PLP) began to crystallise, together with an awakening among sections of the SDF and ILP of the need for a more determined struggle for socialist objectives. In 1911 a merger of the SDF with a number of ILP branches and Clarion Scout groups led to the official launch of the British Socialist Party (BSP) in January 1912.

The unofficial character of the rebellion of 1910-14 struck at the heart of the carefully constructed alliances on which the Labour Party was based. As Haynes points out, "MPs found themselves faced with the choice of defending the officials whose unions paid them or supporting the actions of the workers whose support they rhetorically invoked." Although Keir Hardie declared, "Syndicalism is the direct outcome of the apathy and indifference of this House towards working class questions, and I rejoice at the growth of syndicalism", his was a solitary voice, and many of the current or former union leaders among the Labour Party MPs remained silent. Worse was to come. In 1911 Arthur Henderson, Leader of the Labour Party from 1908-1910, together with other senior Labour MPs, proposed a parliamentary bill to make strikes illegal without 30 days notice. Any worker who went on strike illegally would be fined between £2 and £10 for every day or part of a day they were on strike (at a time when the average weekly wage was £1). Phillip Snowden, elected as Labour MP for Blackburn in 1906 and known as the "English Robespierre" for his radicalism, came out against all strikes and won an accolade from the *Wolverhampton Express* just as the strike wave in the Midlands was building up momentum: "We are

---

35: Haynes, 1984, p104.

quite at one with Mr Snowden in his condemnation of syndicalism and the general strike".[36] The role of the PLP as a bulwark against revolt and revolution was made explicit by Lloyd George. "Socialism", he said, meaning the Labour Party, would destroy syndicalism. "One microbe can be trusted to kill another, and the microbe of socialism, which may be a very beneficient one, does at any rate keep guard upon the other, which is a very dangerous and perilous one. I have, therefore, no real fear of the syndicalist...the best policeman for the syndicalist is the socialist".[37]

Blood on the tracks

In Llanelli the funerals of the shot men were huge affairs, with thousands turning out to pay their respects, and many factories closed as the workers poured onto the streets. On Sunday 10 September the town saw a massive working class demonstration to protest against the use of the military, at which the main, black-edged banner, which had also been carried in a London demonstration, declared that the workers, like others in Britain, had been killed in the interests of capitalism. A crowd of between 5,000 and 10,000 gathered in the town centre—not bad for a town of less than 32,000. In September the impact of the uprising in the local community was reflected in the wave of school strikes, where children from Bigyn, New Dock, Lakefield and Old Road schools walked out and called on others to join them. Even the newspaper boys went on strike. In November a mass meeting held the town's magistrates responsible for the deaths, condemned the use of troops and called for a public inquiry. The Swansea railwaymen and the miners of the Cambrian Combine passed resolutions in support of the soldier who had refused to fire on the crowd and was awaiting court martial. Yet despite the resonance in many sections of the working class, socialists in the town and elsewhere failed to make the shootings an issue around which the left could unite. There had been an ILP branch in the town from 1906, which had, with little trade union support, managed to achieve a respectable vote of nearly 13 percent in the second general election in 1910, with the radical Labour MP George Lansbury speaking at a Llanelli ILP meeting in May 1911. Yet the efforts of the BSP and socialist Victor Grayson, ILP MP for Colne Valley from 1907 to 1910, to set up a branch in Llanelli in the autumn of 1911 were unsuccessful. Candidates at two by-elections in 1912 stood against the shootings but failed to gain credible votes around the issue. In one, the independent socialist candidate Frank Vivian got 149 votes, against the sitting MP's 3,836.

36: Quoted in Haynes, 1984, p106.
37: Quoted in Haynes, 1984, p106.

Although initially some court appearances in Llanelli of individuals charged with riot or looting were attended by noisy crowds cheering the defendants, gradually the continuing official denunciations of rioting and particularly looting began to have their effect. In the absence of an organisation on the ground which was willing and able to counter the "official" version of events, and argue the case for the uprising, Liberal orthodoxy prevailed. Although the Liberals nationally were in long-term electoral decline, this did not happen more quickly in Llanelli than elsewhere. And, as we have seen, despite Keir Hardie's criticisms of Churchill's use of troops, in speeches and in his pamphlet *Killing No Murder*, the rapid growth of militancy scared the living daylights out of most Labour MPs. The dominant narrative in Llanelli became the bourgeois counter-offensive, in which the Liberals joined forces with the chapels and the newspapers first to smear and then to expunge any memory of independent working class action.

The chapel, despite the decline of the Welsh Methodist revival movement of 1904-5, still had influence among older workers. Based fundamentally on the vested interests of property, it saw militant trade unionism as a threat, and as the organisational expression of the Liberal Party in south Wales it denounced movements towards an independent working class politics. The Free Church Council of Llanelli was quick to denounce the "riotous behaviour that brought such a cloud of dishonour on the good name of our town". The *Llanelly Guardian* talked of "a howling, reckless, lawless mob bent on riot, destruction and plunder.".[38] The attitude of the Liberal Party can be seen in the attitude of the MP W Llewelyn Williams, who condemned the rioters as "casual labourers and hooligans".

As for the Labour Party, it faced both ways. Largely irrelevant to the progress of the strikes on a national level, party leader Ramsay MacDonald could say in 1912, "If we had been consulted first of all we should have advised the [strikers] to begin with parliamentary action, both on the floor of the House of Commons, and in ministers' private rooms." ILP leader Bruce Glasier called striking "culpable, incomprehensible fatuity", and the May 1912 issue of the ILP's journal *Socialist Review* described strikes as "an apocalypse" and supporters of direct action as "mentally defective"![39]

Beyond electoral politics

Yet in the events at Llanelli can be seen aspects of the Great Unrest which went beyond the limits of electoralism, pointing the way towards an

---

38: The spelling "Llanelly" was an anglicised form used until 1965.
39: Cliff and Gluckstein, 1988, p49.

insurrectionary challenge both to state power and to the inertia of the reformist leadership in the trade unions and the Labour Party. Two things in Llanelli in particular stand out: solidarity action by other workers and the support of the community in the working class districts. The leading role of the tinplate workers at Llanelli has already been mentioned. The Liberal Party's support for a reduction in US import tariffs meant that politically it retained the support of many tinplate workers in south Wales. Nevertheless, once the railway workers walked out on Thursday 17 August, the tinplate workers—the foremost industry of the town—came out on the streets in numbers. There were only 500 railway workers in Llanelli: yet over the next two days the mass picket numbered ten times as many. Speeches of solidarity were delivered on the all-night picket from the tinplate workers: they were seen as the most militant in their confrontations with the civil authority. At the height of the confrontation a telegram from the military to the Home Office stated, "The trouble [at Llanelli] comes from the tinplaters, not the railwaymen." One of the shot men—John John, who was said to have bared his chest and dared the soldiers to fire—was a tinplate worker at Morewood's mills. The tinplate industry was expanding in Llanelli: new mills were opening in 1911. On average, the tinplate worker's wage was double that of the railway worker.

Haynes stresses the importance of the "changing consciousness" of this period, and says: "For contemporaries the most notable aspect of the explosion of consciousness was the sympathetic strike." There was a "new sense of confidence spreading through informal channels...[particularly benefiting] those workers in parts of industry which had never been able to strike before. Here the victories of the strong gave new courage to the weak".[40] Haynes shows that the average length of strikes in Britain began to fall in this period, especially in the very smallest disputes, where the falls were most dramatic, indicating quicker victories. This registers not just a change in workers' attitudes but also a fall in employer confidence.

What were being developed in places like Llanelli were high profile, high visibility actions that sustained the militancy and gave power to rank and file workers and their supporters, creating a stronger unity than before. Haynes describes the way this was done: "Mass picketing was commonplace, daily strike meetings, frequent demonstrations led by brass bands in a carnival atmosphere and often directed against specific targets." On the streets of Llanelli, as elsewhere, resistance was led by the rank and file. It was from the start the mass picket at the railway crossings that determined the ability of the Great Western

---

40: Haynes, 1984, p97.

Railway Company to run trains. The authority even of the joint union railway strike committee, meeting in Copperworks School, was superseded by that of militants on the ground. The core strikers were railway workers, but others involved in the action—tinplate workers and others—were not. Even on the Friday night the chairman of the strike committee appealed unsuccessfully to the mass picket to let trains through. Democratic control was being thrashed out through the process of confrontation with the railway company and the armed forces of the state. As solidarity action extended, bringing in protagonists not employed on the railway, control passed from the hierarchy of the railway strike committee to the activists on the street.

The "official" account of the uprising, in the newspapers and on the pulpits, spoke of a mindless drunken rampaging mob. But what is clear is that, even more so in Llanelli than elsewhere, the targets for retribution were firmly associated with the civil power. This was not "anarchy": informal groupings were evidently able to decide on a course of collective action, besieging the military in the railway station, storming the police station and attacking the property of the Great Western Railway Company and the magistrates. Clearly decisions were being made at street level, perhaps utilising the "informal channels" Haynes talks about, and attempting to escalate the conflict. For example, a group of young men attempted unsuccessfully to break into the Volunteers Armoury in the Markets area on the Saturday evening: in a number of other British towns Territorial Army weapons were removed for fear they would be turned on regular troops.[41] As the situation polarised, the branch-level union officers were pressurised into attempting to limit the uprising. John Bevan, chairman of the Swansea Branch of the Associated Society of Railway Servants and leader of the strike in Llanelli, was persuaded to intervene after the shootings to dissuade the miners of the Gwendraeth and Amman Valleys from coming to Llanelli in support of the railway workers.[42]

Another factor that augmented the control of informal groupings and strengthened the insurgency was the support of the working class communities. Solidarity with the railway workers came not only from the tinplaters and miners but also from the communities of Glanymor and Tyisha around the railway and the docks. Haynes argues that reactions to strikes in this period very often became community reactions not just because strikers came from those communities but because community issues, such as rent strikes, often linked into industrial struggle. This is what fed the dynamic of the uprisings in Tonypandy, Hull and Liverpool. Strikers often assisted the

41: Haynes, 1984, p99.
42: Edwards, 1988, p79.

process by taking their demands into the communities, holding house to house collections and evening meetings, involving those not on strike, other workers, women at home and schoolchildren. When the state reacted with violence "this only served to intensify solidarity against what was seen as a hostile force whether represented on the ground by troops or the police".[43] In Llanelli this solidarity had a memorable effect: a soldier—private Harold Spiers—refused to fire on the crowd. The initial charge against him, of "desertion while in aid of the civil powers", was commuted to one of going "absent without leave", and he served only 14 days military imprisonment.

Aftershocks

The consequences of the railway strike in immediate industrial terms were disappointing. The uprising in Llanelli terrified the union leaderships and half an hour before the explosion in the railway sidings on 19 August the strike was called off by union leaders after government mediation. All grievances were to be brought forward to a Royal Commission: in the meantime no wage increases were to be offered and the hated Conciliation Boards were to remain intact. This angered many railwaymen, and areas like Manchester and Newcastle stayed out on strike. Even after a general return to work, dissatisfaction with the settlement continued: the syndicalist critique of conciliatory trade unionism was vindicated by the manner of the settlement.

Militancy continued, as did the growth of support for syndicalism on the railways. Swansea and 101 other ASRS branches unsuccessfully called for a special general meeting to discuss the actions of its officials, and ASLEF branches in Swansea and Llanelli were among those censuring their union's executive.[44] At the same time joint action by different grades of railwaymen at rank and file level stimulated the movement towards industrial trade unionism as a means of maximising trade union strength. Syndicalist pressure for one union of railway workers played an important part in the foundation of the National Union of Railwaymen (NUR) early in 1913 as an amalgamation of the ASRS and several smaller unions. It was also out of the struggles of 1911 that the Triple Alliance of miners, railwaymen and transport workers came together in an attempt to maximise union power.

Rob Griffiths traces some of the aftershocks of the uprising and the development of the political consciousness of its protagonists. In November 1913 when Dublin transport workers, led by Jim Larkin, were locked out by their employers, Llanelli railwaymen took action

---

43: Haynes, 1984, p98.
44: Griffiths, 2009, p82.

alongside workers in Liverpool, Birmingham and Yorkshire in support of the Irish workers and in protest at the inactivity of the British Trades Union Congress. On 7 November driver George James was suspended and then sacked at Llanelli for refusing to drive a train laden with Dublin cargo. A few days later his colleague driver Reynolds took action in solidarity with James and was also dismissed. A member of the NUR executive warned the press: "Llanelly is the one district in South Wales where we have had the most trouble recently. The men there are the most advanced in our ranks, and some of them would strike on the slightest pretext." Official and unofficial strikes spread across South Wales, the action winning complete reinstatement for both men. [45]

The political failure of the militants of 1910-14 to mount a political challenge which could oppose the drive to war in 1914 has been widely discussed. The syndicalist ambiguity about politics, and the orientation of its leadership upon a purely industrial militancy meant that they were unable to fuse this together with other political struggles of the time, for example the rebellion in Ireland and the fight for women's suffrage. Nor, despite the opposition to the war of individual syndicalists like Tom Mann, had they built up a network of people who, in 1914, could launch political strikes or refuse to handle war-related goods. But in a sense this is to criticise the syndicalists for not being Bolsheviks. Haynes argues that the problem with looking around at groups and individuals at this time to find the "origins of British Bolshevism" is that it claims both too much and too little:

> It claims too much in the sense that no one had found the model of a revolutionary political party that could steer between the twin dangers of sectarianism and simple liquidation into the parliamentary activities of the ILP and the Labour Party. It claims too little in the sense that it obscures what Bob Holton has called "an indigenous dynamic" that was leading a whole series of diverse rank and file elements towards the need for a political party along the lines of that created by the Bolsheviks in Russia. [46]

The First World War and the Russian Revolution acted as a catalyst to cause these elements to fuse together. But this should not prevent us from recognising the importance of the militancy of 1910-14 in creating the elements in the first place. It was this, together with the growing

---

45: Griffiths, 2009, p97.
46: Haynes, 1984, p110.

revulsion against the war, which created the platform for the next period of revolt in 1919. This took British workers beyond the limits of 1910-14 into being for a time part of a general European revolutionary wave.

References

Cliff, Tony, and Donny Gluckstein, 1988, *The Labour Party: a Marxist History* (Bookmarks).

Edwards, John, 1988, *Remembrance of a Riot: The Story of the Llanelli Railway Strike Riots of 1911* (Llanelli Borough Council/Harcourt).

Griffiths, Robert, 2009, *Killing No Murder* (Manifesto Press).

Haynes, Mike, 1984 "The British Working Class in Revolt: 1910-1914", *International Socialism* 22 (winter).

Holton, Bob, 1976, *British Syndicalism 1900-1914* (Pluto Press)

Hopkin, Deian, 1983, "The Llanelli Riots, 1911", *Welsh History Review*, volume 11, number 4 (University of Wales Press), http://bit.ly/llanelliriots

Kendall, Walter, 1969, *The Revolutionary Movement in Britain 1900-1921* (Littlehampton Books).

Lenin, VI, 1962 [1907], "Preface to the Pamphlet by Voinov (A V Lunacharsky) on the Attitude of the Party Towards the Trade Unions ", *Collected Works*, volume 13 (Lawrence and Wishart), www.marxists.org/archive/lenin/works/1907/nov/00.htm

Trotsky, Leon, 1974 [1925], "Where is Britain Going?", *Collected Writings and Speeches on Britain*, volume 2 (New Park Publications), www.marxists.org/archive/trotsky/britain/wibg/ch01.htm

The relevance of
permanent revolution:
A reply to Neil Davidson
Joseph Choonara

L eon Trotsky's theory of permanent revolution formed in its author's
mind during Russia's 1905 Revolution—between 9 January, when
workers marched to the Winter Palace to petition the Tsar, and the mass
strikes of October that gave birth to the Petrograd Soviet.[1]

In early 2011 the practice of permanent revolution once more
became a burning question as workers took centre stage in movements that
swept away dictators in Tunisia and Egypt. These uprisings seemed to show
the relevance of many of the key features described in Trotsky's theory. The
working class in less economically developed societies played a crucial role
in fighting for democracy; the struggles showed the potential to grow over
into a challenge to capitalism; the international dimension necessary to
allow the achievements of the revolution to become permanent was clear as
struggles spread across different Arab states.

In analysing these events a key point of reference for those associated
with *International Socialism* was the theory of permanent revolution. Indeed,
this theory, along with that of "deflected permanent revolution" developed

1:    Trotsky, 1973, p8. Thanks to Alex Callinicos and Esme Choonara for their comments
on the first draft of this article, and to Peyman Jafari and Anne Alexander for helpful
discussions.

by Tony Cliff in the early 1960s,[2] has been deployed in almost all our writing on struggles in the Global South for over half a century. Readers of Neil Davidson's recent article on the subject in this journal might therefore have been surprised to see "permanent revolution and consequently deflected permanent revolution" described as "historical concepts".[3]

I am confident that Neil shares our broad assessment and analysis of the events in the Arab world this year. So what's in a name? Does it matter if we refer to the patterns of revolution we hope to emerge in such contexts as "permanent"? I believe there is something to be said for stressing the basic continuities connecting the situations and struggles analysed by Trotsky and some of those of our day, and I think that Neil's reasons for stressing the historical break between these contexts are bad reasons.

I will attempt to set out, as clearly as possible, what I think the theory means and what is left when the general aspects of the theory are disentangled from the context in which they were formulated.

Why do we need the theory?

In the *Communist Manifesto* of 1848, Karl Marx and Frederick Engels stressed that capitalism itself was developing the various prerequisites for communism. These boil down to two key elements. First, the forces of production must be sufficiently developed to allow the emergence of a society capable of meeting human needs. Second, the working class, the "gravediggers" of capitalism, must have sufficient weight to be able to enact the "forcible overthrow of all existing social conditions".[4]

If these criteria are applied mechanically, a more economically backward society, possessing a low level of material development and in which the working class are a tiny minority, is in no way ripe for socialism. According to this argument, in such a society the best one can hope for is a revolution that secures favourable conditions for capitalist development, leading, eventually, to a potential struggle for socialism.

This "stagist" approach—first the "bourgeois-democratic revolution" to establish a modern capitalist state and then, at some later stage, a fight for socialism—was a commonplace of Stalinist theory.[5] It is still widely accepted on the left internationally today. I will give just one especially striking example. It is from an interview with Bolivia's vice-president Álvaro Marcelo García

---

2:    Cliff, 1990.
3:    Davidson, 2010, p195.
4:    Marx and Engels, 1985, pp221-231, 246.
5:    Cliff, 2000.

Linera, who, along with President Evo Morales of the MAS party, was carried to power on the back of two major waves of struggle in 2003 and 2005:

Interviewer: Is it your thesis that socialism is not viable in Bolivia today?
Linera: There are two reasons why there is not much chance of a socialist regime being installed in Bolivia. On the one hand, there is a proletariat that is numerically in a minority and politically non-existent, and you cannot build socialism without a proletariat. Secondly, the potential for agrarian and urban communities is very much weakened. There is an implosion of community economies into family structures, which have been the framework within which the social movements have arisen…

Interviewer: In that case, what kind of system does the MAS want to build?
Linera: A kind of Andean capitalism.

Interviewer: What is Andean capitalism?
Linera: It is a question of building a strong state… It is a question of transferring a part of the surplus of the nationalised hydrocarbons in order to encourage the setting up of forms of self-organisation, of self-management and of commercial development that is really Andean and Amazonian… Bolivia will still be capitalist in 50 or 100 years.[6]

What was Trotsky's alternative to such a bleak perspective?

Trotsky's theory

One of the strengths of Neil's article is his detailed discussion of the theory of uneven and combined development.[7] The term was introduced by Trotsky in *The History of the Russian Revolution*,[8] published in 1930, but the concept is, contrary to Neil's suggestion,[9] present in a more or less complete form in his earlier writings on permanent revolution—notably *1905* and *Results and Prospects*.

Late developing capitalist nations do not simply replicate their predecessors. Russia in the early 20th century would not follow the path of pre-existing capitalist powers such as France or Britain. There would not be centuries of painstaking growth of handicrafts and manufactories before the

---

6: Stefanoni, 2005.
7: Davidson, 2010, pp182-195.
8: Trotsky, 1985, p27.
9: Davidson, 2010, p184.

rise of the great factories of the industrial revolution. Under the pressure of external competition—military and economic—from more advanced economies Russia would implant the most sophisticated machinery and techniques. By squeezing the peasantry to raise taxes and by borrowing from European financiers, the Tsarist bureaucracy could import the most advanced factories and railroads onto Russian soil. This created, as Trotsky writes:

> The most concentrated industry in Europe based on the most backward agriculture in Europe. The most colossal state apparatus in the world making use of every achievement of modern technological progress in order to retard the historical progress of its own country.[10]

The uneven development of the world system led to combination, in which the modern and the archaic fused in novel ways. Neil writes that this "usually involves what Michael Burawoy calls 'the combination of capitalist modes of production with pre-existing modes'".[11] However, he adds, there can be extreme disparities in the development of the forces of production *within* the capitalist mode of production itself. So Neil writes of the "immense difference between *industrial* capitalism and previous modes of production".[12]

Uneven and combined development affects not only the shape and pace of advance of the means of production of a society, but also the class structure. In the Russian case it meant a small and weak domestic capitalist class, heavily penetrated by external financiers, a colossal and repressive bureaucracy, and a freshly formed and small, but potentially powerful, urban working class.

This had implications for the coming Russian Revolution. The largest social group, the peasantry, lacked the cohesion or commonality of interest necessary to lead a revolution. It could play a revolutionary role only insomuch as it could connect to a revolutionary class in the cities. The bourgeoisie would not play a revolutionary role, because it feared and was antagonistic towards the working class that it oppressed and exploited.

This posed a problem for the country's socialist movement, which was divided between its Bolshevik and Menshevik factions. For the Mensheviks, the coming revolution would be bourgeois in character. Therefore it would be made by the "democratic bourgeoisie". Workers might assist as part of a democratic coalition of forces, but could at best act as a kind of ginger group

---

10: Trotsky, 1973, p53.

11: Davidson, 2010, pp187-188.

12: Davidson, 2010, p192 (my emphasis). The implication that "industrial capitalism" is a distinctive mode of production is probably a slip of the pen.

assuring certain rights for workers in the ensuing democratic regime.[13] The Bolsheviks, led by Lenin, recognised the need for a militant struggle by workers. In their formulation there would be a "revolutionary-democratic dictatorship of the proletariat and peasantry" which would drive the revolution through. The proletariat would, according to this rather vague scenario, limit itself to the tasks appropriate to a bourgeois revolution.[14] This formulation persisted until 1917, when, in the course of the revolution, Lenin won the Bolshevik Party (which Trotsky had by then joined) to a perspective remarkably similar to that of permanent revolution.[15]

For Trotsky the solution to the problems faced by Russia—an agrarian revolution to resolve the land question, the overthrow or Tsarism and the introduction of democracy, and so on—could only be brought about by workers. This struggle might begin with tasks common to the bourgeois revolutions of the past (the English Revolution of the 17th century or the French and American revolutions of the 18th), "but the principal driving force of the Russian Revolution is the proletariat, and that is why, so far as its methods are concerned, it is a proletarian revolution".[16] Faced with this, "the proletariat is driven by the internal progress of events towards hegemony over the peasantry and to the struggle for state power".[17] Having established a workers' state, it was implausible to suggest that the workers would accept a self-denying ordnance and stop at purely "democratic" or "bourgeois" tasks. On the contrary, they would use their power to wrest economic, social and political control from the old ruling class.[18]

In other words, the revolution could pass directly over into a social revolution leading towards the establishment of socialism and becoming

---

13:    See Trotsky 1973, pp290-329.

14:    See Trotsky, 1973, pp329-333.

15:    On the question of whether Lenin ever actually read Trotsky's writings on permanent revolution, see Trotsky, 1982, pp42-43. In Trotsky's assessment, prior to the 1917 Revolution Lenin was probably only familiar with the theory indirectly, through its citation by other writers. However, Trotsky recalls that Adolph Abramovich Joffe, a member of Trotsky's left opposition in the 1920s, claimed a conversation with Lenin in which the latter acknowledged the correctness of Trotsky's insights. Just before his suicide in 1927 Joffe wrote to Trotsky making the same claim. See Trotsky, 1979, pp558-561.

16:    Trotsky, 1973, p66.

17:    Trotsky, 1973, p72.

18:    Lenin makes a similar point in one of his famous "April Theses" of 1917: "Not a parliamentary republic—to return to a parliamentary republic from the Soviets of Workers' Deputies would be a retrograde step—but a republic of Soviets of Workers', Agricultural Labourers' and Peasants' Deputies throughout the country, from top to bottom"—Lenin, 1917.

"permanent".[19] However, having made such a revolution the working class would face a potentially hostile mass of peasantry, who, having taken control of their land in alliance with the workers, would now have quite different interests. This would mean the eventual overturning of the revolution unless the workers could prove that socialism offered greater potential than private capitalist agriculture. But that meant accessing far greater material and cultural resources than were available in Russia. Successful revolution would again run up against the limits of the pre-requisites for socialism.

For Trotsky, the pre-requisites did not exist on the national terrain. He insisted on the international nature of revolution because the prerequisites only existed on a world scale. Russia must provide the prologue for the European, and ultimately the world, revolution.

As capitalism is an international system, connected both through imperialism and the world market, crises provoking revolutionary situations were likely to be regional or global in scale. The other dimension to the "permanence" of the Russian Revolution was, therefore, that revolutions would have to follow in major European countries. The revolutionary wave that followed 1917 was confirmation of the viability of Trotsky's theory; the ultimate defeat of this wave, which paved the way for Stalinist counterrevolution, was, in a negative sense, also a confirmation.

The discreet charm of the bourgeois revolution

Thus far I think Neil would agree with the basic outlines of the theory as I have presented them. The problems involve the generalisation of the theory, something Trotsky later sought to achieve by applying it to colonial and semi-colonial countries.

It is over this question that I think Neil confuses matters unnecessarily by emphasising that the revolution begins as a "bourgeois revolution". If permanent revolution means the replacement of a feudal society with a capitalist one, then permanent revolution is clearly no longer a historical possibility.[20] There are, of course, no "feudal societies" left. But this was not

---

19: The term "permanent" has an odd ring to it, implying "perpetual" to the modern reader, rather than implying an uninterrupted continuation. A recent collection of writings on permanent revolution clarifies this: "In Russian, the words 'permanent revolution [*permanentnaya revolyutsiya*]' and 'uninterrupted revolution [*nepreryvnaya revolyutsiya*]' are semantic equivalents and completely interchangeable...in his foreword to Marx's essay on the Paris Commune...[Trotsky]...spoke of a 'revolution *in Permanenz*, or an *uninterrupted revolution*'"—Day and Gaido, 2009, pp449-450.

20: Neil is not the first to question the relevance of the theory on this basis. A similar piece by David Whitehouse in the US-based *International Socialist Review* in 2006 prompted a response

what was at stake in Russia in 1905 or 1917 either. As Lenin and Trotsky both emphasise, Russia was a country with considerable capitalist development, even if the pattern of development was peculiar compared to that of Britain or France. The tasks assumed by the Russian revolutions had also mutated considerably from those of the classical bourgeois revolution. For instance, the procession led by Father Gapon to the Tsar's palace spoke of the problem of "unheated factories" and the demand for an "eight-hour day", not just "universal and equal suffrage" or land reform.[21] In other words it took up, from the outset, workers' issues that lay firmly within a capitalist framework. So, when Neil claims that permanent revolution implies a break with "feudal", "tributary" or "colonial" rule, or, later in his article, the overthrow of "absolutism", he ought to spell out carefully what he means.[22]

He further complicates matters by the way he employs the categories "social revolution" and "political revolution". In doing so he claims to be applying Hal Draper's definitions, but Draper's descriptions of political and social revolution are far more illuminating than Neil's:

> *Political* revolution...puts the emphasis on changes in governmental leaderships and forms, transformations in the superstructure. But if such a revolution involves a change in the social stratum even within the ruling class, a social element is plainly entailed. Political revolutions run the gamut, from those involving almost no social side, to those with a very important social element, even if it is within the class boundaries we have assumed.

> If these social boundaries are burst...then we have a different sort of revolution...The outcome is a revolution involving the transfer of political power to a new class; and this change in ruling class tends to entail a basic change in the social system (mode of production). It is this kind of revolution that is most properly called a *social* revolution.[23]

However, this does not exhaust the problem. Draper uses the neologism "*societal revolution*" to describe a long-term transformation of one

---

by Paul D'Amato that vigorously defended Trotsky's theory. Although I agree with much of D'Amato's reply, his claim that "all countries...need a permanent revolution because though the material prerequisites for socialism exist on an international scale, they do not within a purely national framework" robs the theory of any specificity. See Whitehouse, 2006; D'Amato, 2006.

21:   Trotsky, 1973, p90.
22:   Davidson, 2010, pp170, 171.
23:   Draper, 1978, pp18-19.

society into another that changes class or social relations in a fundamental way. He continues:

> We can now narrow our focus to what tends to be called a social revolution in Marx's theory. It is most clearly used for a political revolution that expresses a social-revolutionising drive towards the transference of state power to a new class. It is a "political revolution with a social soul", in Marx's earlier (1844) formulation. By the same token it points in the direction of a societal revolution, regardless of when changes in the social system actually begin to take place… The societal revolution is the realisation of these potentialities.[24]

A crucial insight follows:

> Our aim is not to make a hard and fast distinction between political revolutions and social revolutions but, if anything, the reverse: to recognise how often they are mingled in given revolutionary situations, so that the two elements must be distinguished by analysis. For, especially in modern times, revolutionary events tend to blend both in varying proportions… Thus the relationship between political and social revolution is not static.[25]

Now Neil's definitions seem quite different. In a political, as opposed to social, revolution, writes Neil, "the class that was in control of the means of production at the beginning will remain so at the end…and the class that was exploited within the production process at the beginning will also remain so at the end".[26] By implication, a social revolution must mean that control of the means of production *does* shift from one class to another or that those who are exploited at the beginning are *not* at the end.

I am not sure to what extent his formulation is simply a clumsy one and to what extent it reflects Neil's actual approach. But, given that his argument seems to hinge upon the relationship between bourgeois revolution, social revolution and permanent revolution, it certainly requires clarification.

Consider the actual processes involved in socialist revolutions and in bourgeois revolutions. Communism, as an economic system, does not develop within capitalism. A communist economy can be developed only once the working class has assumed state power. Furthermore, the conscious agency and leadership of the working class are required because socialist revolution,

---

24: Draper, 1978, p19.
25: Draper, 1978, p20.
26: Davidson, 2010, p175.

unlike bourgeois revolution, must be an act of self-emancipation. Socialist revolution implies, therefore, a revolution in which workers break the existing state machine and replace it with a workers' state. This flows directly into a process through which workers take control of the means of production and begin to produce in a communistic manner. The actual transition to communism is therefore a prolonged process following the socialist revolution.

Capitalism, by contrast, develops within the interstices of feudal social relations. France had already experienced capitalist development and the emergence of considerable capitalist class power prior to the Great French Revolution of 1789. It is not true that between 1788 and 1790 or 1795 control of the means of production passed from the feudal ruling class to a capitalist one, or that a different class was exploited at the end of the revolution.

Neil adds that this "social revolution" can be a much more prolonged process, indicating that it sometimes requires subsequent phases such as the 1830 Revolution in France. But in such an account any number of phases might be added without necessarily leading to the kind of change to the class structure of society that Neil seems to make the hallmark of social revolution.

In later examples, in which the process was not driven by the kind of classical mobilisations seen in France, America or England in the 18th and 17th centuries, the situation is even more complex. For one thing, a whole range of different agencies can push for what Draper calls "societal revolution". The revolutionary processes that created the "political conditions of capitalist domination" were driven through "from above" in the cases of German unification or the Japanese Meiji Restoration in the 19th century.[27]

But this is not the end of the story. As the system develops on a world scale and capitalist political domination becomes the norm, subsequent "bourgeois revolutions" can take on an even more disjointed and episodic form in late developing capitalisms. Often it is difficult to specify a moment or even a decisive period in which quantity transformed into quality. At what point, for example, did Bolivia cease to be "feudal" and become "capitalist"? Along with a long societal process of economic development, a whole series of upheavals were required, combining blows struck from below and manoeuvres at the top, through successive political revolutions with a social dimension. This must include the great indigenous struggles of 1780-82 and the liberation from colonial rule in the early 19th century, the various coups and countercoups at the start of the 20th century to the great popular nationalist revolution of 1952 and beyond.

27: Callinicos, 1989, pp116, 151-159.

However, it is certainly true that there is no society today where capital does not rule politically and economically (whether or not members of the capitalist class *directly* exercise their political power). Indeed, according to Trotsky, writing in 1930, this has been the case for some time:

> Then wherein lies the distinction between the advanced and backward countries? The distinction is great, but it still remains within the limits of the domination of capitalist relationships. The forms and methods of the rule of the bourgeoisie differ greatly in different countries. At one pole, the domination bears a stark and absolute character: *The United States*. At the other pole finance capital adapts itself to the outlived institutions of Asiatic medievalism by subjecting them to itself and imposing its own methods upon them: *India*. But the bourgeoisie rules in both places. From this it follows that the dictatorship of the proletariat will also have a highly varied character in terms of the social basis, the political forms, the immediate tasks and the tempo of work in the various capitalist countries.[28]

Today uneven and combined development is best conceived as a drawing together of successive phases—including, crucially, capitalist phases—in novel forms within countries of the Global South. Uneven and combined development poses *peculiar* problems for those societies that may require *revolutionary struggle* in their resolution. This involves a broadening of the scope of the theory, but not a break from it. Trotsky, again and again, uses the terms "peculiar" and "peculiarities" in his writings on permanent revolution. He stresses the need, for instance, to make a "genuine study of the peculiarity of a given country, ie the living interpenetration of the various steps and stages of historical development in that country".[29]

Permanent revolution in this conception involves the combination of democratic and socialist challenges to the existing order of things. The former cover a range of potential demands, including the dissolution of large landed estates across much of the Global South, the introduction of parliamentary democracy in Egypt or Tunisia today, the resolution of the "indigenous question" in Bolivia in the struggles of 2003 or 2005, or the overthrow of colonialism in India in 1946-7. None of these demands are, in themselves, incompatible with capitalist social relations, but achieving these in the context of uneven and combined development can lead to an anti-capitalist dynamic raising the possibility of social revolution.

28: Trotsky, 1982, p129.
29: Trotsky, 1982, p129.

The particular interweaving of the political and social is here a dialectical and fluid "blend", to use Draper's term. Permanent revolution begins, Trotsky writes at one point, with "a far-reaching and burning problem 'for the people'...in the solution of which the majority of the nation is interested, and which demands for its solution the boldest revolutionary measures".[30] It is in this sense that the theory is general to both the early examples that Trotsky deals with and the instances we are faced with today.

It follows that Trotsky and Cliff are quite justified in discussing bourgeois or democratic "tasks", provided such tasks are seen as fluid, as part of a dynamic historical process, rather than a fixed and mechanically applied set of criteria. In this context it is tempting to talk about the "uneven and combined consciousness" of those striving for revolutionary change.

While it is quite true that the introduction of parliamentary democracy with universal adult suffrage was not achieved by any of the classical bourgeois revolutions, it is today a feature of many of the most advanced capitalist countries. For the Egyptian masses to demand this is in the tradition of permanent revolution—they have made it their "democratic task". It may well be that, due to the instability of any liberal parliamentary regime faced with the agrarian problem, the weakness of Egyptian capital, the Palestinian question, etc, a further social deepening of the revolutionary process is required to force through such a change. It may be that, out of such a struggle, a higher form of democracy emerges, leaping ahead of the parliamentary democracies of the Global North. Surely this too is part of the tradition of 1917, which, Trotsky wrote, was "in its initial task... a democratic revolution. But it posed the problem of political democracy in a new way".[31]

We need to remain true to this, the spirit of Trotsky's theory, rather than seeking to apply it formalistically and, inevitably, finding it wanting. Strangely enough, and in contradiction to much of the rest of the article, Neil seems to come to a similar conclusion towards the end of his piece:

Uneven and combined development is therefore likely to be an ongoing process, which will only be resolved by either revolution or disintegration. But in the meantime, China and other states like India and Brazil where growth has been less dramatic remain both inherently unstable in their internal social relations and expansive in their external search for markets, raw

---

30: Trotsky, 1982, p130.
31: Trotsky, 1983, pp35-36.

materials and investment opportunities. *It is in this inherent instability that the possibilities for permanent revolution lie.*[32]

If that is Neil's position, then there is no disagreement.

Cliff's contribution

From this standpoint, Cliff's contribution to the problem of permanent revolution is less ambiguous than Neil implies. Cliff's starting point was the insight that "an automatic correlation between economic backwardness and revolutionary political militancy does not exist".[33] Neil objects that Trotsky never insisted on such a correlation and he adds that uneven and combined development is the fundamental "enabling condition" for workers' militancy.[34]

While it is true that uneven and combined development is one factor destabilising the Global South, and so creating potentially revolutionary situations, this is only one part of the story. Cliff focuses on societies where these kinds of processes lead to revolutionary crises but where workers do not play a revolutionary role. We do not require a single special explanation for the failure of workers to "be revolutionary" in any particular context—a whole range of economic, political and ideological factors will dictate whether this is the case. But I do not see any evidence in what Neil writes that it was the absence of uneven and combined development that prevented workers' militancy taking hold.

Cliff's second point was that, in contexts in which workers do not take the initiative, the sizeable revolutionary intelligentsia could impose a solution to the problems thrown up by uneven and combined development. They could do so alone, as in Cuba in 1958, or, as in China in 1949, at the head of a peasant rebellion. Neil's second objection to Cliff is that China in 1949 was "feudal" and Cuba in 1958 was "capitalist".[35] However, if one accepts Trotsky's claim that China was dominated by capitalist social relations in the 1920s, and it is not clear to me whether Neil does or does not,[36] then the problem vanishes.

Incidentally, Cliff was also more orthodox in his Trotskyism in identifying the intelligentsia as a potentially revolutionary force than is sometimes realised. In *1905* Trotsky contrasts the middle class who, he argues, were central to the French Revolution with the Russian, "'new middle class', the

---

32: Davidson, 2010, p197 (my emphasis).
33: Cliff, 1990, p22.
34: Davidson, 2010, p182.
35: Davidson, 2010, pp174-175.
36: Cited in Davidson, 2010, p188.

professional intelligentsia: lawyers, doctors, engineers, university professors, schoolteachers".[37] However, in the Russian context, this was a relatively small layer. Trotsky argues that they were in fact drawn behind the organisation of the liberal landowners, who resented the Tsarist state's industrial protectionism and the burdens it imposed on the countryside. The Kadet party was "a union of the oppositional impotence of the *zemtsy* [landed constitutionalists] with the all-round impotence of the diploma-carrying intelligentsia".[38] When in 1905 the landowners swung behind the Tsar in the face of rural unrest, the intelligentsia:

> With tears in its eyes, was obliged to forsake the country estate where, when all is said and done, it had been no more than a foster child, and to seek recognition in its historic home, the city. But what did it find in the city, other than its own self? It found the conservative capitalist bourgeoisie, the revolutionary proletariat, and the irreconcilable antagonism between the two.[39]

In the societies examined by Cliff, where the proletariat was not in a revolutionary mood, and where the intelligentsia was sufficiently developed to play an independent role, things were rather different. They also had a model of capitalist development to look to—in its purest form the state capitalist model giving rise to "deflected state capitalist permanent revolution".[40] The more common form involved a combination of private and state capitalism. Sensitivity to these possibilities was of profound importance to the International Socialist tradition. It allowed us to give unconditional support to struggles for national liberation without falsely painting the leadership of such movements as socialists:

> For revolutionary socialists in the advanced countries, the shift in strategy means that while they will have to continue to oppose any national oppression of the colonial people unconditionally, they must cease to argue over the national identity of the future ruling classes of Asia, Africa and Latin America, and instead investigate the class conflicts and future social structures of these continents.[41]

I sympathise more with Neil on the question of the subsequent

---

37: Trotsky, 1973, p58.
38: Trotsky, 1973, pp58-59.
39: Trotsky, 1973, p59.
40: Cliff, 1990, p25.
41: Cliff, 1990, p26.

over-generalisation of Cliff's theory. Chris Harman's *The Prophet and the Proletariat* is an important analysis of the contradictions of political Islam.[42] But Iran's 1979 Revolution cannot be an example of deflected permanent revolution—because here, as Harman shows, the level of revolutionary energy and the potential for self-organisation of the proletariat were magnificent. Unlike Neil, though, I would see this as an aborted process of permanent revolution, which failed to break through for subjective political reasons.

The same applies to John Newsinger's account of the 1952 Bolivian Revolution, which was marked by workers holding effective power in streets of the major cities.[43] The kind of class forces Cliff discussed played an important role in Iran and Bolivia. But here the absence of a revolutionary party with sufficient size and experience is the central problem rather than the non-revolutionary nature of the working class. Trotsky would have recognised the problem of the absence of the subjective element of the revolutionary party.[44]

Goodbye Trotsky?

International Socialism has always prided itself on being part of a living tradition. Permanent revolution cannot, for us, be a dry and lifeless formalism. It is not something that we bolt on to our analysis simply because we require the reassuring familiarity of orthodoxy. For this reason, Neil's contribution and the series of articles in recent journals re-examining elements of our tradition are especially welcome.

However, contrary to what I think Neil is arguing, many of the revolutionary struggles in recent years can still be usefully situated within the framework of Trotsky's theory. This is no substitute for concrete analysis, but permanent revolution, liberated from some of the immediate context in which it was first formulated, remains relevant in guiding our understanding of struggle in the Global South today.

42: Harman, 2010. Harman's analysis was to be especially crucial in the development of Egypt's Revolutionary Socialists who played an important role in the 2011 struggles against the dictatorship of Hosni Mubarak.

43: Newsinger, 1983, p82.

44: For instance, in his 1932 speech "In Defence of October", he situated the need for a revolutionary party in the context of 1917 and permanent revolution—Trotsky, 1932.

References

Callinicos, Alex, 1989, "Bourgeois Revolutions and Historical Materialism", *International Socialism 43* (summer 1989).

Cliff, Tony, 1990 [1963], *Deflected Permanent Revolution* (Socialist Workers Party), www.marxists.org/archive/cliff/works/1963/xx/permrev.htm

Cliff, Tony, 2000, "Democratic Revolution or Socialist Revolution?", in *Marxism at the Millennium* (Bookmarks), www.marxists.org/archive/cliff/works/2000/millennium/chap12.htm

D'Amato, Paul, 2006, "The Necessity of Permanent Revolution", *International Socialist Review 48* (July-August 2006), www.isreview.org/issues/48/permrev-damato.shtml

Davidson, Neil, 2010, "From Deflected Permanent Revolution to the Law of Uneven and Combined Development", *International Socialism 128* (autumn), www.isj.org.uk/?id=686

Day, Richard B, and Daniel Gaido (eds), 2009, *Witnesses to Permanent Revolution: The Documentary Record* (Brill).

Draper, Hal, 1978, *Karl Marx's Theory of Revolution, volume 2: The Politics of Social Classes* (Monthly Review).

Harman, Chris, 2010 [1994], "The Prophet and the Proletariat", in *Selected Writings* (Bookmarks), www.marxists.de/religion/harman/

Lenin, Vladimir Ilych, 1917, *The Tasks of the Proletariat in the Present Revolution*, www.marxists.org/archive/lenin/works/1917/apr/04.htm

Marx, Karl, and Frederick Engels, 1985 [1848], *The Communist Manifesto*, in David McLellan (ed), *Karl Marx: Selected Writings* (Oxford University), www.marxists.org/archive/marx/works/1848/communist-manifesto/

Newsinger, John, 1983, "Revolution in Bolivia", *International Socialism 18* (winter).

Stefanoni, Pablo, 2005, "The MAS is of the Centre-Left: Interview with Álvaro García Linera, Newly Elected Bolivian Vice-President", *International Viewpoint 373* (December 2005), www.internationalviewpoint.org/spip.php?article938

Trotsky, Leon, 1932, "In Defence of October", speech delivered in Copenhagen, Denmark (November 1932), www.marxists.org/archive/trotsky/1932/11/oct.htm

Trotsky, Leon, 1973 [1907], *1905* (Pelican), www.marxists.org/archive/trotsky/1907/1905/

Trotsky, Leon, 1979 [1930], *My Life* (Penguin), www.marxists.org/archive/trotsky/1930/mylife/

Trotsky, Leon, 1982 [1906/1930], *The Permanent Revolution and Results and Prospects (1906)* (New Park), www.marxists.org/archive/trotsky/1931/tpr/

Trotsky, Leon, 1985 [1930], *The History of the Russian Revolution* (Pluto), www.marxists.org/archive/trotsky/1930/hrr/

Whitehouse, David, 2006, "The Fading Relevance of Permanent Revolution", *International Socialist Review 48* (July-August 2006), www.isreview.org/issues/48/permrev-whitehouse.shtml

Anarchism, syndicalism and strategy: A reply to Lucien van der Walt

Paul Blackledge[1]

Lucien van der Walt's reply to my "Marxism and Anarchism" marks a welcome step forward beyond the all too familiar "non-debate" between Marxist and anarchist tendencies on the revolutionary left. Essentially, his argument is that while *International Socialism* and anarchism (or at least the syndicalist interpretation of anarchism outlined in his and Michael Schmidt's *Black Flame*) "converge" in conceiving socialism as a libertarian movement "from below", Marxists such as Lenin and Trotsky represent a different tradition that builds upon more "authoritarian" aspects of Marx's work. This difference is important because Lenin and Trotsky set the "template for Stalin's" regime,[2] and insofar as *International Socialism* fails to break with their ideas it risks undermining its own libertarian aspirations.

If valid this would be a devastating indictment of the SWP and similar revolutionary organisations. In fact, quite the reverse is true. Van der Walt's criticisms rely on a caricatured interpretation of Marxism and a very distorted history of the Russian Revolution that effectively acts as

1:   Thanks to Mike Haynes and Alex Callinicos. Considerations of space prevent me from engaging properly with Ian Birchall's reply to my essay—I shall return to the issues he raises at a later date.
2:   Van der Walt 2011a, pp201-204.

a barrier to learning the lessons of past struggles. This perhaps explains why he attempts no serious engagement with Ian Birchall's comments on the undoubted appeal of Bolshevism to a whole generation of anarchists and anarcho-syndicalists around the time of the Russian Revolution. As we shall see, though a minority of these activists withdrew their support for the regime during the civil war,[3] Bolshevism attracted many syndicalists because it pointed to a socialist alternative to reformism that overcame the limitations of syndicalism in a way that is still of relevance to the left today.

Anarchism, syndicalism and strategy

With regard to van der Walt's comments on Marx's ideas, it is simply wrong of him to claim that *International Socialism* is unusual in stressing the centrality of the concept of working class self-emancipation to Marx's thought. All serious writers on Marx agree that this concept is fundamental to his politics. From the third thesis on Feuerbach in which Marx writes that "the coincidence of the changing of circumstances and of human activity or self-changing can be conceived and rationally understood only as revolutionary practice", through *The German Ideology* where he and Engels insisted that revolutions were necessary not merely to remove the old ruling class but also, and much more importantly, to make the working class fit to rule through its own activity, to the rules of the First International in which Marx wrote that "the emancipation of the working class must be conquered by the working classes themselves" this idea was his lodestar. What is more, this concept is no mere political add on to the rest of Marx's social theory. For, as he insists in *Capital*, we can only understand capitalism as a totality, and therefore conceive of challenging it as a totality, from the standpoint of working class struggles.[4]

There is a tacit acceptance of this perspective amongst those anarchists, such as Todd May and Ben Franks, whose critique of Marxism extends to a rejection of *strategic* thinking for a supposedly more democratic form of *tactical* politics.[5] Writing from a similar perspective, Saul Newman points to the link between the movement away from strategy to tactics and the rejection of the idea of revolution. Because (postmodernist) anarchists cannot conceive capitalism as a totality, they dismiss the idea of revolution as a totalitarian project. Consequently, politics (of all colourations) in a fragmented world is reduced to a plurality of tactical forms.[6] Simon Critchley

---

3: Avrich, 1967, p196.
4: Marx, 1976, p732.
5: May, 1994, pp1-15; Franks, 2006, p98.
6: Newman, 2001, p2.

suggests that for anarchists this means embracing an "infinitely demanding" but ultimately forlorn anarchist "commitment to a politics of resistance".[7] For all its supposed radicalism, this perspective is congruent with modern liberal ideas that change is possible so long as it is of a very minor and local variety, and in fact resembles a more pessimistic version of the reformism against which syndicalism rebelled at the end of the 19th century. This was a period when the nominally Marxist parties of the Second International (1889-1914) combined revolutionary rhetoric at their annual conferences with a day to day practice that limited politics "to the question of tactics".[8] And while theorists such as Karl Kautsky tried to cover the growing gap between theory and practice with an increasingly disconnected version of Marxist rhetoric, the actual practice of these organisations was best summarised by Eduard Bernstein, the most influential reformist critic of Marxist revolutionary politics at the turn of the last century, who argued that for socialists the movement is everything, the goal nothing.[9]

By contrast with thinkers who reduce anarchism to a plurality of tactical approaches, it is a great strength of van der Walt and Schmidt's book that they attempt to conceptualise anarchism as a revolutionary strategy. However, while welcoming this attempt to think through the issue of moving from resistance to revolution, we should not shy away from addressing problems with their proposed syndicalist strategy for socialism

These problems are obscured in van der Walt's method of reply to the criticisms of anarcho-syndicalism levelled in my original article. He argues that it is incoherent of me "to condemn all anarchist experiences (as in Spain) as due entirely to ideology, not context, but to exonerate all Marxist experiences (as in Russia) as due entirely to context, not ideology".[10] Any reader of my original article should immediately recognise that this is less a response to my arguments than an attempt to avoid the issue by means of a sleight of hand. I shall return to the issue of objective circumstances presently. With respect to the power of ideas, the contrast between Russia and Spain related to the problem of how revolutionaries should relate to the mass of workers who are still as yet under the influence of one or other form of reformist politics. I suggested that in two comparable revolutionary situations, Spain in 1936 and Russia in 1917, the Bolsheviks and the Spanish anarchists responded in two very different ways to this problem. I did not

---

7:　Critchley, 2007, p89.
8:　Cliff, 1975, p254.
9:　Bernstein, 1993, p190.
10:　Van der Walt, 2011a, p203.

touch upon the material constraints affecting the Bolsheviks after 1917 because this issue was irrelevant to the political lessons I was highlighting.

My argument was clear. Because the Bolsheviks had a concept of dictatorship of the proletariat (as real democratic control by the working class) they were able to frame their "united front" with Kerensky's bourgeois regime against Kornilov's attempted coup in September 1917 in a way that allowed them to avoid taking an ultra-left abstentionist position on the coup while nevertheless maintaining their independence from Kerensky's bourgeois government. If this approach paved the way for the October Revolution, anarchism's rejection of the concept of the dictatorship of the proletariat meant that it was far more difficult for the CNT in Spain to do something similar. It is all well and good to say that the CNT broke with anarchism when they joined the Republican government. At a theoretical level this is perfectly true. The point is, though, that when the CNT leaders joined the government they were reacting to a real problem, and unless their critics point to a viable alternative course of action then their criticisms remain at a purely abstract level. The anarchists in Spain were right to defend the Republic against Franco, but without something like the concepts of united front and dictatorship of the proletariat they had no adequate answer to those Republican politicians who said that because war demanded a unified military structure they should join the Republican government.

The beginning of an answer to this problem was formulated by various anarchists in the 1930s. Interestingly, Diego Abad de Santillán, who in 1936 had been one of the first anarchists to justify joining the government in order to help win the war against Franco, was by 1940 amongst those anarchists who had come to the conclusion that the strategy had been a disaster: "We sacrificed the revolution itself without understanding that this sacrifice also implied sacrificing the aims of the war".[11] Because, in essence, Trotsky shared this critique of the Popular Front government, the arguments of Santillán and other similar anarchists open up the possibility of a fruitful dialogue between Marxists and anarchists. Nonetheless, because Trotsky's argument involves a defence of the concept of the dictatorship of the proletariat, for such a dialogue to be meaningful it must involve discussion of this idea.[12]

11: Broué and Témime, 2008, p208.

12: On Spain Trotsky wrote, "We can and must defend bourgeois democracy not by bourgeois democratic means but by the methods of class struggle, which in turn pave the way for the replacement of bourgeois democracy by the dictatorship of the proletariat. This means in particular that in the process of defending bourgeois democracy, even with arms in hand, the party of the proletariat takes no responsibility for bourgeois democracy, does not enter its government, but maintains full freedom of criticism and of action in relation to all

To this end, it is interesting that van der Walt should claim that anarchism does not suffer from the weaknesses over the issue of democracy that I laid at its door. This is not because I agree with the detail of his arguments—on the contrary I think he has a procrustean tendency to force the messy plurality of real anarchisms into an ideal version that he'd prefer anarchism to be. Nevertheless, when he counters my charge that anarchism has great difficulty with the concept of democracy by pointing to Wayne Price's anarchist engagement with this issue, this at least has the benefit of opening a door to debate on the thorny question of the dictatorship of the proletariat.[13]

In *The Abolition of the State*, Price argues that "anarchism is democracy without the state".[14] More concretely, he suggests that while "it will be necessary for the oppressed to take power" in a revolutionary situation, it would be "a mistake for the oppressed to take state power".[15] It is to Price's credit that he recognises that this position was, in essence, shared by Marx and Lenin. They too rejected the idea, often mistakenly associated with their names elsewhere in anarchist and autonomist circles, that socialists should "seize the state". In its place they insisted that the revolution should be defended through workers'' own democratic organisations.[16] In an interesting comment in the longer online version of his critique of my essay, van der Walt runs with this idea. In regard to my and Leo Zeilig's rehearsals of the Marxist understanding of the dictatorship of the proletariat as a form of extreme democracy he writes: "*If* (and I stress, only if) we concede [such] definitions, then we *must* argue that Bakunin, Kropotkin, as defenders of working class power and it's armed defence, were *for* a 'workers' state' and a 'dictatorship' of the proletariat. Indeed, it would follow that the majority of the broad anarchist tradition were *for the state*."[17]

Clearly, this statement takes us beyond sectarian non-debate. It is also safe to say that it would be very contentious in anarchist circles—even Price insists that Lenin's "libertarian interpretation of Marxism is contradictory to the totalitarian state" he developed.[18] Nonetheless, given that neither Zeilig

parties of the Popular Front, thus preparing the overthrow of bourgeois democracy at the next stage"—Trotsky, 1973, p257.

13: Van der Walt, 2011a, p198.

14: Price, 2007, p172.

15: Price, 2007, p10.

16: Contra van der Walt, Price also recognises that whereas Marx was clear that the dictatorship of the proletariat was the concrete modern form of democracy, "the historical relation between anarchism and democracy is highly ambiguous—Price, 2007, pp49; 165.

17: Van der Walt, 2011b.

18: Price 2007, p50.

nor I wrote anything particularly controversial or new about the concept of the dictatorship of the proletariat, van der Walt's comments suggest that once we escape caricatured readings of Marx there is a real potential for dialogue between anarchism and Marxism. Concretely, it opens the door to a discussion of the means through which we should fight for democracy.

On this issue, van der Walt and Schmidt argue that syndicalism emerged as the revolutionary opposition to the reformism of the Marxist movement at the turn of the last century. There is an element of truth to this argument. However, in his eagerness to conflate Marxism with social democratic reformism van der Walt ignores the way that the practice of these socialist parties was informed by an important break with Marx's theory of the state. By disregarding Marx's critique of the Gotha Programme and Engels's similar critique of the Erfurt Programme—in which they insisted it was a grave mistake for the German party to claim that the transition to socialism could be won without smashing the old state through a revolution—the leading socialist intellectual of that period, Karl Kautsky, defended a practice whereby socialist parties aimed to represent all the disparate elements of the working class in one organisation. The problem with this type of organisation was that unity among disparate tendencies could only be maintained by overlooking divergent political practices within the working class, and in particular the increasingly conservative practice of the bureaucratic leadership of the trade unions and parliamentary party. In practice it meant reining in the left of the party so as not to alienate the right.[19]

Syndicalism developed as a radical working class response to the conservative consequences of this kind of politics. In an attempt to correct what anarcho-syndicalists such as Alexander Berkman regarded as the entirely rotten "game of politics",[20] syndicalists insisted that socialists should orientate on the "the primacy of industrial struggle and militant trade unionism".[21] This approach, or so Berkman argued, overcame a contradiction within Marxism between Marx's claims, on the one hand, that revolution is necessary to create a new society and, on the other hand, that "the proletariat must get hold of the political machinery, of the government, in order to conquer the bourgeoisie".[22] According to van der Walt and Schmidt, this change of focus meant that whereas "classical Marxism tended to pose a strict dichotomy between a "political field" (centred on the state, and engaged by

---

19: Harman, 2004, p31; Schorske, 1983, p115.
20: Berkman, 1989, p60.
21: Darlington, 2008, p233.
22: Berkman, 1989, p77.

the revolutionary party through political action) and an "economic field" (dealing with wages and working conditions, and relegated to the unions, but led by the party) the syndicalists saw the revolutionary union as *simultaneously* undertaking both political and economic functions".[23]

This argument is both problematic and suggestive. We have already noted that among anarchists Price recognises that the interpretation of Marxism repeated by Berkman is simply wrong: neither Marx nor Lenin believed that socialism could issue from the capture of the bourgeois state machine.[24] More specifically, van der Walt's argument is problematic because Marxists have been the most important theorists to recognise that the separation of economics and politics was a problem for the workers' movement. Van der Walt's claim to the contrary relies upon a reduction of Marxism to social democratic reformism. This has the important consequence of obscuring the fact that a powerful Marxist response to Second International reformism grew alongside the syndicalist challenge. More pertinently, these Marxists complemented their critique of reformism with a critique of syndicalism. And though they welcomed syndicalism as a revolutionary current within the working class, they argued that it was unable to point beyond the limits of reformist socialism.

This is where van der Walt's comment on overcoming the separation between economics and politics is suggestive. For if anarchists and Marxists can agree that we are struggling for a real democratic alternative to capitalism, that is for a form of democracy that isn't confined merely to the "political" level but which gives us social control over economic decisions, this can act as a focus for a real dialogue about how this can be achieved. If we can also agree that socialism cannot be won by seizing the state (either through insurrection or parliamentary vote), then we should move forward to discuss the kinds of political practice that complement the idea of socialism from below.

If Marxists and syndicalists agree that trade unionism will play a fundamental part in the struggle for socialism, we also need to take on board Rosa Luxemburg's critique of the limitations of trade unionism. At a time when trade union bureaucrats were exercising increasing power in the German socialist movement, Luxemburg caused great consternation by pointing out that trade unionism is enmeshed in capitalist social relations.[25] This is because, at a day to day level, trade unionists tend to focus on negotiations to improve

---

23: Van der Walt and Schmidt, 2009, p141.
24: For a recent academic anarchist defence of the similarities between Marx and the anarchists on the question of the state see Karatini, 2005, pp165-184.
25: Luxemburg, 1970a, p72.

the conditions of sale of labour power. This practice informs the emergence of a layer of professional negotiators, and because this bureaucratic layer exists to negotiate terms and conditions of work *within* capitalism it tends to become a conservative barrier against struggles which point beyond the parameters of these negotiations.[26] This is relevant to the issue of syndicalism because, though syndicalist leaders tend to be more militant than the average trade union leader, they essentially play the same role and thus experience similar pressures towards conservatism. Indeed, the actions of the leaders of the CNT in 1936 reflected this situation.[27]

Van der Walt and Schmidt are aware of this tendency to conservatism, but rather than provide a historically specific sociological explanation of it in terms of capitalist relations of production they tend to turn it into a law of nature, appealing to Robert Michels's famous "Iron Law of Oligarchy"—with the caveat that Michels's law is counteracted by an opposite "tendency toward democracy".[28] Whereas Marxists explain the conservatism of the trade union bureaucracy in terms that are specific to capitalist social relations, Michels explains this tendency in a way that effectively makes capitalist social relations universal. Indeed, he argues that it is a "natural love of power" which gives rise to "immanent oligarchical tendencies in every kind of human organisation".[29] The key implication of Michels's thesis is the impossibility of democracy, and to the extent that van der Walt and Schmidt, alongside many other anarchists, accept his claims they weaken their own arguments for the possibility of a real democracy. This is the basis for the point I made in my original article about anarchism's tendency to flounder when confronted with the problem of democracy.

So while the attempt to rethink anarchism as a democratic theory by van der Walt, Price and others is to be welcomed, to realise this project requires breaking with the liberal assumptions about the universality of individual egoism that are embedded within Michels's critique of democracy. Specifically it means breaking with his transhistorical account of the tendency to oligarchy and replacing it with a social and historical account that is able to grasp the concrete roots of oligarchy in particular reformist institutions that develop within capitalism.[30]

This would allow them to come to terms with the real strengths and limitations of syndicalism. In his classic 1938 defence of anarcho-syndicalism,

---

26: Cliff and Gluckstein, 1986.
27: Darlington, 2008, p224; Hallas, 1985, p82.
28: Van der Walt and Schmidt, 2009, p189.
29: Michels, 1962, pp326; 50.
30: Barker, 2001.

Rudolf Rocker argued that syndicalism grew as a "reaction against the concepts and methods of political socialism". This did not mean that he rejected politics altogether, but rather that he insisted the focal point of struggle should be "in the economic fighting organisations of the workers". A similar point can be found in Earl Ford's and William Foster's *Syndicalism* (1912). This book combines a powerful critique of social democratic reformism with a defence of direct working class industrial militancy. Ford and Foster point out that because the latter represented "real power" it was the real source of reforms whereas the former was merely an "expression of public sentiment".[31]

In a gesture of solidarity with this general perspective, Trotsky insisted that Bolshevism had more in common with syndicalism than it did with social democracy. However, he argued that the Bolsheviks differed from the syndicalists insofar as they took seriously the problem of how the militant minority within the working class was to win the rest of the working class over to the kind of direct strike action advocated by syndicalists.[32] That this is a real problem for syndicalism is evident in Rocker's tacit assumption that workers became united in a more or less automatic process: "the whole development of modern capitalism...can but serve to spread this enlightenment more widely among the workers".[33] There is a similar problem with Berkman's discussion of working class reformism. He sees this merely in terms of the existence of false ideas within the working class.[34] The corollary of this argument is a propagandistic (of the deed) approach to winning workers to socialism.

But if working class reformism is rooted in the struggle to improve the conditions of sale of labour power (wages and conditions) which underpins the emergence of a reformist and oligarchic labour bureaucracy, then syndicalism severely underestimates the social basis of reformism. It was because of this that, although the Bolsheviks agreed with syndicalist criticisms of reformist political parties, they nevertheless insisted that new forms of political organisation were necessary to win the majority of workers away from the influence of reformism. This project builds upon fundamental insights from syndicalism. For instance, British syndicalists a century ago laid the basis for all subsequent revolutionary work in the unions: "We will support the officials just so long as they rightly represent the workers, but we will act independently immediately they misrepresent them".[35] But it also involves a break with syndicalism.

31: Ford and Foster, 1990, p20.
32: Hallas, 1985, pp35-37.
33: Rocker, 1989, pp85, 116, 124.
34: Berkman, 1989, p63.
35: From the Clyde Workers' Committee 1915, quoted in Cliff and Gluckstein, 1986, p34;
See also Darlington, 2008, p221.

Ralph Darlington explains that the Bolsheviks pointed to a contradiction at the heart of syndicalism between "trying to build *both* revolutionary cadre organisations and mass trade unions".[36] In contrast both to syndicalism and to reformist (statist) socialism, the Bolsheviks pointed to a new form of organisation that transcended the opposition between direct action and politics. Like the syndicalists, the Bolsheviks aimed to organise the real fighting minority within the working class. This meant that, unlike the reformists, when the Bolsheviks oriented on taking political power they did not mean to seize the state but rather to smash it and replace it with real organs of workers' democracy. In this way Bolshevism went beyond not only the limits of political reformism but also the limits of direct action within capitalism, and hence of syndicalism. As Darlington argues, though "syndicalism clearly represented a significant step forward from parliamentary reformism...the exclusive emphasis on the industrial struggle meant that in practice it represented the mirror image of reformism, with its separation of economics and politics".[37]

It was because Bolshevism pointed beyond these limits that many syndicalists, including the main author of *Syndicalism*, William Z Foster, came over to Bolshevism after 1917. Van der Walt and Schmidt recognise this fact, but don't think through the fundamental questions it poses for their defence of syndicalism.[38] For all its strengths, syndicalism's rejection of parliamentary politics did not succeed in informing a practice that overcame the separation between economics and politics, and therefore did not provide an adequate revolutionary alternative to reformism. To the extent that syndicalist struggles don't orient towards a challenge for political power, they, like all forms of direct action, remain trapped at the level of civil society, and therefore effectively remain as a subset of reformism.

Beyond the myths about Leninism

It was one of Lenin's great contributions to revolutionary theory to point towards the practical measures necessary to move beyond a situation where the left was leading a myriad of local fragmented struggles that did not challenge for power. His fundamental strategic contribution to socialist theory involved an attempt to think through the practical political problems associated with realising the socialist goals immanent to the real movements from below for freedom. Thus in *What is to be Done?* he argued that if Russian socialists, who had succeeded in winning real local leadership within the

---

36: Darlington, 2008, p167.
37: Darlington, 2008, p245.
38: Van der Walt and Schmidt, 2009, p13; Darlington, 2008.

workers' movement, were to realise the full potential of this movement they needed to create a unified network of activists through which to combine these various struggles into a challenge for power.

A decade and a half later, on the basis of a return to Marx's writings on the Paris Commune, Lenin made a root and branch critique of the way that reformist (statist) socialism reproduced the capitalist separation between economics and politics. Concretely, he argued that this situation could only be transcended by the emergence of new forms of democracy that were simultaneously economic and political. He insisted that the Russian soviets or workers' councils in 1905 and again in 1917 represented the real spontaneous basis for such a democratic order. By actualising a real democratic alternative to capitalism these structures prefigure socialism. It is because similar organisations have emerged at high points in the class struggle over the 20th century that Marxists insist they continue to act as the concrete utopia against which we can judge capitalism.[39]

Nevertheless, because the working class is fragmented and workers' struggles tend to be sectional, the idea that workers' councils represent a more democratic form of social organisation must be won inside the workers' movement against those who deny it. This implies the need for some form of political organisation whose aim it is to win the majority over to socialism. Such an organisation cannot prefigure socialism because by its victory it begins to create the conditions for its own dissolution. Of course, we could dogmatically assert that any such organisation would not dissolve but would attempt to fix its own power. However, as I noted in my original essay, arguments such as this imply a pessimistic because ahistorical model of human nature that undermines *any* model of socialism.

The key problem with the vehement tone of van der Walt's criticisms of Lenin is that it acts as a barrier to a serious discussion of these strategic issues. Specifically, van der Walt follows well trodden anarchist ground in damning Lenin by reference to the nature of the regime in Russia after the October Revolution. Against Zeilig and me, he argues that if we admit that Lenin played a pivotal role in 1917 we should also accept that he played a similarly key role in the revolution's degeneration after 1917.[40]

At one level this argument is obviously true: of course Lenin and Trotsky made a difference both before and after the revolution. The difficulty is to grasp how much of a difference they made and the possible alternatives open to them. To give one example, the key Bolshevik slogan in 1917

39: Gluckstein, 1985; Barker, 1987.
40: Van der Walt, 2011a, p203.

was "Bread, peace and land: all power to the soviets". This encapsulated their argument that the only way to feed the cities (bread) involved ending the War (peace) and redistributing the land to the peasants (land), and this could only be done if the workers' councils (soviets) took power from the bourgeois government. The huge assumption in this argument was the success of a revolution in Germany, for otherwise the German army would keep fighting. In negotiations with the German imperialists from December 1917 to March 1918 the Bolsheviks had to choose between peace on the one hand and bread and land on the other. In the end they compromised by handing over massive grain producing regions for the sake of peace. Many anarchists, and some Bolsheviks, argued that they should have continued to fight. Clearly this decision made a difference, but what kind of difference? Any adequate answer to this must consider the choices open to the Bolsheviks in this period.

Economic crisis led to an unprecedented narrowing of the parameters of what was possible. The problems facing the Bolsheviks were of almost unheard of severity. Russia was a relatively backward country at the outbreak of the First World War, and war and then civil war made matters much worse. So by 1920 the value of industrial production had declined to about 13 percent of the already very low level it had been in 1913, while over the period from 1913 to 1921-2 the number of waged workers had dropped from 11 million to 6.5 million with the number of industrial workers more than halved.[41] This incredibly harsh context meant that sheer physical survival was the primary goal both for ordinary Russians and for the new revolutionary regime. So while it is obviously true that what the Bolsheviks did mattered, more than anything else this terrible context that shaped the new Russian state.[42] As Peter Sedgwick wrote, "the 'objective' social circumstances of Russia's revolution and civil war contain sufficient conditions for the collapse of the mass revolutionary wave, without recourse to causal factors stemming from the 'subjective' deficiencies of Lenin's early formulations".[43] In this situation Lenin's tragedy was that his nominal position of power coincided with a keen awareness that there was no internal *socialist* solution to the grave problems facing the regime. The problem with van der Walt's comments on these issues is that he gives no sense of the narrowing boundaries of the possible. This changing context meant that whereas Lenin's choices had been decisive in 1917, in the civil war and afterwards the opposite was true: he floundered before unbeatable odds.[44]

41: Nove, 1992, pp89-110.
42: Lewin, 1968, p17; see also Harman, 2008, p427; Mayer, 2000, p49.
43: Sedgwick, 1992, p13.
44: Harris, 1968, p152.

Indeed, in the post-revolutionary context Lenin responded to the increasingly grave internal and external threats to the revolution in a more or less *ad hoc* manner. As E H Carr wrote, "Almost every step taken by [the Bolsheviks in the civil war] was either a reaction to some pressing emergency or a reprisal for some action or threatened action against them".[45] One example of van der Walt's misleading methodology is his comments that in the five years after 1917 there were 20 times more executions than there had been in the previous 50 years under the Tsarist *Okhrana*. Van der Walt doesn't compare like with like: civil wars are endemically violent, and as there hadn't been a civil war over the previous 50 years comparing these periods is close to nonsensical. The Bolsheviks were involved in a civil war in which they were compelled to respond to a "bloody attempt by the old order to restore its reign".[46] While individual decisions should always be open to criticism, to condemn them for their general use of violence in this context is not merely absurd, but also effectively amounts to an attack on the revolution itself. We might equally dismiss Abraham Lincoln's Emancipation Proclamation because it went hand in hand with the deaths of 625,000 Americans in their civil war (about the same number of Americans as were killed in the First and Second World Wars and the Korean and Vietnam wars combined!), or reject the gains of the English Revolution when we discover that, as a percentage of the English population, three times more people died in the civil wars of the 1640s than did in the First World War. More to the point, we could deploy a similar methodology to reject anarchism because of the role of anarchists in the executions of tens of thousands in Spain's Republican Zone in the first few weeks of their civil war?[47]

Similar criticisms could be made of van der Walt's claim, noted above, that "the Lenin-Trotsky regime" was a "template for Stalin's". The problem with this comparison is that once again the discussion of violence is abstracted from its social context. This is of fundamental importance. The earlier use of violence was in response to genuine military threats to the revolutionary regime from counter-revolutionary armies—"the terror of 1917 to 1922 was, in the main, a fact of civil war fuelled by the dialectic of revolution and counterrevolution".[48] But violence in the later period was deployed to crush the last vestiges of the revolutionary ideology that could trace its roots back to 1917: the Stalinist regime "needed that bloodletting in order to install firmly

---

45: Carr, 1950, pp161, 168 and chapter 7 more generally; Mayer, 2000, p258.
46: Haynes and Husan, 2003, p49.
47: Durgan, 2007, p80.
48: Mayer, 2000, pp312, 253, 13, 239, 309-313.

the new class created by the 'new' method of production".[49] By abstracting these two periods of violence out of their social context, van der Walt effectively makes history meaningless except as a series of forms of domination.

Indeed, in his eagerness to attack Lenin, van der Walt goes so far as to regurgitate the old right wing smear, first spread as early as October 1917, about the use of rape by the Bolsheviks. Though van der Walt doesn't repeat the original stablemate of this slander—the claim that Bolsheviks had passed a decree nationalising women!—this is perhaps because not even the most right wing ideologues can get away with this absurd accusation any more. As it is, van der Walt's comments on rape are paraphrased from the writings of the controversial right wing historian Vladimir Brovkin. While this provenance of the rape claim would normally trouble a socialist (would we trust a Reaganite to give a honest account of an anarchist demonstration?), van der Walt actually accentuates the anti-Bolshevik tone of Brovkin's argument by replacing the word "often" with "routinely" to describe Bolshevik use of rape. Thus, whereas Brovkin wrote that "beatings, torture, intimidation and rape were often used", van der Walt changes this sentence to "beatings, torture and rape were routinely used". This is doubly misleading because Brovkin doesn't actually cite any specific cases of rape to substantiate this claim.[50]

Elsewhere in his book where he does cite actual rape cases his evidence comes from the archives of Bolsheviks who were prosecuting the rapists—ie, it was evidence that, far from deploying rape as a means of terror, the regime was trying to stamp it out! Moreover, his key argument is not that the Bolsheviks were rapists, but rather that rape became widespread after the revolution because the Bolsheviks challenged the sanctity of religion and the family. He thus blames what we might call the feminist aspect of Bolshevik policy for increasing violence against women: "The problem the Bolsheviks did not want to face was that the debunking of religion and attacks on courtship, the family, and the private sphere necessarily encouraged a 'utilitarian' attitude to women".[51] This kind of reactionary nonsense is a commonplace amongst conservative critics of the liberation movements of the 1960s and we on the left should be debunking it rather than pretending those who regurgitate it are reliable critics of revolutionary movements. The fact that van der Walt not only cites Brovkin as an authority on the revolution but also reinforces the anti-Bolshevik bias of the language of this Cold War warrior suggests that he

---

49: Dunayevskaya, 1988, p227.
50: The sum total of evidence cited for the claim that the Bolsheviks used rape is this: "numerous instances are cited in 'TsKa: Ko vsem chlenam partii, ko vsem mestnym organizatsiyam', Iz Partii No 4 (May 1923)"—Brovkin 1998, pp24, 227.
51: Brovkin, 1998, p119.

is less interested in obtaining a rounded picture of the Bolsheviks' practice than he is in repeating any accusations that might be used to damn them, however outlandish they might be, and irrespective of their origin.

A more balanced summary of the practice of the Bolsheviks in the civil war was suggested by William H Chamberlain in his pioneering social history of the Russian Revolution. Commenting on comments from an officer who had deserted the Red Army to join the Whites only to find their behaviour appalling, Chamberlain writes that "not all communists, certainly, were saints or puritans. But their general behaviour and morale seem to have been better than those of their opponents".[52] To recognise this does not imply, as van der Walt suggests, that Marxists believe everything Lenin and the Bolsheviks did in this period was right; clearly that would be absurd. Rather it is to recognise that, despite occasionally making a virtue of necessity, the Bolsheviks acted to defend the revolution in a situation in which the only solution lay beyond their control in the success or failure of socialist revolutions outside Russia. So while it is legitimate to criticise them for the decisions they made in this period, the reality is that famine, disease and decimation of the working class meant that a "third revolution" replacing them with a system to their left was simply not a realistic political perspective at the time.[53]

The choice in 1917 was between the Bolsheviks on the one hand and the proto-fascists in the White armies on the other (before October the provisional government merely maintained a precarious balance between these two social forces), and this remained the choice in the early 1920s.[54] This situation is reflected in the fact that, for all the (abstract) moral power of their criticisms of the Bolsheviks, the anarchists remained largely isolated in Russia. Indeed, as Paul Avrich points out in the conclusion to his very friendly history of Russian anarchism, it was in part because the anarchists "paid scant attention to the practical needs of a rapidly changing world" that anarchism remained a "visionary utopia" of a "small group of individuals who had alienated themselves from the mainstream of contemporary society".[55]

So though it is true that Bolshevik rule in the immediate post-revolutionary context did come to resemble aspects of the Jacobin regime at the height of the French Revolution in 1793-4, it is doubly important not to conflate this process with Stalinism. First, Stalin's rise to power went hand in hand with the purging of the Bolshevik Party—by 1939 only

---

52: Chamberlain, 1952, p461.
53: Haynes and Husan, 2003, pp49-61.
54: Haynes, 1997; Mayer, 2000, p244.
55: Avrich, 1967, p253.

1.3 percent of party members could date their membership back to 1917, 93 percent of those who had been members in 1917 were no longer members, and 70 percent of party members had joined since 1929.[56] Second, and perhaps more importantly, to reduce Bolshevism to a variant of Jacobinism obscures the way that in the run up to the October Revolution Lenin had built a party that was able to win a majority of Russian workers to socialism.

Conclusion

Unfortunately, rather than debate the substantive issues raised by my original article, van der Walt has chosen to erect and reject a straw man version of Lenin (and Marx). While in this response I have had to deal with these distortions, I want in conclusion to return to the main strategic debates between anarchists and Marxists. I suspect that van der Walt would agree that though the world is a very different place today than it was when the left engaged in many of the debates touched upon in this essay, in its essence capitalism is still built upon the systematic exploitation of wage labour. In turn, this means that Rosa Luxemburg's claim that socialist organisation must be rooted first and foremost in the working class retains all its validity: "Where the chains of capitalism are forged, there they must be broken".[57]

Such a project demands political organisation, and the nature of political organisation presupposes some model of its function: we can only decide what kind of parties we want by working out what we want them for. If reformist parties are organised around electoral districts and parliamentary calendars with a view to winning elections, insurrectionary parties merely organise a more militant approach to the same goal of seizing the state. Because direct action by contrast aims to prefigure a libertarian model of socialism, anarchist "parties" will be organised along very different lines. While seeming opposites, in practice these two approaches—statism and direct action—actually reflect two sides of the same coin of the modern capitalist separation of politics and economics: both approaches fetishise an emasculated politics.

Van der Walt's argument that Marxist parties are statist parties assumes that we too are trapped within these parameters. In my original article I showed via a contrast between Marxism and Jacobinism/Blanquism that we are not. Our aim is not to seize the state but rather to win the majority of workers to socialism and to smash the old state and replace it with our organs of democratic authority. This process will involve the use of a variety of

---

56: Harris, 1978, p272; Harman 2008, p477.
57: Luxemburg, 1970b, p419.

tactics, some electoral and some direct action. Strategy, from this perspective, is best understood as a project aimed at the conquest of power that is rooted in lessons learnt from previous and ongoing struggles as generalised in theory and as creatively applied and developed in a practice.[58]

For all of its undoubted strengths, syndicalism could neither escape the pressures towards bureaucratisation nor provide an adequate account of the relationship between the revolutionary minority within any union and the union more generally. The strength of Bolshevism, by contrast, was that it provided a clear distinction between party and class that allowed it to conceptualise the process by which the socialist minority were able to win over a majority of the working class to the soviet idea during the Russian Revolution. This experience obviously includes lessons from which socialists would do well to learn. Similarly, the experience of the Comintern in its revolutionary period—the first four congresses—provides an indispensible resource for contemporary activists.

The key problem with the caricatured interpretation of Lenin's (and Marx's) politics reproduced in van der Walt's essay is that it acts as a barrier to our assimilation of lessons from these movements. Conversely, it is a key strength of his essay that he attempts to conceptualise anarchism as a strategy for the realisation of real democracy through revolution. While I stand by my claim that the elements of liberalism embedded within anarchist theory act as a barrier to a full embrace of democracy, I can only welcome van der Walt's attempt to point beyond this impasse.

In response to this project we should respond, good, let's fight together for real democracy, discuss our differences as comrades in struggle, and try to formulate a strategy adequate for the socialist transformation of society.

References

Avrich, Paul, 1967, *The Russian Anarchists* (Princeton University Press).

Barker, Colin, (ed), 1987, *Revolutionary Rehearsals* (Bookmarks).

Barker, Colin, 2001, "Robert Michels and the 'Cruel Game'", in Colin Barker, Alan Johnson and Michael Lavalette (eds), *Leadership and Social Movements* (Manchester University Press).

Berkman, Alexander, 1989, *What is Communist Anarchism?* (Phoenix Press).

Bernstein, Eduard, 1993 [1899], *The Preconditions of Socialism* (Cambridge).

Broué, Pierre, and Emile Témime, 2008, *The Revolution and Civil War in Spain* (Haymarket).

Brovkin, Vladimir, 1998, *Russia After Lenin* (Routledge).

58: Cliff, 1975, pp253-254.

Carr, Edward Hallet, 1950, *The Bolshevik Revolution, volume I* (Penguin).

Chamberlain, William Henry, 1952, *The Russian Revolution, volume II* (Macmillan).

Cliff, Tony, 1975, *Lenin: Building the Party* (Pluto).

Cliff, Tony and Donny Gluckstein, 1986, *Marxism and Trade Union Struggle* (Bookmarks).

Critchley, Simon, 2007, *Infinitely Demanding* (Verso).

Darlington, Ralph, 2008, *Syndicalism and the Transition to Communism* (Ashgate).

Durgan, Andy, 2007, *The Spanish Civil War* (Palgrave).

Ford, Earl, and William Foster, 1990, *Syndicalism* (Kerr).

Franks, Benjamin, 2006, *Rebel Alliances* (AK Press).

Gluckstein, Donny, 1985, *The Western Soviets* (Bookmarks).

Hallas, Duncan, 1985, *The Comintern* (Bookmarks), www.marxists.org/archive/hallas/works/1985/comintern/index.htm

Harman, Chris, 2004, "Spontaneity, Strategy and Politics", *International Socialism 104 (autumn)*, www.isj.org.uk/?id=12

Harman, Chris, 2008, *A People's History of the World* (Verso).

Harris, Nigel, 1968, *Beliefs in Society* (Penguin).

Harris, Nigel, 1978, *The Mandate of Heaven* (Quartet).

Haynes, Mike, 1997, "Was there a Parliamentary Alternative in Russia in 1917?", *International Socialism 76* (autumn), www.marxists.de/russrev/haynes/

Haynes, Mike, and Rumy Husan, 2003, *A Century of State Murder* (Pluto).

Karatani, Kojin, 2005, *Transcritique* (MIT).

Lewin, Moshe, 1968, *Lenin's Last Struggle* (Monthly Review).

Luxemburg, Rosa, 1970a, "Reform or Revolution", in Mary-Alice Waters (ed), *Rosa Luxemburg Speaks* (Pathfinder), www.marxists.org/archive/luxemburg/1900/reform-revolution/index.htm

Luxemburg, Rosa, 1970b, "Speech to the Founding Convention of the German Communist Party", in Mary-Alice Waters (ed), *Rosa Luxemburg Speaks* (Pathfinder).

Marx, Karl, 1976, *Capital* (Penguin), www.marxists.org/archive/marx/works/1867-c1/

May, Todd, 1994, *The Political Philosophy of Poststructuralist Anarchism* (Penn State Press).

Mayer, Arno, 2000, *The Furies: Violence and Terror in the French and Russian Revolutions* (Princeton).

Michels, Robert, 1962, *Political Parties* (Collier Books).

Newman, Saul, 2001, *From Bakunin to Lacan* (Lexington).

Nove, Alec, 1992, *An Economic History of the USSR: 1917-1991* (Penguin).

Price, Wayne, 2007, *The Abolition of the State* (AuthorHouse)

Rocker, Rudolf, 1989, *Anarcho-Syndicalism* (Pluto Press).

Schorske, Carl, 1983, *German Social Democracy 1905-1917* (Harvard University Press)

Sedgwick, Peter, 1992, Introduction to Victor Serge, *Year One of the Russian Revolution* (Pluto Press).

Trotsky, Leon 1973, "Is Victory Possible in Spain?", *The Spanish Revolution* (Pathfinder).

Van der Walt, Lucien 2011a, "Debating Black Flame, Revolutionary Anarchism and Historical Marxism" *International Socialism 130* (spring), www.isj.org.uk/?id=729

Van der Walt, Lucien 2011b, *Anarchism, Black Flame, Marxism and the IST: debating power, revolution and Bolshevism*, at http://lucienvanderwalt.blogspot.com/2011/02/anarchism-black-flame-marxism-and-ist.html

Van der Walt, Lucien, and Michael Schmidt, 2009, *Black Flame* (AK Press).

Zeilig, Leo 2010, "Contesting the Revolutionary Tradition", *International Socialism 127* (summer), www.isj.org.uk/?id=674

Talkin' 'bout a revolutionary

Joseph Choonara spoke to Ian Birchall, author of Tony Cliff: A Marxist for his Time (Bookmarks, 2011), which looks at the life of the founder of the International Socialist tradition

You have made your biography of Tony Cliff as objective as possible, standing back from episodes that you were personally involved in and setting out both sides of arguments. So I wanted to start with a subjective question: how did you first encounter Tony Cliff?[1]
I first heard Cliff in February or March of 1963. I had joined the Socialist Review Group a couple of months earlier but I was actually far from being convinced about state capitalism.[2] I heard Cliff speak on the subject and I don't think I have had any reservations since then. I was enormously impressed by him as a speaker.

Cliff discovered that I knew various foreign languages, so I was given the job of reading foreign magazines, translating and so on. It was clear that as soon as he got his teeth into my neck he was going to start sucking blood. At that time he was absolutely remorseless in getting hold of people and pulling them in. When I joined the wretched organisation I thought it was a discussion group. Over the next six months or so I discovered it was something very different!

1: A longer version of this interview can be found on our website: www.isj.org.uk
2: Cliff's theory that the Soviet Union was "state capitalist" rather than a "degenerate workers state" or a socialist society, and the detailed picture of the society that he derived, was one of his major contributions to Marxist theory. See Cliff, 2003. The Socialist Review Group was the forerunner of the International Socialists, which later became the Socialist Workers Party.

What kinds of people were drawn towards his group?
I met people like Colin Barker, Sandra Peers, Richard Kirkwood, Peter Binns and Richard Hyman. It was an organisation where you could feel at home, which took itself seriously but didn't take itself too seriously as an organisation of 100 people. We didn't think we were going to be the vanguard of the revolution in two or three years.

One thing which I kept being reminded of when doing interviews with people from the 1960s is that Mike Kidron was at that time almost as important as Cliff. Kidron had come to Britain in 1953 and was pulled in almost immediately. If you read *Socialist Review* from that period Kidron wrote about half of some issues under three pseudonyms. That lasted till about 1964-5, when Kidron started to distance himself a bit. But during the period from 1953 to 1965 Kidron was essential. To me he seemed phenomenally clever—that man really seemed to understand how the world worked. Cliff came across as much more rooted in the tradition and would talk about the Russian Revolution a lot; Kidron would talk about modern developments in capitalism. I think Kidron also had an enormous influence on Cliff. The period when he was working closely with Kidron was one of the most creative in his life.

Before he came to Britain in 1946 Cliff was active in a Trotskyist group in Palestine. The chapters that look at that period are among the most fascinating in your book. How much of that was a revelation to you?
Oh quite a lot. Cliff would make occasional references to his time in Palestine and we knew he'd been in jail there but he didn't talk about it a lot. I managed to track down ten people who had known him in Palestine, all of whom of course were pretty old and three of whom have died since I interviewed them.

I think I've got a reasonable picture of the sort of activity he was involved in even though some things were hard to pin down. For example, in the articles he wrote in 1938 for the *New International* he's still in favour of unrestricted Jewish immigration into Palestine; by 1945 he's completely reversed that position. What nobody seems to remember is when exactly that reversal came and how it happened.

The group in Palestine was very small, with at most about 30 members. It was semi-clandestine and everybody had pseudonyms. I believe Cliff was the only native born Palestinian—Jewish Palestinian—in the group. Everybody else was an exile from Europe. There were a few Arab members. The only one I know anything about was Jabra Nicola, a remarkable individual who I think later ended up on the executive of the

Fourth International and died in 1974. The group did apparently publish in Arabic as well as Hebrew, although Cliff didn't know much Arabic.

How important were those early experiences of building a small Trotskyist group?
I think they were crucial. The thing that struck me was just how isolated he was. In the 1930s if you wanted to know what the Trotskyist movement said about Britain or Spain or Germany there were these bloody great volumes of writings by Leon Trotsky. On the Middle East there are occasional interviews where Trotsky is asked about it and he says, "Sorry I don't know much about the Middle East."

So Cliff had to work it all out for himself. And likewise if you look at his early stuff, in particular his book on the Middle East,[3] it is basically Cliff trying to apply the theory of permanent revolution to the Middle East.

Cliff was essentially driven out of the British section of the Fourth International by Gerry Healy. Obviously Cliff had developed a different analysis of Soviet Russia and a particular account of world capitalism. But to what extent was it inevitable that Cliff would have to form his own political organisation?
It's hard to establish that because there are very few people who I've been able to talk to who were involved at that time. Cliff doesn't seem to have made any real effort to form a faction within the RCP, which had dissolved in 1949, or what replaced it, which was called "The Club". There were all sorts of problems with senior people such as Jock Haston becoming disillusioned and dropping out. Healy was becoming increasingly influential and running the thing in an extraordinarily bullying manner. So there were dissident groups, notably in Birmingham where a group of half a dozen people or so were becoming dissident—although not necessarily over the question of state capitalism.

If you look at the Fourth International and the way various groupings broke away from it in the period, I think probably it was inevitable that Cliff would have to split. But in a sense the way Healy handled things probably made Cliff more successful than he would otherwise have been, because many people were disgusted by the way Healy was behaving.

How important was the theory of state capitalism in holding the group together? And how much was down to Cliff's organisational ability, his bloody mindedness and so on?
State capitalism was important. However, I think if you look at the earliest

---

3: This fascinating and hitherto unknown document is now available in the Cliff section of the Marxists Internet Archive—www.marxists.org/archive/cliff/works/1946/probme/index.html

period, the group basically saw itself as orthodox Trotskyist but with a state capitalist position. It's only in the mid-1950s that Cliff and Kidron start broadening out the perspective. It's after the uprising in Hungary in 1956 that Cliff starts writing about subjects other than state capitalism. There are one or two articles, including an appalling article on Puerto Rico which you wouldn't class among Cliff's great achievements, but generally he was very much focused on developing the theory of state capitalism with his books on Eastern Europe and then on China.

The China book is where I think he first develops his theory of deflected permanent revolution.[4] And I think around that time he also produced articles on the arms economy and on the labour aristocracy.

When you talk about holding the group together, actually relatively few of the initial group survived—you're talking about Cliff and Chanie Rosenberg, Ray Challinor, Geoff Carlsson and one or two others. A number of the people who had been involved in the foundation, including of course Duncan Hallas who was very important in the first few years and then moved away for many years, a lot of those people didn't last through the 1950s.

There was also a heated internal argument about the question of the Labour Party, because some of the people in the Socialist Review Group saw it as a kind of Labour Party ginger group. There is a polemic, ostensibly signed by London branch secretaries but clearly written by Cliff, in which he was very hard on this. He said, "We are in the Labour Party because it's a good place to met people, not because we want to reform it. We are in there because we want to build a revolutionary party."

I was struck by the fact that many people in the group rose quite high in the Labour Party.
Remember Labour was much bigger and more active than it is now. It was also more open. Stan Newens, who left the group in 1959, became a Labour MP in 1964. Sid Bidwell became a Labour MP in 1966 and was expelled almost immediately, not for being an MP but for the way he waged his campaign in Southhall. John Palmer ran as a Labour candidate in 1964 and then in 1966 was removed by the Labour executive for being politically unacceptable. The constituency party were instructed to reselect and they reselected Palmer, so he had a real base there. So yes, up to 1968 people were heavily implanted in the Labour Party. I think Cliff was always a bit suspicious about this but he didn't push the point. I remember him saying

---

4:    Gluckstein, 1957. On deflected permanent revolution, see Cliff, 1981.

to me that he didn't really approve of people becoming Labour councillors but nobody ever disciplined anybody. Ray Challinor was a Labour councillor for a number of years and afterwards was very critical of what it is possible to achieve as a councillor.

You've written in this journal about Cliff's role in 1968.[5] What seems to emerge out of that year is something a great deal more like the Socialist Workers Party (SWP) today.
Yes, although it happened gradually. But generally 1968 was when we became an open membership organisation rather than existing in a slightly clandestine form in Labour. There had been some witch-hunts against us in the Labour Party although not very serious. I tried very hard in 1967 to get myself expelled from Labour and failed. I've got the correspondence somewhere. I was saying "come on expel me" and they didn't have the nerve. The Labour Party was very different in those days.

Cliff goes back to Lenin in 1968. On top of everything else he was doing, I remember visiting him at his home in Stoke Newington and he had the complete works of Lenin piled up on the floor. This was the beginning of his work on his Lenin book.[6] The question of the Leninist party is a bit problematic because, maybe not everyone understands it this way, but one of the fundamental lessons I've always taken from Cliff's Lenin is that there is no such thing as "the Leninist party". Lenin had six or seven different concepts of the party according to the situation he was in. But yes, in terms of democratic centralism, that was carried through in 1968.

Frederick Engels writes somewhere that, while Karl Marx might not have had the sharpest vision at every point, in moments of revolutionary struggle Marx was always the one with the finest instincts. You get the impression that Cliff was likewise someone who thrived on workers' struggle. Is that fair?
Oh yes. I think he says in his autobiography that he was never happier than between 1968-74. You go back to state capitalism and, while it is very important, it's a negative. It's saying what socialism isn't. I'm not saying that wasn't an enormously important point to make, but then when you get the Saltley pickets and the Pentonville five and so on, this is what the emancipation of the working class looks like, and I think for Cliff that was always what was more important.[7]

5:   Birchall, 2008.
6:   Cliff, 2010.
7:   Saltley was the crucial battle in the 1972 miners' strike when trade unionists shut down the largest coke depot in the country. The Pentonville Five were dockers jailed for their activity in a 1972 strike who were released after a wave of union struggle.

You describe the late 1970s as a period of "moving on up but with complications". It is also a period in which the party is riven with arguments. People leave, there are expulsions and so on. It must have been one of the more difficult bits of the book to write, both in terms of trying to give an objective and balanced account and assessing the strengths and weaknesses of Cliff.

Yes, I think particularly the 1975 split, when the Birmingham engineers were expelled and a number of other people left to form the Workers League. I think about 150 people left, but probably we lost more because a lot of people just dropped out. I talked to a number of people, including those who left, and I've tried to give a balanced account.

I get the impression that the period of the downturn—although there are very important struggles, for example the 1984-5 miners' strike where Cliff played a crucial role going to meetings with Paul Foot and so on—lasted far longer than Cliff or anyone else anticipated. I think you mention somewhere about him scanning the back pages of SW looking for any indication that struggle is reviving.

I don't think that when Cliff started talking about the downturn in 1979 he had any notion of how long it would last. He was always looking for possibilities. The miners' strike was crucial there. Cliff clearly did believe that the miners could have won, and that if they had won, things might have shifted. I think Cliff was depressed by the outcome of the miners' strike very briefly. But the remarkable thing about Cliff was not that he was depressed by that, but that although he was nearly 70 he didn't say, "Well I've done my bit. I'm going to write a couple of books but I'm going to pull out of taking a leading role in the party." I don't think it crossed his mind for more than a couple of days.

I think Cliff's concern always was to not miss an opportunity. There's a danger that you see opportunities when there aren't really opportunities and so you wear people out. But I don't think we did that. For example, the 1992 pit closures led to a few weeks in which there was a phenomenally transformed mood, with all sorts of people you would not have thought of as even mildly political saying "a general strike would be a good idea". That mood was real and we did relate to it. But it dispersed quickly; it had vanished by Christmas. That was always Cliff's attitude, that you're always alive to possible opportunities.

What was it the made you feel you had to write this book?

Cliff had been an enormous influence on me personally; my whole life would have been very different if I'd never met him, and I knew that was true of a lot of people. I thought that a good biography of Cliff should be written and obviously it had to be done relatively soon because people would die. If you look in the front of the book you'll see the number of people in the acknowledgments who have little daggers by their name, meaning that they have died since I interviewed them.

Then I was talking to Paul Foot at a party and I mentioned casually that I would like to write Cliff's biography. I was unsure about it, partly unsure if I was up to the job and also unsure whether the SWP central committee would let me! Paul was enthusiastic and encouraging.

Paul Foot would have been the other obvious candidate to write a biography after Cliff died.
Remember though, Foot had been very ill. He'd already been in a coma for a period and I don't think he felt up to it. He would have done something very different from what I've done. It would have been much better written obviously, much more lyrical! Whether Foot would have spent as much time as I did chasing up obscure internal documents I'm not sure. But Foot and Cliff's partner Chanie were enormously encouraging to me. And, somewhat to my surprise, the central committee didn't veto it.

A final question—if an 18 year old who had just joined or was thinking of joining the party asked you "Why should I be reading a book about Tony Cliff?"—how would you respond?
There is a wonderful quotation in one of Cliff's meetings towards the end of his life where he said, "If we stand on the shoulders of giants we see a long way. If our eyes are closed, we don't see much at all." I think that's always the essence of Cliff. Sticking by the fundamental principles of Marxism, in particular the self-emancipation of the working class which is the core of the whole thing, but a willingness to constantly explore what is changing in the world.

And I would say to this 18 year old: "Don't take what Cliff has said as gospel—Cliff did it, as my title suggests, for his time. You've got to do it for your time, and your time will be very different from anything Cliff experienced."

References

Birchall, Ian, 2008, "Seizing the Time: Tony Cliff and 1968", *International Socialism 118* (spring 2008), www.isj.org.uk/?id=426

Cliff, Tony, 1946, *Middle East at the Crossroads*, www.marxists.org/archive/cliff/works/1946/me/index.htm

Cliff, Tony, 1981 [1963], *Deflected Permanent Revolution* (International Socialism Reprints), www.marxists.org/archive/cliff/works/1963/xx/permrev.htm

Cliff, Tony, 2003 [1948], *The Nature of Stalinist Russia*, in *Marxist Theory After Trotsky: Tony Cliff Selected Writings, volume 3* (Bookmarks), www.marxists.org/archive/cliff/works/1948/stalruss/

Cliff, Tony, 2010 [1975], *Lenin, volume 1: Building the Party (1893-1914)* (Bookmarks), www.marxists.org/archive/cliff/works/1975/lenin1/

Gluckstein, Ygael [Tony Cliff], 1957, *Mao's China: Economic and Political Survey* (Allen & Unwin).

Book reviews

Behind the masks
Peyman Jafari

Hamid Dabashi, **Brown Skin, White Masks** *(Pluto Press, 2011), £14.99*

Hamid Dabashi is a prolific writer and an engaged scholar. He has written extensively on Iran, Islam and cinema. Recently, many have come to know Dabashi through his relentless support for the pro-democracy struggle in Iran against its authoritarian rulers.

Dabashi's writings and political engagement, however, do not fit in the categories of "exile" or "diaspora". This is not a minor point if one really wants to understand his most recent book, *Brown Skin, White Masks*, and especially the anger that has compelled Dabashi to write it. Towards the end, Dabashi explains the very mundane and yet consequential reason why he and many others no longer belong to these categories:

"Not when—immigrant or citizen—your tax money builds bombs and drops them on your brothers and sisters halfway around the globe, in Afghanistan, Iraq, Lebanon, and Palestine... I am here [the US], and here is home—unfetishised, deromanticised, cut loose from all nostalgia—and I am here to stay, for my children are here, and here I have a fight to fight." For Dabashi, home is where you "above all raise your voice in defiance and say no to oppression".

Dabashi has made himself feel at home in the US by resisting the belligerent empire building of its rulers. This, and of course not his opposition to the autocrats in Tehran, has earned him a place among the "101 most dangerous academics in America", a list compiled by the neo-conservative supporter of Israel David Horowitz. I would argue that home is not only the place where one raises her voice against oppression in general, but especially the site where the oppressor resides. Dabashi operates within this logic of the "home" (the Dabashi reader published last year is titled *The World Is My Home*) and is thus not indifferent to and certainly not disengaged from the struggles against the evils in his immediate surroundings.

Every sentence in *Brown Skin, White Masks* is an indictment of one of the greatest injustices of our times—the dehumanisation and humiliation of Muslims and Arabs in order to justify imperialist wars waged by the US and its allies. To hammer his point home, Dabashi begins by contrasting the reactions in the American media to two terrorists. When a violent group murdered at least 173 people in Mumbai in November 2008, the media and politicians reacted with outrage. Many blamed Islam as a driving force behind this act of violence, and stigmatised and criminalised 1.5 billion Muslims. Assuming collective guilt, many demanded that Muslims denounce publicly what they called "Islamic terrorism". However, when in December 2008 Israel started a bloody war against Gaza and murdered more than 1400 Palestinians in three weeks, the media and mainstream politicians showed no indignation. No one talked about

"Jewish terrorism" or demanded that all Jews publicly denounce it—rightly so, as Dabashi stresses.

Dabashi asks: "What could account for this discrepancy—outrage at criminal acts when the perpetrators are Muslims, yet complacency toward far worse acts when they are aimed against Muslims? How would one understand this systematic dehumanisation of Arabs and Muslims—as being capable only of criminal acts (when a mere handful have perpetrated them), coupled with disregard for their sufferings when millions of them are victims?"

His answer is that "in present-day North America and Western Europe—and by extension the world they seek to dominate—brown has become the new black and Muslims the new Jews". This involves a recodification of racist power relations which no longer revolves around colour but mainly around an Islam as the essential, unchanging hallmark of a whole people. Dabashi dissects this ideological construction, which dehistoricises Muslims in order to justify the expansion of the American empire by means of war and occupation.

Dabashi's critical narrative is built on three intellectual sources, which he further develops to analyse a reality that has changed due to transformations in the functioning of global capitalism. First, taking his cue from William Kornhauser's "mass society" and Guy Debord's "society of the spectacle", he asserts that we have arrived in an "ideological society", which designates "America and her allies' systematic consensus building for military adventurism around the globe on the threshold of the twenty-first century". According to Dabashi, the "ideological society" is "unprecedented by history" and is held together by "ideological convictions and assumptions". The main assumption is that we live in the era of the "clash of civilisations", as formulated by Samuel Huntington, an ideology that sanctifies everything in the West and vilifies everything in the Muslim countries. Added to this is the centrality of Carl Schmitt's notion of "the enemy" to neoconservatives—a role fulfilled by "Islam".

Although Dabashi is right to recognise the "clash of civilisations" as the ideological foundation of the dehumanisation of Muslims, I think he exaggerates the role of ideology, which has played an important role in legitimising imperialism, in its anticommunist form during the Cold War for instance. His focus on ideology also tends to orient him towards Toni Negri and Michael Hardt's flawed concept of Empire as capitalist power without a centre, and to disregard Marxist analyses provided by, for instance, David Harvey and Alex Callinicos. However, these are secondary issues as Dabashi's main goal is to analyse ideological aspects.

Dabashi's second intellectual source is Franz Fanon's *Black Skin, White Masks* (1952), which he uses to reevaluate the relationship between racism and colonialism in its new manifestations. Fanon argued that the colonial apparatus "successfully manufactures a profound sense of inferiority in the colonised subjects that leads them—actively or passively, consciously or unconsciously—to identify with and seek to reserve the colonial agency". The subjects of Dabashi's critique, however, are not those intellectuals in colonial countries who helped legitimise colonialism. He sets out to explain how those who emigrated to the heart of empire assist it in a certain mode of knowledge production that justifies imperialism and criminalises resistance to it. Dabashi thus extends Fanon's insights to the age of War on Terror.

Edward Said, Dabashi's third intellectual source, had identified the "exilic intellectual" as a locus of dissent at the heart of empire that had managed to squash critical public intellectuals. Dabashi, however, sets out to explore the "darker side of intellectual migration". He writes about how from "the selfsame cadre of exiles…are no longer telling their imperial employers what they need to know but rather what they want to believe in order to…convince the public that invading and bombing and occupying the homelands of others is a good and moral thing".

Dabashi calls these immigrants who service empire "native informers" and "comprador intellectuals". After developing these concepts in reference to anthropological and historical studies, Dabashi explores in some detail the modus operandi of comprador intellectuals. A chapter on "Literature and Empire" concentrates on Azar Nafisi's *Reading Lolita in Tehran*, while another chapter on "The House Muslim" delves into the writings of Ibn Warraq who has been celebrated in the media as a "dissenting voice" and an "ex-Muslim". Tapping into his extensive knowledge of literature and the history of Islam, Dabashi provides a devastating critique of these comprador intellectuals.

At times Dabashi's (justified) sense of irritation hampers the flow of his argument, when for instance he repeats a point too often or sneers at what he takes for granted instead of explaining. Overall, however, *Brown Skin, White Masks* is a well-structured, eloquent and worthy continuation of the intellectual tradition of Franz Fanon and Edward Said that provides a timely cultural criticism. It is also a powerful reminder that despite the presence of the comprador intellectuals in the Western media, there are those who chose not to inform the rulers of the US empire, but those who want to resist it in order to bring an end to war, occupation and racism.

Interrogating empire
G Francis Hodge

Gopal Balakrishnan, **Antagonistics: Capitalism and Power in an Age of War** *(Verso, 2009) £14.99*

Reading *Antagonistics* is a contradictory experience. Written by US academic Gopal Balakrishnan, currently on the editorial board of *New Left Review*, the book is on one hand a theoretically dense interrogation of several contemporary (and some not so contemporary) thinkers on international politics. On the other, it is a frustrating exercise in mining through prose so turgidly impenetrable as to render its potentially excellent essays virtually inaccessible to all but academics and specialists.

The book is a collection of review articles written between 1995 and 2007, the bulk of them having appeared in *New Left Review* in the early years of the new millennium. Balakrishnan covers a lot of intellectual ground through the course of these essays, from territory occupied by non-Marxist theorists on the left, to that dominated by commentators on the political right. Chapters interrogating works on figures as diverse as the well-known Jürgen Habermas, Antonio Negri and Alexis de Tocqueville cohabit with thoughts on Machiavelli and several lower-profile theorists such as Israeli Security Studies specialist Azar Gat and Philip Bobbitt, former advisor to US President Bill Clinton. In each review, Balakrishnan attempts, in his own words, "a reconstruction of the overall argument of a work, which explores the possibility that its logical, empirical and even stylistic failures arise from ideologies embedded in its framework".

Balakrishnan interrogates both politically conservative and progressive writers in order to find "the authentic insights" they may have to offer and to polemicise against them. In so doing, he provides a rigorous survey and critique of recent writing by several key theorists, though one not without problems.

The survey of conservatives presented in *Antagonistics* is an excellent introduction to the assumptions underlying much of establishment thinking since the early 1990's. In his reviews of Bobbitt and Gat, Balakrishnan commends the ambition of each writer and effectively summarises the arguments made, before thoroughly dismantling their central claims. Azar Gat's point in *War in Human Civilisation*, that the history of human conflict can be understood largely as an expression of evolutionary biology, is shown to be critically flawed. Likewise, Balakrishnan offers a sharp critique of Philip Bobbitt's *The Shield of Achilles* and *Terror and Consent*. He demonstrates that while both books combined offer a broad overview of the debates that have shaped American foreign policy since the collapse of the Stalinism, they substantially fail to engage with or even acknowledge the role played by the US in propagating the international conflicts in which it is currently engaged. He points out that nowhere in *Terror and Consent* is there a serious discussion of the actual causes of Islamic terrorism or the motivations of those who identify as Islamic terrorists.

As incisive as he is with those far from his politics, Balakrishnan does not spare those who might be considered his allies. In his critique of *Afflicted Powers* by the Retort Collective, first published in *New Left Review* in late 2005, Balakrishnan does a fine job exposing the problems associated with theorising the international system in mechanistic terms.

The Retort Collective attempt to explain the current geopolitical situation by referring to Marx's concept of primitive accumulation,

"the earth-shaking use of force to create or restore the social conditions of profitability". They portray post-9/11 US foreign policy as a response to the economic difficulties faced by US capitalism at the end of the boom of the 1990s, rather than making any "reference to the structure and history of the capitalist, or more specifically, the American state". In the view of the Retort Collective, the drive to militarise US foreign policy can be understood as an attempt to seize capital and force open new parts of the globe to American capital investment, an attempt to secure the conditions for the ongoing expansion of capitalism.

This conception, as outlined by Balakrishnan, misses the complex connection between economic competition and geopolitical rivalry, reducing geopolitical competition between states to simply economics. Balakrishnan rightly argues that there are problems with the Retort Collective's formulation. He notes that the process of capital accumulation and economic restructuring that took place from the 1980s onwards actually occurred "without any significant bouts of organised violence from above", a fact which suggests there is more to capital accumulation than simply the use of force and coercion. He also points out that the world now being organised exclusively on the basis of nation-states, "impedes the open use of military coercion to acquire or retain spheres of influence". Simply put, the world is now organised in such a way as to make military coercion less straightforward than in the era of classical imperialism and empire-building. This suggests there is more to the connection between military force and capitalism than is suggested by the Retort Collective's argument.

Balakrishnan is right when he takes the Retort Collective to task for an economically deterministic conception of the connection between war and capitalism.

However, he throws the entire Marxist baby out with his critique of deterministic bathwater. He does not convince when he remarks that "there are no theories that explain in general terms what advantages accrue to major states in the current world market environment from possessing more military power than their peers or competitors".

Almost 100 years ago, Nikolai Bukharin argued that geopolitical competition between states and economic competition between rival firms based in those states was becoming increasingly fused together. National states were thus compelled to act for a complex mix of geopolitical and economic reasons. This classical Marxist theory of imperialism has been developed in the decades since, not least in the pages of this journal. One example is Alex Callinicos picking up the thread in 2002 when he wrote "The Grand Strategy of the American Empire", arguing that while there were economic motives contributing to the decision by the Bush administration to invade Afghanistan the primary motive was geopolitical, "focused on reasserting [US] global hegemony after 11 September".* Callinicos is at pains to argue that one cannot simply reduce the geopolitical to the economic or vice versa. This theory of imperialism, appropriately developed and applied, goes some way to answering the question posed by Balakrishnan. *Antagonistics* would be much improved if it incorporated a closer examination of this theoretical tradition.

Balakrishnan's short critical examination of multiculturalism in many ways sums up both the strengths and weaknesses of *Antagonistics*. A pugnacious and determined look into the limits of multiculturalism as a vehicle for human emancipation—"its treacly pieties are incompatible with any political élan against the established order"—at the same time the essay fails to acknowledge that the idea of multiculturalism, whatever its limits, must be defended when attacked by that same established order. In a context of governments throughout the industrialised world looking to scapegoat immigrants and racialised populations, a call to defend the basic inclusiveness that multicultural policy protects seems necessary, whatever the content of one's own critique of those policies. In fairness to Balakrishnan, the essay was written in early 2001, before the attacks on the World Trade Centre and the ensuing US Global War on Terror. However, its inclusion in a collection appearing in 2009, with no mention of that changed context, makes one wonder exactly who is the intended audience for *Antagonistics*.

In his quite favourable remarks quoted by the publisher, Slavoj Žižek writes of *Antagonistics* that "it is a book for *everyone*". Would that this were true. The book might have been an excellent primer for specialist and non-specialist alike on several key contributions to political thought since the collapse of the Soviet bloc. Problems aside, it remains a useful resource for specialists and students requiring a theoretically dense interrogation of post-Cold War intellectual history. The shame is that *Antagonistics* is a bit of an opportunity missed. Its opaque prose, coupled with the decision on the part of the writer to avoid direct engagement with the struggles of the day, limits the potential appeal of the book to only those academics and specialists already versed in the ideas to which it contributes.

* http://pubs.socialistreviewindex.org.uk/isj97/callinicos.htm

This time it's personal

Simon Englert

Illan Pappe, **Out of the Frame: The Struggle for Academic Freedom in Israel** (Pluto, 2010), £13

In this excellent book, the Israeli academic Illan Pappe breaks from his usual style to offer a mixture of personal stories, general overviews, historical insights and fictional accounts to paint a clear and damning picture of the state of critical thought in Israel.

Pappe guides the reader through the last 30 years of political and academic history in Israeli society. From the opening up of internal debate following the first intifada through the Oslo talks and the shutting down of dissenting voices by the end of the 1990s, Pappe describes in a vivid, personal and resonant language his journey to anti-Zionism and his attempts to hold those politics inside Israel and its academia.

Using examples such as the 2006 second war on Lebanon and the assault on Gaza which began in December 2008, Pappe argues that a clique of generals have managed to take over key aspects of Israeli society. Many key politicians, media bosses and political commentators are former generals in the Israeli military. The ability of this clique to shut down dissenting voices and organise public and academic debate while simultaneously setting and implementing policy is described with a chilling clarity.

An interesting question is raised through the accounts of personal and political attacks against the author, namely, whether a consistent and viable anti-Zionist politics is possible inside Israel itself. Pappe seems to have answered that question by deciding that the most helpful thing for him to do was to leave the country (after huge professional and political pressures) and to throw his energy into promoting and spreading the boycott, divestment and sanctions campaign. It is also worth noting that Pappe's break with Zionism began while he was studying in England and was accelerated through contact with Palestinian activists, freedom fighters and revolutionaries. Pappe's emphasis on the need to apply pressure upon Israel from the outside and isolate it as a rogue state suggests that he sees only a limited possibility for internal dissent for the time being.

While the politics of *Out of the Frame* are generally solid, towards the end the author describes Zionism as being born originally from a progressive impulse to oppose anti-Semitism. Although a minor point in the book, I think it is inaccurate. Early Zionists, who were indeed reacting to anti-Semitism, were a small minority of Jews. They felt European racism could not be fought and that the Jews should emigrate. But at the same time thousands of Jews were actively involved in anti-racist, anti-fascist and revolutionary politics. As a matter of fact, in his book *The Jewish State*, Theodore Herzl argued Zionism would deal with both anti-Semitism and the strong influence of socialism on the Jewish masses. Zionism was a reactionary ideology from its inception and should be remembered as such.

Science and industry

Amy Gilligan

David Knight, **The Making of Modern Science** (Polity, 2009), £17.99

There prevails in society the notion that the practice of science is somehow objective and neutral. However, when we look at the way funding is allocated and what research is undertaken it quickly becomes clear that this is not the case. By looking at the history of science we can see this is not a new development.

David Knight's book *The Making of Modern Science* provides an interesting and thorough overview of the development of science between 1789 and 1914. The French Revolution saw the development of a salaried body of scientists in the Académie du Sciences in Paris, the École Polytechnique, and something that could be termed a "career" in science. Through the 19th century state support for research, predominantly in universities became more common. Change came to England later than other places in Europe (including Scotland); science persisted as "a hobby chiefly for inquisitive if dotty professors, gentlemen of leisure and country parsons", and grants were only awarded to universities in 1889.

The differences between England and other countries must be seen in the context of the industrial revolution and the rise of capitalism. Britain had already advanced rapidly industrially, was the dominant naval power in the world at that time, and had a significant number of colonies, providing a market and a source of raw materials. This meant that, in order to compete, there was pressure on France and Germany to develop scientific education to inform industry, which led to commercial success in many fields.

Things in Britain eventually began to change. The Great Exhibition in 1851 was a huge display of scientific and industrial development in Britain and the empire. Coming so soon after the revolutions of 1848, it seems likely that part of the motivation for the exhibition was to generate national pride and a sense that things were going well. However, for many scientists there was a realisation that Britain had a lot to learn from other countries in terms of mass production, standardisation, higher education and design. Wars in the US, France and Prussia also served to highlight how power, influence and progress depended on science and technology.

Changes to the kind of scientific enquiry taking place saw science move from the homes of wealthy individuals to large laboratories. Laboratories were increasingly necessary for experimental physics, and in the biological sciences for dissection and microscope work. This led to further changes, as laboratory environments made it possible to undertake experiments under controlled conditions to test theories. There are parallels between changes in the locus of scientific enquiry with those in other forms of manufacturing, with scientists increasingly being employed for a wage.

One of the most interesting aspects of 19th century science, and a significant theme running through *The Making of Modern Science*, is how scientific developments interacted with wider society. The theory of evolution by natural selection, developed simultaneously by Charles Darwin and Alfred Russell Wallace, was, of course, hugely scientifically significant in its own right. But it was also important in strengthening the developing materialist conception of the world. In the late 18th and early 19th century, materialism within science was often shunned, in part because the ruling class saw it was being intimately connected with the French Revolution. Joseph Priestley, a scientist who attempted to reconcile religion with materialism, was forced to flee Britain for Pennsylvania after a mob burned down his house and church.

Science at the start of the 19th century in Britain was to a large extent the preserve of a wealthy elite, or of those who could find a patron, as there were no other ways of being able to buy the necessary equipment and to support oneself. Science begins to open up in this period as the ruling class realise that scientific research is crucial in the drive for profit. The language used in science, however, means that it can often seem no less elitist; the increasing role of mathematics in science developed in the 19th century, making science, at times, seem quite remote for many people.

The Making of Modern Science is a useful source for linking the development of science to social changes occurring through the 19th century, although at times some of these links could be a little more explicit. By looking at how research was conducted during the period it forces the reader to examine why particular research is conducted today, a key question that must be asked when seeking to understand the impact science has on our lives.

Karl Marx in Wonderland
Luke Evans

Simon Choat, **Marx Through Post Structuralism: Lyotard, Derrida, Foucault, Deleuze** *(Continuum, 2010),* £65

In this book, Simon Choat analyses the relationship between the ideas of four "post-structuralist" thinkers—Jean-Francoise Lyotard, Jacques Derrida, Michel Foucault and Gilles Deleuze—and the works of Karl Marx.

The key concerns of post-structuralism arose from what is called the "linguistic turn", after which the development, use and study of language became a key focus for philosophers and other social scientists. Documenting, criticising and challenging social issues became a matter of observing how language and discourse contained inherent asymmetries of power, and post-structuralists held that attempts to aspire to a radical, revolutionary truth could not overcome this distorting and mystifying character of language.

Post-structuralism was in many ways a response to the bastardisation of mainstream Marxism, in both its Stalinist and social democratic forms. At some level it was a genuine attempt to overcome the limitations of the politics that held back the great revolutionary moment in Europe after 1968.

Choat's book does not shirk from engaging critically with the post-structuralists. Nor does he seek to diminish the legacy of Marx's work in favour of academic fashion. The book is written in a thorough and meticulous fashion, with no argument left ambiguous or seeming ill-thought through.

Choat rightly points out that the shift in post-structuralism thought can be surmised as the move from Hegel to Nietszche in terms of philosophical ancestry. This means moving from the idea of contradiction or conflict shaping and changing the social whole, to the proliferation of isolated, and unique moments of difference as a force for social change.

Choat is right to point out that the post-structuralists he discusses sought to engage with Marx without sticking to any party orthodoxy or branch of Marxism. But the resulting alternative method becomes the scholastic one—poring over Marx's *Collected Works*, finding meaning in every turn of phrase or remark in a margin he ever made. Choat calls this the "event-Marx", rather than the historical set of politics called Marxism. This method actually reinforces one of the key ideological threads within bourgeois ideology—the idea of the individual as the most basic unit through which we compose and understand society as a whole.

A keen and vociferous engagement with Marx's prose is never a bad thing. But basing one's engagement on an abstract fidelity to the letter of his text assumes that Marx's words, and the subsequent response proffered by the analyst of his work, somehow possess a truth beyond their social and material context. This reinforces the Marx of the dead word—a Marx from the past, trapped in his manuscripts. When Marx's work is engaged with simply as the author of texts, not as a living body of political thought (ie Marxism), innovation within his legacy becomes the sole preserve of the masters of novel or idiosyncratic readings of his work. This relegates advocates and agents of Marxist politics to the role of ignorant passengers of history, awaiting the word of god from cognoscenti with plenty of free time.

From a critique of orthodoxy and the evasion of the dreaded party-line, the post-structuralists actually end up repeating the practices of the most hard-line sectarians, deeming their Marx of a more authentic and liberated character than the Marx of the party.

Choat concludes by highlighting the point where post-structuralists are weakest when dealing with Marx—class.

As Choat rightly highlights, the post-structuralists do not engage effectively with the complexity of Marx's conception of class struggle as the motor of historic change. The problem is that Choat takes from his work the idea that class is not an objective reality, but is only present in the context of class struggle. Whilst it is true that struggle between oppressor and oppressed defines the development of history, this does not mean that there are not classes that exist objectively based on their relationship to the means of production. By neglecting the notion that the working class is the agent of change, Choat ends up affirming a kind of "if it fights, it's class struggle" idea that can slip easily into movementism or autonomism.

The dialectic of class struggle means that the working class, because of its social position, is sometimes compelled to fight against its exploiters—through this process, it can come to understand the power it has to do away with this whole sordid system.

Pick of the quarter

Making sense of the Arab revolutions is an urgent priority for the radical left. *New Left Review* 68 carries two pieces that seek to address this task. The first, by Perry Anderson, has a strange title, "On the Concatenation in the Arab World", that maybe symbolises his distance from the upheavals. Anderson is caustic about the Western intervention in Libya, describing the vanguard role of France and Britain as "re-running the spool of the Suez expedition". His complaint that "anti-imperialism is the dog that has not—or not yet—barked in the part of the world where imperial power is most visible" ignores the extent to which opposition to American domination and solidarity with the Palestinians ran deep certainly in the Egyptian Revolution. This has become more visible since the article appeared in April with protests outside the Israeli embassy in Cairo and the military regime's decision to re-open the border of Gaza.

The same issue also carries a long interview about Egypt with Hazem Kandil. This contains much interesting detail (though friends in Cairo have queried some of its accuracy). Kandil concludes that, "if the movement remains as it is now, moderate and pragmatic, we will have a much better Egypt than existed before, not a perfect democracy." Pressing for more radical change might provoke "an authoritarian backlash". The problem is that it's not impossible to freeze the situation where it is. The economic crisis presses the ruling class to clamp down, and workers, peasants, and the poor to fight for their own demands. Simply to defend the gains that have been already won will require the movement to fight for deep political and economic change.

The latest issue of *Historical Materialism* (19,1) carries a symposium on Chris Wickham's great book *Framing the Early Middle Ages* edited by Paul Blackledge. Poignantly, the contributors include the late Chris Harman, whose piece is a model of clarity and erudition. Among the others are Jairus Banaji, Neil Davidson, John Haldon and John Moreland, and Wickham himself responds in a characteristically open but tough-minded way. The exchanges offer an impressive display of the quality contemporary Marxist historical scholarship.

The June issue of *Monthly Review* contains an interesting piece by the Chinese academic and former political prisoner Minqi Li which examines the changes within the Chinese working class in recent years and social unrest that has resulted. Although the article proceeds from the highly dubious perspective that the Chinese Revolution of 1949 and the Maoist period that followed it were socialist in character, it nonetheless offers an interesting snapshot of the contradictions and imbalances of the economic situation in China as well as a very optimistic view of the possibilities for the development of working class struggle.*

AC & JJ

---

* http://monthlyreview.org/2011/06/01/the-rise-of-the-working-class-and-the-future-of-the-chinese-revolution

RETHINKING INVASION ECOLOGIES FROM THE ENVIRONMENTAL HUMANITIES

Research from a humanist perspective has much to offer in interrogating the social and cultural ramifications of invasion ecologies. The impossibility of securing national boundaries against accidental transfer and the unpredictable climatic changes of our time have introduced new dimensions and hazards to this old issue. Written by a team of international scholars, *Rethinking Invasion Ecologies from the Environmental Humanities* allows us to rethink the impact on national, regional or local ecologies of the deliberate or accidental introduction of foreign species, plant and animal.

Modern environmental approaches that treat nature with naïve realism or mobilise it as a moral absolute, unaware or unwilling to accept that it is informed by specific cultural and temporal values, are doomed to fail. Instead, this book shows that we need to understand the complex interactions of ecologies and societies in the past, present and future over the Anthropocene, in order to address problems of the global environmental crisis. It demonstrates how humanistic methods and disciplines can be used to bring fresh clarity and perspective to this long-vexed aspect of environmental thought and practice.

Students and researchers in environmental studies, invasion ecology, conservation biology, environmental ethics, environmental history and environmental policy will welcome this major contribution to environmental humanities.

Jodi Frawley is a Discovery Early Career Researcher Award Fellow in the Department of Gender and Cultural Studies, University of Sydney, Australia.

Iain McCalman is a Professorial Research Fellow in History, University of Sydney. He is Co-Director of the Sydney University Environment Institute, Australia.

The *Routledge Environmental Humanities* series is an original and inspiring venture recognising that today's world agricultural and water crises, ocean pollution and resource depletion, global warming from greenhouse gases, urban sprawl, overpopulation, food insecurity and environmental justice are all *crises of culture*.

The reality of understanding and finding adaptive solutions to our present and future environmental challenges has shifted the epicentre of environmental studies away from an exclusively scientific and technological framework to one that depends on the human-focused disciplines and ideas of the humanities and allied social sciences.

We thus welcome book proposals from all humanities and social sciences disciplines for an inclusive and interdisciplinary series. We favour manuscripts aimed at an international readership and written in a lively and accessible style. The readership comprises scholars and students from the humanities and social sciences and thoughtful readers concerned about the human dimensions of environmental change.

Rethinking Invasion Ecologies from the Environmental Humanities
Jodi Frawley and Iain McCalman

The Broken Promise of Agricultural Progress
An environmental history
Cameron Muir